D1294457

The Standard Theatre of Victorian England

Frontispiece: The City of London in 1851. The site of the Standard theatre is near the right edge of the engraving in the low buildings between the church towers. *From A.S.J.*

THE STANDARD THEATRE

OF

VICTORIAN ENGLAND

Allan Stuart Jackson

Rutherford•Madison•Teaneck
Fairleigh Dickinson University Press
London and Toronto: Associated University Presses

Associated University Presses
440 Forsgate Drive
Cranbury, NJ 08512

Associated University Presses
25 Sicilian Avenue
London WC1A 2QH, England

Associated University Presses
P.O. Box 39, Clarkson Pstl. Stn.
Mississauga, Ontario,
L5J 3X9 Canada

The paper used in this publication meets the requirements
of the American National Standard for Permanence of Paper
for Printed Library Materials Z39.48–1984.

Library of Congress Cataloging-in-Publication Data

Jackson, Allan Stuart, 1934–
    Standard Theatre of Victorian England / by Allan Stuart Jackson
    p.   cm.
    Includes bibliographical references.
    ISBN 0-8386-3392-7 (alk. paper)
    1. Standard Theatre (Shoreditch, London, England) 2. Theatre—England–
–London—History—19th century. 3. Shoreditch (London, England)—History. 1. Title
PN2596.L7S736   1993
792'.09421'209034—dc20   89-46134
                                                                          CIP

Printed in the United States of America

CONTENTS

ILLUSTRATIONS

10

PREFACE

While browsing some years ago in a London shop, I came upon a bundle of watercolor paper bound up in a tattered roll. Through the grime I could dimly see a stamped name and address: "Richard Douglass Painting Rooms next the Grand Theater London N.11." Without opening the roll, I purchased it for a nominal price and hurried away with my undisclosed prize. Upon examination, the bundle was found to contain several small water colors of the area of Shanklin labeled "the Chine" [ravine]; designs for two "act drop" curtains; six eight-foot-long panoramas of English and Scottish landscapes and castles; and a five-foot-long design for a moving panorama. This last item showed a change of place, time, and weather for the opening of a Christmas panto of *Robinson Crusoe*. (See figs. 130 and 189 through 200).

I found that researching Richard Douglass, the artist, was a surprisingly difficult task. There was little mention of him in the basic sources about Victorian theatre—just a few tantalizing facts. A number of other Douglass family members were mentioned along with their connection to the Standard Theatre in Shoreditch High Street. Even this theatre was a shadowy institution in the major sources.

Several facts did stand out. The Standard was considered the largest theatre building in London, perhaps in all of Europe. The founder of the Douglass theatrical family, John, was considered the chief rival of the famous actor of nautical roles, Thomas Potter Cooke. Finally, in the 1880s spectacular staging at the Standard included realistic railroad scenes, cataracts and ponds of real water, fox hunts, hansom cabs, and excellent Christmas pantos.

Threading through the biographies of the major performers of the last half of the nineteenth century were a constant, yet undeveloped, references to the Douglass family and performances at the Standard Theatre. The operations at the Standard appear to have been a microcosm of the Victorian theatre. Yet there was no major source covering its history in depth. Wilson's *East End Entertainment* devoted chapters to the theatre, but they are only a brief introduction.

As a fabric of small facts accumulated, some partial answers to this mystery appeared. Unlike so many other London theatres, the primary materials pertaining to the Standard's history were widely and thinly scattered. The building stood in a part of the city that was considered unfashionable. The major members of the Douglass family, unlike so many other nineteenth century theatrical figures, did not write memoirs of their accomplishments. The two small paperbound books printed in the twentieth century by Albert Douglass, a nephew, were privately printed and circulated. Because of this, they are not readily available or widely known.

From the sources one fact clearly emerged: The Douglass family and the Standard Theatre had not been treated in proportion to their place in the Victorian theatre. It is to this end that this work was begun. Over the past years a considerable amount of original documents have been accumulated by me. These include pictures, playbills, programs, and other ephemera. In addition, the materials in the London theatre collections have been sifted. This has brought together the facts in thousands of documents, thus providing a day-to-day study of the operations at the Standard Theatre from 1835 to 1889.

I have been given much friendly assistance by the staffs of the various theatre collections. I wish to take the opportunity to thank Mr. Tongue and his assistants at the Rose Lipman Library in Hackney where the best group of playbills is housed. The archivists of the Enthoven Collection served me very well as always. The staff at the Westminster Central Reference Library was particularly kind to put up with me for weeks. The curators of the beautiful Guildhall Library were exceptionally helpful. The efficient arrangement of their holdings and their wide knowledge reflects credit on them all. Mary Speaight and the librarians of the Museum of London in the Barbicon went out of their way to aid me in my project. Mr. Webb at the Bishopsgate Institute, and the reference librarians at the Hackney, Tower Hamlet, and Islington libraries gave me a number of useful suggestions. At the Greater London Council Architects Department, in Middlesex House, Mr. Pollard gave me useful advice, as did the staff of the Department of Architectural Planning in Hackney, and the District Surveyor's Office in Shoreditch. My research in England has always been made most pleasant by the ministrations of Barbara, John, George, and Mary, and my friends the Winlows.

ACKNOWLEDGMENTS

The following institutions are to be acknowledged for materials or illustrations identifed as part of their holdings: The Enthoven Collection, Crown Copyright; The Rose Lipman Library, London Borough of Hackney Library Services Copyright; The London Museum, Trustees of the London Museum copyright; Guildhall Library, City of London copyright; The British Library, Trustees of the British Library copyright; Harvard Theatre Collection, Harvard College Library copyright; The Lilly Library, Indiana University Libraries copyright.

INTRODUCTION

Recent writers have made a plea for the reassessment of the Victorian arts. Joseph Donohue, in his splendid study, *Theatre in the Age of Kean*, destroys with great clarity a number of prejudices against late eighteenth-century and early nineteenth-century theatre.[1] He also presents a number of important arguments for new attitudes about the Victorian theatre. J.C. Trewin, in his rollicking book on the Edwardian theatre, and Donohue bracket the Victorian period with fresh studies in the new spirit of critical thinking.[2]

Donohue points to the statement in G. Kitson Clark's book, *The Making of Victorian England*, that best summarizes the new approach. Researching the masses of ephemera from the mid-nineteenth century produces "new details that . . . may not seem to have been worth the trouble to unearth, since they so often relate to obscure persons, places and events that may claim at most a secondary importance. Yet it is exactly from sources like these that large changes will eventually come in our understanding of the history of that age."[3]

Doctor Johnson was correct when he said, "The stage but echoes back the public voice." The late Victorian critics and more recent writers alike have refused to listen to this "public voice" of the mid-Victorian popular theatre in their assessment of it. In addition there has been a distressing tendency to confuse upper-class West End attitudes with virtue or quality. This has produced a ranking of dramatic productions in which the day-to-day plays of the Elizabethan, Restoration, and even the eighteenth-century, have been considered superior to the Victorian. This is despite the fact that far more people saw, and appreciated, the productions of the mid-nineteenth century than in all previous eras put together.

As to the Victorian dramatists themselves, they spoke as clearly to their age as previous writers had. But critics of Victorian writing so often raise the phrase "lacking in timelessness." In any well-constructed work of artistic merit, from any time period, an expert can find "timelessness." On the other hand, to the majority of our contemporary theatregoers the impact of works from the past increas-

1.   Joseph Donohue, *Theatre in the Age of Kean* (Bowman and Littlefield, New Jersey 1975), pp. 157-169 (audiences), 177 (theatrical techniques), 183 (importance of Victorian theatre).
2.   J .C. Trewin, *The Edwardian Theatre* (Bowman and Littlefield, New Jersey 1976).
3.   G. Kitson Clark, *The Making of Victorian England* (Cambridge, Harvard University Press 1962), p. 3.

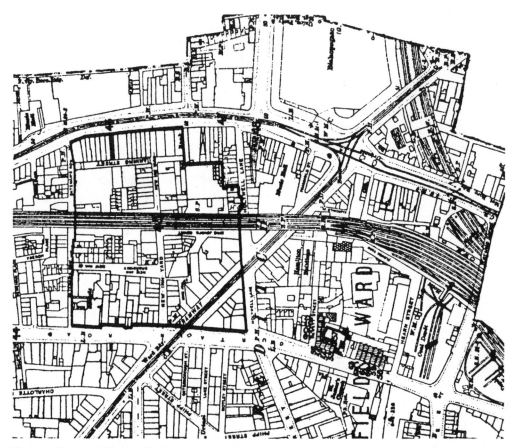

Fig. 1. Map of Shoreditch as it was between 1890 and 1915. The Standard Theatre is labeled "Music Hall," and is just above the diamond crossing, and union of the horse-drawn street tram tracks, just below Holywell Lane. *From A.S.J.*

ingly dissipates as human experience and language evolves. Less and less will audiences be able to enjoy Elizabethan and Baroque dramas.

This has happened before when, in the Hellenistic age, of all the classical dramatists, only Euripides was accorded more than a rare revival in the public theatre. Eventually even his works came to be known only to experts of the Byzantine academies. Euripidean production was seen in a steadily diminishing amount for about five hundred years. Finally the language and life he depicted no longer seemed "timeless" to the general theatregoer.

The Elizabethan drama has been the primary model for the serious drama for the last four hundred years. But one can see a time in the not- too-distant future when the evolution of human life and language will make even Shakespeare inaccessible, except to the coterie and academics.

In fact, already his works have been translated into the modern idiom of English, just as Euripides and his fellow fifth-century playwrights must be translated for the modern Greek audience. Even though these works have been the pattern for modern dramatists, they are less and less seen in the commercial public theatre. This is because their language and subjects seem no longer central to the concerns of the contemporary audience.

Very few plays have lasted on a commercial basis for more than two centuries. Perhaps most plays that were successful in their own time dealt with issues that are resolved or become unimportant. The longer-lived dramas may, by chance, deal with as yet unresolved issues. Or, perhaps these dramas provide such attractive vehicles for performers that they, or producers, continue their stage life by sheer force of artistic will.

All through the history of theatre its aesthetics reflect a swing from an emphasis on emotional content in one period, to an emphasis on intellectual content in the next, and then back again. The younger Victorian drama critics, who were on the leading edge of the aesthetics of naturalism, criticized the romantic theatre for the things that were basic to its nature. It was a form centered on emotion. "Feeling" was vastly more important than "common sense," "accuracy," or "logic." Of course, the intellectual-centered theatre of naturalism was to emphasize just these things.

The audience of the romantic plays greatly enjoyed the "what if" nature of the plots and characters. The extraordinarily long arm of "coincidence" was virtually mandatory. Impossibly complex and illogical series of events were considered thrilling. Characters who acted in ways not generally thought typical of normal human beings were intoxicating to transfixed audiences. Blazing lights, glittering scenery and costumes, dark and mysterious ruins by moonlight, and storms, all provided the play upon emotions so central to the mid-Victorian audience.

Now in the mid-twentieth century, naturalism in all its forms and distortions has run its course, the elements of common sense, accuracy, logic, and all the rest of its intellectually centered components are being criticized in their turn. The

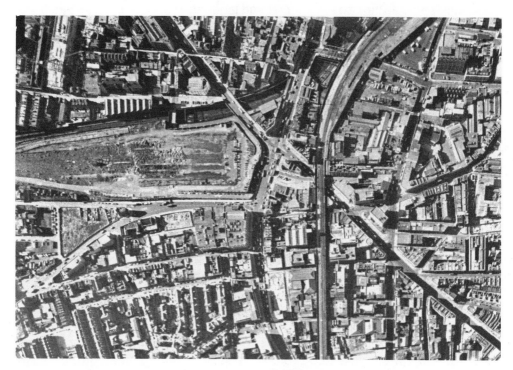

Fig. 2. Aerial map of Shoreditch in 1971. The site of the Standard Theatre is just across from the derelict, bombed-out Great Eastern Railway Station at the lower right. *From the Rose Lipman Library, Hackney.*

closer to reality art comes, the less art it contains. Now a new emotion-centered aesthetic is forming. This neoromantic, or neo-baroque age will undoubtedly have an aesthetic form centered on emotion, in which logic and reality will be less important. Perhaps in light of these natural changes in emphasis, late twentieth- century critics and audiences will be able to view Victorian theatre with a less jaundiced eye. Therefore, a plea must be made for methods of criticism of dramatic production that deal with how well a play handles the issues of its time, speaks to its audience, represents the human condition, and presents the most ethical attitudes of the majority of the people. By this means Victorian theatre can be revaluated. It is to be hoped that the idea that everything written or produced between Sheridan and Shaw was "insignificant" art can be rejected, then replaced with a more sympathetic evaluation.

One example of the topics, which needs this revaluation deals with a catchword that has been traditionally applied to Victorian theatres and dramas. This is the term "minor." Unfortunately, the term "minor" carries a degrading connotation similar to that of the word "provincial." It should be dropped by modern writers and only selectively applied when it is really appropriate. As a substitute the term "suburban" could be used when referring to the theatres not considered to be in the West End. The reason for this change is that "minor" does not reflect accurately the character of theatrical institutions like Sadler's Wells, the Brittania, the Standard, the Surrey, or the Grecian. Many of these were larger, better managed, and better attended than the Theatres Royal. The plays developed for the suburban houses were often artistically successful, better presented, and better performed than anything in the West End. Avant-garde techniques that later proved their artistic worth were pioneered in the suburban productions. The best performers and their best plays were cheered by the local audiences. Above all, the suburban houses were often the only theatrical operations successful at the box office. They thus provided the members of the theatrical profession with their chief income, and kept the performing arts afloat.

Another example of subjects that need revaluation is the place in social and artistic history of London's suburbs. The East End of London suffers a similar fate in the hands of historians that the theatre has at the hands of the critics. By the accounts of the few brave writers who have ignored fashionable attitudes, the rich and varied fabric of East London life is worthy of a great deal of attention. Charles Dickens presented it in short stories and in *Oliver Twist* and *Nicholas Nickleby*. Israel Zangwill's turn-of-the-century novels and plays are considered fascinating and accurate views of life around Bishopsgate. Zangwill principally depicted life of the Jewish community. Other writers and dramatists covered subjects of interest to the Irish minority.

As the central European, Jewish and Irish immigrations swelled the population of the area north of the London docks, thousands were forced to move north and east into rural Islington, Shoreditch, and Hackney. *The Hackney Official Guide* indicates this spectacular increase in population between 1811 and 1900.

DATE	SHOREDITCH	HACKNEY
1811	43,930	16,771
1841	83,432	37,771
1851	109,257	53,589
1861	129,364	76,687
1871	127,164	115,110
1881	126,591	163,681
1891	124,009	198,606

To crowd a total of 129,364 people into Shoreditch, an area about one-half mile square, made it standing room only. It is small wonder that after 1861, large amounts of housing were rushed into completion further north. Then the population of aging Shoreditch began to decline.

The rise and fall of the fortunes of the theatres in the East End follows the population patterns. The ethnic character (because some groups went to the theatres more than others) had some impact on them as well. Finally, the arrival of the railroads, the horse-drawn trams of the streets, and eventually the underground, increased the ebb and flow of potential audiences.

In 1835, John Gibson, a mast maker, decided to branch out and build a house of entertainment. By a stroke of good fortune, he choose a site, in the growing suburb of Shoreditch, that was destined to become one of the great crossroads of transportation. This was to make his little theatre one of the most accessible to the public of all the theatres in England.

On 1 July 1840, the Eastern Counties Railway (later the Great Eastern) pushed its five-foot broad gauge rails across costly brick viaducts, over the river Lea's marshes, between Bow and Stratford, through Romford and Brentwood, into the unfinished terminus in Shoreditch. This station was directly across the street from Gibson's "Royal" Standard Theatre, as he began to style it (figs. 1 through 5).

Destined for extensive redevelopment, the elevated site of this station is still extant. It was a major freight terminal during both World Wars, and received heavy bomb damage, especially during the "blitz." In the mid- nineteenth century this station was the principal eastern railway terminal for the city of London until 1865, when the present Liverpool Street Station, a few blocks to the southwest, was opened.

Fig. 3. The Great Eastern Railway Station in 1977, looking at the south east corner, that was just across the street from the Standard Theatre. *From A.S.J.*

From the Shoreditch station (later called the Bishopsgate Goods Depot when it became freight only), tens of thousands of potential theatregoers passed the facade of the Standard Theatre. Many passengers, whiling the hours between trains, must have welcomed the family entertainment available just across the street. Later horse-drawn street trams further added to the developing audience.

Before the arrival of the railroad this area was one of bedrooms, light manufacturing, and cottage industries. The most extensive of the latter were furniture making, boxes, colored glass beads for foreign trade, match and tobacco, and most of all, brick making. With the arrival of the waves of Jewish immigration, the clothing trades became preeminent.

Farm products flowed into the city of London through the rail terminus. The foreign goods from the London docks began their distribution to the north and east from here. It was to this dynamic suburb that several theatrical entrepreneurs came to try to pick what seemed a plum. The saga of the Standard is a major part of this development.

Fig. 4. The Great Eastern Railway Station in 1977. *From A.S.J.*

Fig. 5. The yard throat and signal tower. *From A.S.J.*

The Standard Theatre of Victorian England

1

THE ROYAL STANDARD THEATRE 1835

In the year 1835, despite the supposed monopoly of the three Royal Patent Houses, there were at least twenty places of entertainment that could be called theatres in the greater London area.[4] In the city center and Westminster, for theatrical purposes together considered the "West End," were the Adelphi (1806); Theatre Royal Drury Lane (1812); the Little Theatre Royal in the Haymarket (1821); the King's Theatre Haymarket (1818); the Lyceum (1834); the Olympic Pavilion (1806); the St. James's (1835); the Strand (1832); and the Royal Opera House Covent Garden (1809).

South of the River Thames were Astley's Ampitheatre (1831); the Royal Victoria (1818); and the Surrey (1809). North and west of the city center were the theatres eventually called the

Marylebone (1832); and the West London (1810). The latter was also known as the Queen's and the Fitzroy. The northern suburbs were served by the elderly Sadler's Wells (1765), in Finsbury. Down the Thames, in the far eastern docks area, was the East London (1834), and the Pavilion (1828). Nearer the tower of London was the Garrick (1831).

Due north of the Tower, but still in the "East End" were the Grecian (1832), the City of London (1835), and the Standard. These last three buildings were considered to be in an area known as Shoreditch, although only the Standard was in Shoreditch High Street (fig. 1). The Grecian was a little to the northwest in City Road, and the City of London was in Norton Folgate. This is a short jog in the area where the

---

4.   The dates given for the theatres is the date the building was built, that was standing in 1835, rather than the date of founding a theatre on the site.

Bishopsgate once stood. It forms the connection between Shoreditch High Street and Bishopsgate to the south.

Shoreditch High Street, named after King Edward IV's unfortunate mistress who was found dead there in the ditch in 1527, is the most venerable theatrical area in England. It was the site of the first two public playhouses of Elizabethan times, The Theater (1576), and the Curtain (1577). Later, after the great fire of 1666, the area around Curtain Road and Holywell Street be-

Fig. 6. The Royal Standard Theatre about 1835. *From the London Museum.*

came one of the dumps for the cleared debris. The resulting mound is to be seen to this day in the rise and fall of the grade in the streets. (See fig. 2 for the general area).

Virtually all the theatres listed above stood inside a circle three miles in radius from St. Paul's Cathedral steeple. A vast majority were within a mile and a half, and one could walk from one to its nearest neighbor in about fifteen minutes.

Easily accessible to the London docks, but consisting of inexpensive land because of its reputation as a dump, Shoreditch became a suburb of minorities, inhabited by the Jewish and Irish immigrants who poured into London in the mid-nineteenth century. The Jews fled from the vicious, and increasing pogroms of central Europe, to the open, and rising commercial society of England. The Irish fled the equally dangerous potato famine of the eighteen thirties, and forties.[5]

By 1835 the large population of Shoreditch made it an attractive area for investment. New public houses, saloons, and pleasure gardens appeared. John Gibson, a mast maker, had a small theatre, one-shop-front in width, constructed about the center of the west side of the High Street (figs.6 and 7). A playbill in the Guildhall Library Collection describes the opening of the "Royal Standard Theatre," as it was called. The appellation "Royal" could hardly have been

5.   Milicent Rose, *The East End of London* (London, 1951), pp. 198–213.

official since Gibson had no license, and there is no reason to believe any member of the Royal family had any connection with the enterprise.

Perhaps Gibson was merely anticipating his Middlesex magistrate's saloon or music license. In any case "Royal" it was, and continued to be for fifteen years, until the new larger building was constructed in 1850.

The playbill describes the opening scheduled for Monday, 12 October 1835:

> With entire new scenery, dresses decorations, and a talented company. The splendid drop scene and magnificent curtain painted by Mr. Marshall of the Theatre Royal Covent Garden, and the rest of the scenery by Mr. Willett of the Theater Royal Drury Lane, Mr. Moon, W. Remmington, and assistants. The machinery by Cove and Son, decorations by Mr. Blamire of the Theatres Royal, properties by Mr. Phillips of the Victoria Theatre, dresses by Mr. and Mrs. Gay of Sadler's Wells, leader of the band, Mr. T. Brown of the English Opera House.

According to the playbill, most of London's theatrical population was involved. The capacity of the "remodeled" theatre was stated to be two-thousand two hundred and twenty in 1845. But this number must have represented some expansion of the building and was based on the extreme crowding that occurred at the time of the Christmas pantomimes. The capacity was given as four hundred in newspaper articles written in 1866. This seems more realistic.

The playbill goes on to describe the new structure as having "commodious entrances, and a colonade capable of holding nearly as many persons as the theatre itself, being 100 feet in length."

The ground plan of the site indicates that what Gibson did was gut a shop that fronted on the High Street to make the long narrow lobby and part of the auditorium, while the stagehouse must have been constructed in the yard behind the row of shops that faced the street.

Illumination was by the exciting, newly introduced, gas method, and there was a handsome saloon. The purpose of the theatre was to: "offer amusements that could be in every respect moral and intellectual." The ceremonies and performances of the opening night were to be:

**An opening address and introduction
of the stock company
"God Save the King."**
Henry Grattan's Drama *Minerali,or,the Dying Gift*, and his original mythological extravaganzical musical burletta in one act, *Diana's Revenge*. The whole to conclude with the laughable farce, *A Slight Mistake*.

The author of this last play is not named, although it might have been C.C. Eames, whose play of this title is normally dated 1840.

The performers of the company for this auspicious occasion were:

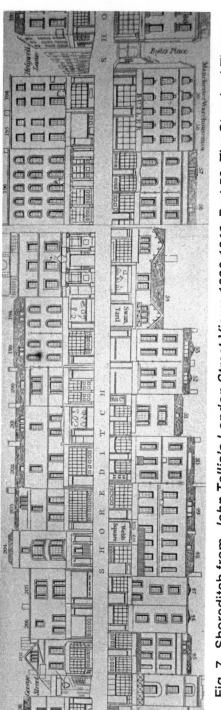

Fig. 7. Shoreditch from *John Tallis's London Street Views 1836-1840*, Part 59. The Standard Theatre is number 204. The Eastern Counties Railway Station of 1840 was built across the street. Because it is not shown, the map must date from about 1838. *From the Rose Lipman Library Hackney.*

J. Parry, producer and director,
late of the Victoria and Sadler's
Wells Theatre.
Montague from the York Theatre
H. Grattan from the Norwich
Theatre
Lawrence from Astley's
Harwood
Worrell from the Queen's
Wilton from the Queen's
Herbert from the Brighton
Payne from the Queen's
Chester
Pickering
Mrs. J. Parry of the Garrick
Theatre
Miss Byron of the Victoria
Miss Farrar
Mrs. Whorrell, Miss Barker
Mrs. Chester, Mrs.Weston
Mesdames Godenhaus,
Martin, Sharpe, and Shepherd.

Prices were doubled for the opening, but soon returned to the average for the smaller theatres of the time:

Boxes two shillings, pit one shilling, gallery sixpense; later reduced to one shilling for pit and sixpence for gallery, children under twelve half price.

John Parry, the theatre's first manager, was only twenty-five. In fact, the whole company was young and inexperienced despite the listed connections with other theatres.

Parry, born in 1810, was educated to become a merchant in shipping, and banking. At the age of nineteen he ran away and joined a stock company in Leeds. After six years of apprenticeship in the touring companies of the North, he came to London to debut at the Royal Victoria Theatre.[6] After a brief connection with the Standard in 1835 and 1836, he went on to become the stage manager at the Queen's. Pascoe described Parry's musical training, and comic or mimic abilities, although the details are at variance with a short newspaper biography published in 1847 (fig. 8).[7]

Gibson, despite the fact that as yet he had no license, did not seem troubled that he was opening with a play, with spoken dialogue, as well as the normal musical-style productions usually found at the outer theatres. He must have taken the attitude that he was opening a regular provincial theatre that could be licensed for all types of performances, because of the Acts of 1751 (25 George II) and (28 George II). These legal Acts provided for regulation of places of entertainment in London, Westminster, and twenty miles outside, and for the licensing by local magistrates.

Later evidence showed that Gibson did not get the license, but he continued to perform anyway. In fact, a notice for

6.   C. E. Pascoe, *Our Actors and Actresses, the Dramatic Life* (London, 1880), p. 410 ff.
7.   *The Theatrical Times*, no. 61 (Saturday, 3 July 1847).

Fig. 8 John Parry as Cromwell in *The Secret Witness*, from the *Theatrical Times*, no. 61, 3 July 1847. *From the Rose Lipman Library, Hackney.*

December of 1836 announced "Monday, George Lillo's *George Barnwell*, Tuesday and Friday, Rowe's *Jane Shore,* and Milman's *Fazio, the Italian Wife* for Wednesday and Saturday." These were to be followed each night by the Christmas Pantomime *The Bronze Horse; or, Harlequin and the Cloud King.*

The Middlesex Sessions Report of 19 October 1837, describes Gibson's further attempts to gain his license. He had asked for permission to have music, and dancing performed. The record stated that the license had been refused both of the previous Octobers (1835 and 1836) because: "The construction of the theatre was defective, and there was no certificate of architects to guarantee the safety of the edifice. Second, there was something irregular in the conduct of the party in the management of the theatre, and thirdly, there was a want of neighborhood to form an audience."

Fig. 9. W. Wood with his dog Bruin, in *The Dog of the Alps*, 2 August 1836. *From the Rose Lipman Library, Hackney.*

Fig. 10. W. Wood with his dog Bruin in *The Foulah Slave*, 18 July 1836, and *The Knights of the Cross*, 21 July 1836. *From the Rose Lipman Library, Hackney.*

By 1837 two of the objections had been removed. Twelve hundred local signatures were obtained on a petition requesting the granting of the license. A certificate of a surveyor had been obtained for the building. But that left the third problem: the illegal performances of 1835 and 1836.

The irregularity of the management had been that Gibson had operated without a license. He explained that as engagements had been made with performers in anticipation of a license in 1835, they "would have come down on him if he had not performed . . . the moment he had discharged his obligations towards those performers he closed his theatre."

A Mr. Phillips opposed the license on the grounds that there already was a licensed theatre within four hundred

Fig. 11. John Charles Freer (1802–1857), tinsel print. *From the London Museum.*

Fig. 12. The interior of the Standard Theatre about 1837, by Robert B. Schnebbelie. *From the Guildhall Library.*

had paid Gibson for the use of the building.

After further wrangling over whether the City of London or the Standard had been built first (the Standard was); and whether the proximity of two licensed theatres was of any moment, when there were "half a dozen theatres at the West-end, all within a-compass of four hundred yards"; and whether it was fair for one theatre operator (Mr. Cockerton) to try to suppress the other (Mr. Gibson) for purely monopolistic reasons (applause); the magistrates granted the license by a vote of thirteen for and twelve against (upon which there was further applause).

Earlier in the hearing, magistrate Sir J. S. Lillie had stated that: ". . . the court did not acknowledge theatrical establishments, and that they had only to give music licenses. He did not see therefore how anything about theatrical performances could come in, or how the objection founded, as it was on theatricals could hold good."

It is clear that Gibson operated, and continued to operate, by means of the loophole that existed because of the vagueness of the theatre acts of 1737, 1751, and 1755. Because his building was outside the walls of the medieval boundaries of the city, and in a suburb that harboured animosity toward the "swells" of western, and central London, and the theatre was small, and obscure, he had taken a chance. The Standard presented little competition to the great institutions of the city. Even so

yards of the Standard (the City of London), that Gibson had performed during two separate seasons without a license (in contempt of court), and even up to within ten days before the hearing.

A magistrate said he had talked to Gibson the night before the hearing and Gibson assured him that they had not performed for the last six months. Later testimony showed that what Gibson meant was public performance. There had been performances by amateurs, who had issued free tickets to their friends. On the other hand, they the closeness of the vote indicates he probably obtained his license because of political reasons rather than because of legal correctness.

His case was weak. He knowingly: had operated illegally without a license, and; claimed he had to operate because he had contracts with performers, that, of course, he had made at a time when he was merely hoping to get one. Apparently the magistrates, conveniently, did not discuss the point raised about the difference between theatre performance, and musical performance, and the type of license they were permitted to issue.

By authority of the new license, the performances at the Standard over the next eight years were intermittent, and of a mixed character. A letter in the *Hackney Express and Shoreditch Observer*, from an old Shoreditch inhabitant, said of these early days:

> . . . the first to seek patronage was 'little Grundy.' It was a little affair in every way. It had a little entrance, a little price for admission, a little house, and very little to see when you got in. He had a kind of variety entertainment that seemed to please . . .[8]

Included in the thirty-two different ᵣoductions that are known to have been produced in this first eight years are: melodrama, burletta, Shakespeare (with added songs), ballet, and typical plays (*Brutus*, *Jane Shore*, and *George Barnwell*). W. Wood, and his dog, Bruin, were very popular, beginning in

Fig. 13. Richard Nelson Lee (1807–1872). *From the Rose Lipman Library, Hackney.*

1836 (figs. 9 and 10). The principal performers and managers were Mr. and Mrs. John Parry. In 1836 Charles Freer (fig.11) as a guest star was seen in a number of serious dramas. Freer at this time was thought to be an important rising young talent. He had been in the stock company of the Pavilion theatre in 1828, and the Garrick in 1831. By 1835 he had moved into management; and eventually, in 1838 he assumed sole operation of the Garrick. Despite a good reputation and popularity, his career soon plunged.

8.   *Hackney Express and Shoreditch Observer*, (12 February 1898), p. 3.

38

At the Garrick the books didn't balance. Alcohol got the best of him. His wife wrote scandalous attacks on him for the newspapers. He replied in playbills. A tour to America collapsed because of his illness, and he only performed once. He tried to carry on; but by 1857 he was unemployable, and committed suicide. About 1840, John Grundy became manager for Gibson at the Standard. Playbills and newspaper advertisements for this period are rare. Money was dear and hand-printed posters stuck up on the theatre front may have been the normal way of

Fig. 14. The rebuilt Standard Theatre in 1845, with *The Eagle Rider of the Desert. From the Rose Lipman Library, Hackney.*

advising the audience of the program to be seen inside.

Illustrations of the building are equally difficult to find. One that may show the interior about this time is in the Guildhall Library. It is attributed to Robert B. Schnebbelie (1790–1849).[9] There are similarities between this water color (fig. 12), and a view dated 1845 (fig. 14). However the 1845 print depicts a renovation with an enlarged stage. The curved dome shown in the second view represents quite a variance between the two illustrations. This feature is particularly singled out in the article, and thus probably embodys a new feature.

The Licensing Act of 1843 (6–7 Victoria) repealed all previous Acts that controlled theatrical activities. As manager John Grundy received the new license for the Standard on 29 September 1843. For this 1843–44 season, little production information is available. Gibson was looking for some experts to take advantage of the expanded license, and make his investment pay. Grundy was out. His five seasons had not been profitable.

Something of the haphazard character of Grundy's management may be seen in John Coleman's description of the way he broke into show business:

Somehow or other I got to know that some one was wanted at the old Standard theatre in Shoreditch, a little place about the size of the Royalty [cap. 657]. Off I went, and tackled

Fig. 15. E. F. Saville(1811-1857) as Joe Hatchaway, in *Union Jack*, tinsel print. *From the London Museum.*

the manager, a little man named Grundy. At first he wouldn't listen to me, but when I explained that my views were accommodating, that I would do anything or everything, take anything or nothing (for the company were on shares), he relaxed and consented to my joining his small but efficient troupe. There were two or three excellent actors who afterwards became celebrities, and a beautiful being in the shape of the heroine, to whose blandishments I succumbed, and whose bond-slave I immediately became. Of course, she was twice my age; but what did that matter? Boys always fall in love with their grandmothers.

9.   Iain Mackintosh and Geoffrey Ashton, *The Georgian Playhouse* (Hayward Gallery, London, 1975), Plate 340.

Really and truly I found in this charming creature something like maternal solicitude.

I had pitched my tent at Camden Town, and had to walk from thence to Shoreditch and back twice a day. During the whole of my engagement I never received a shilling for my services. To be sure, I was to have a benefit, and as all my amateur acquaintances from Gough Street had promised to act and to take tickets, I might reasonably anticipate a fair house. My Dulcinea must have had a pretty good idea of the state of the land, for after a prolonged rehearsal of Joan of Arc (what a gorgeous creature she looked in her golden spangled armour!) she invited me to take tea. Her mother, a charming old lady, and her brother, a lad of my own age (afterwards a distinguished American manager), gave me a cordial welcome and delicious mutton chop, for the actor's tea in those days meant dinner as well. These dear, kind creatures took compassion on my loneliness and desolation, and from this time forth I was daily expected at tea-time.

At the theatre I was occasionally entrusted with parts which the more important members of the company declined to study. One effort in this direction brought my engagement to an abrupt and sensational termination. I had the temerity—or shall I say the folly?—to attempt, in an emergency and at a few hours' notice, Count Romaldi in The Tale of Mystery—a 'villain of the deepest dye,' who gives about two hundred music cues for a mysterious dumb man to pantomime to. This wretched count is bullied and insulted by everybody, and finally found out, and handed over to justice. There had been

a breakdown somewhere. The old birds fought shy of M. le Comte; but it needed little persuasion to induce me to make a fool of myself. I was righteously punished for my presumption, for I broke down ignominiously, was chaffed most unmercifully by the gods, and held up to ridicule by the actor who played the 'exempt.' This noble youth who afterwards became a distinguished man of letters, had to read a proclamation offering a reward for my apprehension. He availed himself of the occasion to describe me 'a young gentleman with straight hair and curly teeth, who had the additional advantage of being knock-kneed, bandy-legged, and generally imbecile!' Of course, the audience roared at the delicate irony of this description.

My insulter stalked into the green room. I was about to follow, when she muttered through her white teeth, 'Thrash him, John, thrash him within an inch of his life.' 'I will' I replied, and I did thrash him there and then; and I am bold to say I gave him a most beautiful beating. The cad had some occult influence with management, and the result was that I was dismissed there and then, and, worse still denied my benefit, because forsooth, I had broken the rules of the theatre.[10]

The next license holders, men with experience in theatre management, were to do better than Grundy. They were Richard Nelson Lee (1806–1872), and his partner, a stage struck tradesman, John Johnson (?–1864).

---

10. John Coleman, *Fifty Years of an Actor's Life* (London, 1904), pp.110–112.

Nelson Lee (as he was called) was one of the most enterprising theatrical entrepreneurs of the mid-century. His parents had intended him for a naval career. However, he became acquainted with the performers at the Victoria Theatre, and his infatuation with the stage began. Lee went through the difficult apprenticeship of a provincial actor.

Later he worked at Richardson's Booth at the fair. Eventually he joined the company at Elliston's Surrey Theatre. There he performed in the Christmas pantomimes. At this time he became one of the writers of pantos. By the time he was fifty-four (1860), he claimed to have composed 209 successful scripts (fig.13).

After Richardson died in 1837, Johnson and Lee joined forces in the management of the Booth. Following some success, they went into regular management, successively leasing the small Marylebone (1838–39), then the Pavilion (1840–44), the Standard (1845–48), and finally the City of London where they remained for the next twenty years.[11]

John Gibson leased the Standard to Johnson and Lee on the 20 January 1845. The lease lists the fittings as they were on this date:

Chandeliers; 10 pairs of flats; 32 wings; 17 borders including the proscenium; one roller, and act drop; three traps; a green curtain; seats; gas fittings; frames, shafts, drums,– one large shaft and two drums–under the roof over the stage; a large iron frame; six winches and iron handles.

Johnson and Lee began their first season with the Christmas panto, several melodramas, and a farce or two. But they had big plans afoot, as the

Fig. 16. Harvey Leech as "What is it?" from *The Wild Man of the Prairie*, 2 November 1846. *From the Rose Lipman Library, Hackney.*

---

11. *The Abstract and Brief Chronicles of the Time*, ed. Wilfred Wisgast, vol. 1, no. 18 (Saturday 28 April 1860).

Illustrated London News explained:

THE NEW STANDARD THEATRE

The East-enders have now their amphitheatre, or Cirque Olympique, for equestrian performances, which the proprietors of the New Standard Theatre had just provided for in a novel and ingenious manner.

This little temple of the drama was erected a few months since, on the site of twelve houses, adjoining "the Standard Theatre," by Mr. John Gibson, for the proprietors, Messers Johnson and Nelson Lee. It faces the Terminus of the Eastern Counties Railway, in Shoreditch. The interior is of the horseshoe form, and a domed roof, a construction peculiarly well adapted for the transmission of sound. The proscenium is 30 feet wide and 30 feet in height; the auditory has a circle of ten private, and fourteen public boxes which, with the pit and gallery, will accommodate 2200 persons. It is lit by a cut glass chandelier; the fronts of the boxes are coloured in two drabs, relieved with gold mouldings, pilasters, equestrian medallions, etc.

The equestrian performances were the holiday novelty of Monday last: they are not given in the area of the auditory, but in the place of the stage; for which purpose the flooring is, by ingenious machinery removed upon a kind of railway, the proscenium boxes are made to recede, and a ring is presented 39 feet in diameter, wherein Mr. Cooke and his Stud first exhibited on Whit Monday [of 1845]. Our illustration is a scene from an equestrian spectacle, also then produced, [on the stage, not in the ring] and entitled *The Conquest of Tartary; or The Eagle Rider of Circassia, and Her Monarch Steed of the Desert!* wherein Mrs. R. B. Taylor's performance is very striking.[12]

Fig. 17. N. T. "Bravo" Hicks (1811–1873) as Claude Duval, tinsel print. *From the London Museum.*

The stage floor moved into the wings on tracks, and the proscenium sides, with boxes, moved back to enlarge the sight lines for the circus ring. The illustration accompanying the article above shows not this, but rather a standard hippodrama with a chase-on-horseback sequence from one of the

12. *Illustrated London News*, (17 May 1845).

plays that was presented in the first half of the evening's entertainment. The scenes in the circus ring were after the interval. The availability of the horses led to a series of hippodramas (fig. 14).

In May of 1845 the newspapers announced "A circus and equestrian season for the summer." The old "summer" license granted to Foote at his Little Theatre in the Haymarket in 1767 was for the period from May 15th to September 15th. This established the pattern for the London theatres. The legitimate dramatic season began in mid-September and ran to mid-May of the next year. Many theatres closed for the summer. Others relied on foreign performers, circuses, light operas, and eventually the minstrel shows to produce revenue during the off season.

A number of variables affected this pattern. The date of Easter, bad weather, or small houses could cause earlier closings in the spring. The popularity of the Epsom races, or a political event could greatly increase or decrease the size of the potential audience. In 1845 the choice was circus, hippodrama, and the first of the minstrel shows. Productions announced included: *St. George, and the Dragon, England's Monarch, or the Wars of Cromwell, and the Royal Oak*, and *The Battle of Waterloo*. In August, The Ohio Ethiopian Serenaders was among the first acts to bring the new, evolving American form to London.

In the autumn E. F. Saville (1811–1857) was the premier actor for the melodrama season (fig. 15). One of the plays produced, influenced by the proximity of the railroad no doubt, was T. E. Wilks' "interlude," *The Eastern Counties Station, or a Rail-Road Adventure*. Similarly the 1845–1846 Christmas panto featured a moving railway locomotive in. (Fig. 46 shows another of these in the panto of 1854.)

W. D. Broadfoot, the famous equestrian, led the performers; and A. Cooke, clown and mimic, demonstrated a series of characters from Dickens' *Pickwick* (on horseback). In the ring, rope dancing, and animal acts were shown. The autumn season of 1845 had a guest star in the person of Henry Howard (1820–1853). His portrayals of Richard III, Shylock, and Hamlet were the first real attempts at serious legitimate drama at the Standard.

The season of 1846–47 continued this same pattern. The Ohio Minstrels, circus, hippodrama, in the summer followed by melodrama, Henry Howard in *The Fatal Dowry*, and *Virginius* by Sheridan Knowles, *Hamlet, Macbeth, Merchant of Venice*, and *Richard III,* in the autumn. The Christmas panto finished out the year. The most peculiar production of the season was in November when *The Wild Man of the Prairie, or What is It?* appeared. A three-foot, five-inch tall dwarf, called Signor Hervio Nano (actually Harvey Leech), had from time to time been displayed in public, dressed as an insect or monster. As an insect he slid down ropes, and climbed all over the interior architecture. As a monster he was exhibited in a cage roaring, devouring supposedly raw

Fig. 18. George Wilde (1805–1856), and Fanny Williams in their comic entertainment *Very Suspicious*, 4 December 1854. *From the Rose Lipman Library, Hackney.*

Fig. 19. The Playbill for the week of 14 February 1848, at the Standard Theatre. *From the Rose Lipman Library, Hackney.*

carcasses, and scaring the ladies. This melodrama was devised to use his peculiar talents. He dressed in a shaggy costume with enormous claws on his hands (fig. 16).[13]

Johnson and Lee operated in this pattern through the 1846–1847, and 1847–1848 seasons. The guest star of the autumn "legit" period was now N. T. Hicks (1811–1873). He was called "Bravo" Hicks because of his broad style, and popularity in melodramatic roles (fig. 17). The plays in his repertoire were *Othello, Macbeth,* and *Romeo and Juliet.*

More importantly, for Lee's December 21st benefit night, John Douglass, a young actor who was growing famous for his portrayal of nautical roles, was imported to perform Joe Hatchway in William Rogers' *Union Jack* (1843). Douglass had been the lessee of the Marylebone Theatre from 1842 to June of 1846. At that time he sold the rest of his seven-year lease because of the discouraging business there.

Nautical drama had long been a feature at Sadler's Wells Theatre. Gradually these plays, which featured an idealization of the British sailor, became a major part of the repertoire of the greater London theatres.

Douglass had been moving from one to the next in his specialty, and was at the peak of his popularity. It was at this point that he developed an interest in managing the Standard.

Johnson and Lee's final spring season at the Standard was in 1848. From the panto onward they produced melodramas; then, there was a two- week engagement of Henry Betty, Jr. He was the son of the notorious infant star Henry West Betty who had vanished from the theatrical scene in 1811.

The son appeared in *Macbeth, Hamlet, Othello, Richard III, Virginius,* and *Esmeralda.* This last item was based on the *Hunchback of Notre Dame,* and was by either C. Z. Barnett or Edward Fitzball (1834). Young Betty seems to have given acceptable performances. The critic in the *Era* for 26 March 1848, gave him a thoughtful and positive review. However, Betty was never able to build a theatrical career of importance. Just before the this engagement, Lee purchased the old crimson velvet drapes from the Royal Italian Opera House in the Haymarket. This spruced up the auditorium and boxes.

The next novelty was the appearance, for the first time at the Standard, of the Irish husband and wife comedy team, of George Wilde (1805–1856), and Fanny Williams (fig. 18). But, despite all the activity, Johnson and Lee gave up their lease at the end of May, and by August had taken over the City of London, just a few blocks south. Perhaps the Standard was too small a house, or too poorly constructed for their plans. The City of London was a little closer to the city center; it was

---

13.   Unpublished scrapbook, *Pleasure Gardens and Taverns*, Guildhall Library.

somewhat larger,[14] and they could buy the property. What ever the reason, they were gone, and the Standard stood empty until September 1848.

Johnson and Lee had done something for the reputation of the house. In October of 1847, the critic of the *Era* had written of the Standard: ". . . this out of the way but not obscure place of entertainment . . . is as popular in the East as our greater houses in the West, and deservedly so. A more elegant little temple of its kind cannot be mentioned."[15]

In summary they had just begun to produce a few nights of higher drama, about ten per season. The only new script produced was the anonymous *The Lancashire Witches, or the Lass of Dewsbury Hill* (LC. 28/2/47). This was probably an adaptation of Shadwell's 1681 play. Some of the melodramas were recently written, but licensed for other houses first. The hippodramas were pageants that usually didn't require licenses. The circus acts soloists, comedians, and minstrels were not considered legal theatre. Therefore, before 1849, except for the novel machinery that converted the stage to a circus ring, there was little to distinguish the Standard from a multitude of other theatres (fig. 19).

At least it had not gained an evil reputation for disreputable drama, or criminal-infested audiences. A few of the plays presented significant moral subjects, such as: national pride, anti-slavery, anti-gambling, and pro-temperance.

Of the performers, Howard, Saville, Hicks, and Betty presented Shakespeare; G. Hodson, and T. Lee, the Irish comedians, provided scenes from the "old sod" for the homesick; *The Merchant of Venice* was presented as a tragedy, providing the Jewish members of the audience with a serious dramatic character for their pleasure.

An audience was being created and the building newly refurbished. The new lessee would have something with which to work.

---

14. John Anderson stated in his biography that in 1852 the City of London held between two and three thousand.
15. The *Era*, (17 October 1847).

2

JOHN DOUGLASS BECOMES PROPRIETOR

The story of the rise in the fortunes of the Standard Theatre is the story of John Douglass (fig. 20). He was born 17 March 1814, into a huge family of twenty-one brothers and sisters. There were few advantages there. His Uncle William was the gas-lighting engineer at the Theatre Royal, Covent Garden. Because of this, young John was able to get a position as one of the Christmas pantomime children in 1825. The pay for this humble role was eighteen pence per night. Farley, the manager of the pantos, chose John to be his principal imp in a new production being planned because of the serious attention and energy he displayed. This led to a humorous series of events that E. L. Blanchard recounted in later years:

Oberon—the name at once conjures up a vision of fairyland and fills the air with echoes of Weber's delicious melodies—still has an attractive look in a playbill. As Leigh Hunt could never see a flower without recalling all

that poets had thought concerning it, so the monarch of that Elfin-Kingdom can hardly be spoken of by an imaginative playgoer without a rush of memories accompanying the source. As one who had the good fortune to be present at Covent Garden Theatre on the night when the opera was first produced and who can perfectly well remember the impressive face and figure of the great composer who conducted on that occasion, I find *Oberon and* Weber are always inseparably associated. It is impossible to write the one name without the other coming into my mind: and then amidst dreamy recollections of delightful music, I hear the voices of Braham, Miss Paton, and Madame Vestris, and see before me a dark cavern through which the substantial spirits of the storm came trooping forth in hundreds, whilst the numbers appeared to be interminably multiplied by the fitful illumination of a crowd of fiends painted in transparency at the back. And then came the beautiful scene of the calm, where the troubled waters were gradually lulled into repose, and on the transparent surface of the waves came floating a couple of majestic swans, who curved their necks and changed their positions with a wonderful completeness of mechanical contrivance. On the fourth night I saw the opera again, but the conductor was absent, and a whisper went sadly around the house that Weber was dying. Unhappily for the world of art the intelligence thus conveyed was mournfully verified, and the audience would have gone gloomily away that night but for one ludicrous incident, that for a time produced as loud a shout of laughter as I ever remember to have heard within the walls of a theatre. One of the imps of the storm, dancing about with a lycopodium torch, suffered his zeal to outrun his discretion. Full of the excitement of the moment, and absorbed in the importance of the pantomime character he had to enact, and which I think was the first he ever played, the juvenile demon exceeded his instructions and danced madly about the stage by himself long after the rest of his demoniacal brethren had disappeared. Until the enthusiastic little storm-spirit had exhausted his energies, it was manifestly impossible for the music or scene to change, and the waters had to keep on rolling to the unusual accompaniment of stormy voices, which began to be audible even above the sonorous notes of the bassoons in the band. It was in vain the members of the orchestra tried to engage the attention of the excitable little imp. Perhaps his mask rendered him insensible to the wild gesticulations of the violin players in front, who alternately directed their bows away from their instruments in the direction of the wings, and gave, by nods and becks

and anything but wreathed smiles, significant hints that his continued presence on the stage was not desirable. Then amidst this prolonged storm a strange phenomenon appeared. Long arms with clenched fists began to emerge from the side-entrances, and threatened terribly the unruly urchin lately belonging to the land of storm-spirits, and who now was raising the wind entirely on his own account. In the midst of his gambols the small fiend became conscious of something wrong, and that he was in more personal danger than Sir Huon had been on his wave-tossed vessel. Eagerly he looked from side to side to see where he could break through this cordon of the enemy. Not a chance of escape presented itself. To his terrified gaze the arms and fists seemed multiplied in all directions, and pointed toes, suggestive of summary chastisement, were ominously wherever he turned. There was only one refuge, and of that he availed himself. Clearing the footlights at a bound, he jumped into the orchestra and vanished beneath the stage, to be seen and heard no more during that evening. As the mask effectually concealed his features, there was a difficulty in discovering the exact boy who was the offender on the occasion: but I am enabled to state, for the gratification of the curious, that the zealous little pantomimist grew up to be an excellent actor, and most enterprising manager, and that he now bears the respected name of Mr. John Douglass, lessee of the Standard Theatre.[16]

William Douglass, the uncle, was killed in the gas explosion at Covent

---

16. The *Era*, (8 February 1874).

Fig. 20. John Douglass (1814–1874), as Ben the Boatswain, and looking like Popeye, tinsel print. *From the London Museum.*

Garden Theatre, 18 November 1828. But young John had made enough contacts to continue his apprenticeship in the company. By 1833, when he was nineteen, he had something of a reputation as a performer. However, he had already realized that few actors achieved the artistic satisfaction, property, security, or social status accorded the administrators of the theatres. Therefore he resolved to go into theatre management. His first attempts were in truly minor enterprises. They were more like saloons that had entertainments bordering on theatrical production. The first was a small theatre in Gravesend; then in London, the City Theatre, Milton Street; the Grange Street Theatre; the Clarence (a cabinet) at King's Cross; the Yorkshire Stingo (the Marylebone Baths) in the New Road; the East London, Whitechapel Road in Stepney (called the Effingham Saloon by 1834); the Queen's, Windmill Street (called the Argyle Rooms) in the Haymarket; and finally a real theatre, the Marylebone in Church Street, where he came to be by 1838.

The new licensing act gave John Douglass the first hope of becoming a licensee himself. He took over the Marylebone in September of 1843 where he continued until 8 September 1847. By the age of twenty-nine he had amassed enough capital to attempt the dangerous speculation of operating a licensed house. The story of this period is documented in Malcolm Morley's monograph on this theatre.[17]

The actors Douglass hired for his enterprise were a combination of established favorites at the suburban theatres and young novices. Charles Freer was the leading man. Tom Lee, the tubby and short purveyor of Irish characters, was for comedy. J. B. Johnstone was pantaloon, playwright and supporting actor all-in-one. Emily Butler was the heroine.

The repertoire of this company was a mixture of musical entertainments, nautical plays, melodramas, and, pantos. Shakespeare was occasionally given. Freer played Macbeth, and E. W. Elton Richard III. Striking-looking Charles Dillon joined the company in the spring to play the melodramatic leads. W. Coney, and T. Blanchard, the dogmen, brought their canine heroes each season for some of their special plays.

Morley tells the story from this period of the singer Joseph Cave. Cave saw an American named Sweeney play a secret stringed instrument. Cave obtained the secret from a prop man. Douglass heard Cave play, and brought him to his audience on 5 June 1843. This was when the banjo was introduced to the British public.

The Marylebone season of 1843–1844 was sprinkled with novelties. Barnum brought General Tom Thumb, the midget, in the spring; a red indian band, a cataract of real water, and

17.   Malcolm Morley, *The Old Marylebone Theatre* (St. Marylebone Society Publications, no.2, 1960), pp. 15–23.

Madame Wharton's living statues of whitened humans, and horses were also featured. The actors of the company were Dillon, and his wife; Tom Lee, and his exuberant wife Kate Martin, Clara Conquest, and Mrs. W. West. Douglass played his sailor roles, and his wife was in the company. One unusual actor in the group was Edward Edwards, who is chiefly remembered for his portrayal of vampires.

The 1844–1845 and 1845–1846 seasons were similar. Douglass brought several new members to the company, who were later to become regulars at the Standard. They were John Neville, the stage manager, Henry Hughes, Joseph Rayner, and Mr. Lickfold. The Douglass family ghost story comes from this theatre in 1845. Picture the interior of the Marylebone illuminated solely by a flickering T–shaped gas night light screwed into the footlights:

At the time mentioned, [John Douglass] was fulfilling an engagement at the Britannia saloon, at the other end of the town, and his nightly custom was to see the curtain up at his own theatre, and to drive as quickly as possible in 'a curricle' to the east. After having delighted the gods of Hoxton as a nautical hero, with three or four terrific broadsword combats against dreadful odds, after having slaughtered pirates by the score, knocked down a dozen bailiffs with a single quid of tobacco, the actor-manager would return to his own establishment to settle up the nightly accounts, arriving, as a rule, before the curtain fell.

On the evening on which the events took place which I am about to relate, the manager was far beyond his time, and when he did arrive, he was by no means in an amiable temper.

Two days earlier the groom Jones (who had been over five years in his employ), whilst detaching the horses from the vehicle, received a kick, which, although not apparently dangerous, yet necessitated the sufferer's removal to the hospital.

Jones was what is called a handy man; careful of his horses, a good coachman, sober, civil, and obliging, and was only too delighted, when the opportunity offered, to act as dresser to his master. As he was clean and active, and thoroughly understood the celerity required in the necessary 'protean changes,' small wonder he soon became a great favourite with his employer, who sincerely regretted the accident, and had on the morning now referred to, called early at the hospital, seen the patient, and been assured by the house surgeon he was progressing satisfactorily.

In the meantime another coachman had to be found, who on this particular evening, having whilst waiting outside, taken more than was good for him, finished up by disabling the curricle, and so compelling the manager to take a cab to return to the Marylebone, as it was, figuratively speaking, raining cats and dogs at the time. It was not surprising, therefore, that his temper was a little ruffled, and that several obnoxious expressions were interspersed with prayers for Jones's speedy convalescence.

When the manager arrived it was past midnight, and the stage and front of the house presented the usual gloomy, indescribably desolate appearance, so well understood by all acquainted with things theatrical. Dimly lighted by the familiar Tee-light in front of the stage, the auditorium beyond looked like a huge black mass, wherein it was impossible (until the eyes became accustomed to the gloom) to distinguish the outlines of the several tiers. The creaking of the cordage, as the hempen ropes adjusted themselves to the rapidly decreasing temperature of the flies, the wind rushing thro' the half-opened windows on the stage, the steady patter of the rain against the glass outside, combined with the dreariness and weirdness of the deserted theatre within, were enough to impress even the strongest nerves with superstitious awe. Close to the before mentioned Tee-light was a small table, set ready for the stage-manager's use at the rehearsal in the morning. Against the table stood the housekeeper, Mr. White, a stoutish built man between 45 and 50 years of age, who, shading his eyes with his hand, was endeavoring apparently to penetrate the black veil that hung pall-like over the interior. Near to him was his wife, the direction of her eyes and her anxious manner conveying the impression that the same mysterious object occupied the attention of the woman and her husband.

In order that the reader may fully comprehend the details of this narrative, it will be as well here to give a brief description of those portions of the premises more immediately concerned. The reader, then, is supposed to be upon the stage facing the audience. On the left hand or prompt side of the stage was a small door marked 'Private,' and mostly used by the manager or his representative to pass to and from the front of the house. On the same side, but in the audience portion of the theatre, was a wooden staircase leading from the pit to the gallery level, whence a small passage entered the domains of the Marylebone gods. The door covering the main outlet from the gallery could be seen on the right-hand side: beyond that the way out ran down a long passage, thro' a green-baized door, and on to the main staircase direct to the street. The lower or outer end of this staircase was protected from trespassers by a heavy iron gate, which shut closely into the opening, and was always kept locked except during performance.

'Hulloa, hulloa, White! What's the matter?' said Douglass, when he reached the table under the Tee-light. 'What are you looking at, eh?' 'Oh, Governor,' meekly responded the female, turning to her employer. 'Just look up in the gallery. There's a man there and he won't move. We've called to him and he takes no notice.' 'Haven't you been round, White?' said Douglass, interrupting the housekeeper's wife. 'Yes, sir, an hour ago,' was the rejoinder. 'Then how came you to overlook him? He must have fallen asleep during the performance,' continued the manager--adding in an undertone, 'Tho' I can't for the life of me understand how any man could sleep thro' Hicks's Pizarro, especially if N.T. was in good voice.'

Perhaps this is a mistake for either Dillon or Freer both of whom had very strong voices, and were in the company at this time.

'I've been twice after him,' said the housekeeper angrily, 'and he hides away, tho' it's a funny thing where he gets to, but he hasn't moved now for a quarter of an hour.' White's explanation was here cut short by a terrific clap of thunder, which seemed to shake the building to its foundations. Hardly had the echoes died away before Douglass was startled by a cry from the female. 'There, sir! there, sir!' shrieked the woman, pointing a long bony finger towards the centre of the gallery. 'He's moving, sir! Look, sir! He's taken off his hat to you.' 'He knows you,' chimed in the housekeeper. 'And I'll sware he wasn't in the gallery when I went round first, as I had my lantern, and the chandelier was well up, whilst the officers were putting the cloths on the seats.'

Douglass immediately bent forward over the footlights, so as to be in front of the gas jets, and distinctly saw a stranger leaning on the front rails of the gallery, quite undisturbed by the trouble he was causing and heedless of the manager's scrutiny. 'Oh, he won't move won't he?' said Douglass. 'Now then, you sir, whoever you are! What business have you there? Go out directly!' The manager shouted the last words, and his voice seemed to come back to him with a strange, indefinable echo– a wail of distress, a stifled cry, as from a sorely stricken soul.

In after years, whenever the manager recalled the events of that night, the peculiar sepulchral echo was looked upon as a warning–a message from an unknown land– tho's what it was and whence it came must be left to scientists to discover. I but relate the absolute facts, leaving the explanation of the phenomena to abler heads and pens.

'He'll be obliged to come down this way,' said White, pointing to the little wooden staircase. 'I locked up the front when I turned off the gas in the passage.' 'Do you mean to move?' shouted the manager again, thoroughly roused, 'or do you want me to give you in charge?' Still no word from the intruder, but he drew himself up to his full height, and his arm was raised in a menacing way. This was quite enough for Douglass, so, pulling off his overcoat and handing it (with his hand-bag) to the housekeeper, he muttered, 'We'll soon see about this,' and quickly made towards the little private door. It was locked! 'Never mind,' he said. 'I can get across the orchestra.' Suiting the action to the word, he sprang from the stage to the private box and dropped from the box into the pit (there were no orchestra stalls in those days). 'Oh, Governor, take the keys,' said White from the stage, at the same moment throwing the bunch. The sound of the falling keys on the pit floor was accompanied by a vivid flash of lightning, and rapidly followed by a tremendous peal of thunder, for the storm was now at its height. The flash illuminated the pit under the tiers sufficiently to enable the manager to see his way to the foot of the stairs, whilst the man White and his wife by the same brilliant agency discovered the mysterious stranger preparing either to resist capture or make good his escape.

The staircase by which the manager sought to reach the gallery was what is generally known as a transfer staircase, i.e. one not used as a main entrance or exit, but simply to enable the 'overflow' of the gods for a small extra fee to transfer to the pit without going out at the front of the theatre, and in again at the regular pit entrance. The staircase was not absolutely dark, and as the light from the Tee-piece on the stage assisted the manager's ascent, he soon gained the gallery level. To unlock the door leading from the staircase across the passage was but a moment's work. He was now on a level with the intruder he was in search of, who had boldly turned, and faced him. It was, however, but a momentary resolve, as the next instant saw him in full retreat to the door opposite to that by which his pursuer had entered the gallery. 'I have you now,' said the manager as he saw the stranger close to the door on the right hand leading to the main staircase. 'That door is locked if White has done his duty.' So saying, he pressed forward with rapid strides, speedily gaining on the fugitive. A few feet only separated them when the astonished manager saw the man unfasten the door, and disappear. 'The devil!' muttered Douglass between his teeth. 'You're no stranger. Keys for my doors as well. I'm determined now to know who you are.' Another step brought him to the door, which stood ajar, and there in front of him stood the object of his chase nearing the green-baize-covered door at the end of the passage. Reckless as to results, the manager dashed after the retreating figure, who, with both arms extended, seemed to invite the attack. Gathering all his strength for the fray, and with an exclamation of rage, Douglass threw himself upon the stranger, intending to grapple him by the throat, but his fingers closed on space, the materialized form became air, and the would-be assailant fell heavily to the ground, the impetus of his onward movement having been suddenly arrested by forcible collision with the strongly secured door in front of him.

But the stranger? Where was he? The solution of this problem occupied Douglass's mind as he retraced his steps until once more found himself by the prompter's table on the stage.

'Ah, he's gone out, sir! I wonder who he is.' asked the housekeeper, addressing the astonished lessee; but observing the latter's changed expression, he added, 'You're not ill, sir? Did he strike you, sir? 'No, no!' said his employer pettishly. 'What do you mean by saying he has gone out? Have you seen anyone since I left you?' White's reply fairly staggered the manager. 'Yes, yes' he said eagerly. 'The man you followed crossed the stage just after you went through the gallery door, and walked leisurely thro' the hall and into the street. I tried to stop him, but I couldn't. And,' added the housekeeper reflectively, 'how he got over the front gate I don't know."

The next morning early a messenger from the hospital arrived at the manager's residence, bringing the news that Jones, the groom had died, a little past midnight; in his last moments expressing an earnest desire to see his master, having a secret of great importance to disclose to him.

I have narrated only the facts as they were on many occasions told me by my father, and confirmed by the housekeeper and his wife, who were alive and well a few years ago. Cynics say a disordered brain conjures up ghostly visitations, and thoughts running on a particular subject sometimes invest that subject with the appearance of a material form. But here we have the wonderful fact that three distinct brains conjured up the same phantom at the same time and place. Three pairs of eyes saw that airless essence materialized in human shape—not in the darkness of the night to one nervous victim did this thing only appear, but (with a moderate amount of gas illuminant about) to three independent observers. If it was neither phantom, ghost, nor spirit, the eye-witnesses declare it could not have been of this world, for no human being could have passed the iron gates at the gallery entrance on one side of the theatre, and yet have disappeared at the stage door on the other side at the same moment.[18]

Putting aside the interesting story itself, this account, with its description of the auditorium, and passages, when compared with the early prints of various suburban theatres, gives a glimpse of rarely mentioned sections of the theatres from the early gas-lighting era. It also presents the sounds and sights that can, at least slightly, help us recover something of the sensual experiences a person would have while in a theatre of the time.

To return to our protagonist, John Douglass, his reputation as a performer was high. His skills indicate what was required of the mid-nineteenth century performer. He was an excellent dancer of country dances, jigs, and sailorly steps.

He was a fine acrobat and proficient broad-swordsman. And he had developed his skill in several stock character types, particularly the stage sailor. His pictures indicate that in this role he looks the prototype for Popeye.[19]

In 1924, Albert Douglass expanded this description from his childhood memories:

He was a kindly, open-hearted man, devoid of unnecessary pride, very sensitive, and never known to turn a deaf ear to the cause of charity.

Much controversy raged the best exponent of this typical character [the stage sailor]— many voted for T.P. Cooke, whilst others loudly acclaimed John Douglass as the better of the two; H. Rignold (father of George and William) was also in the running for the nautical stakes. Without prejudice I have read many criticisms, and by carefully weighing up the evidence have arrived at the conclusion that whilst T.P. Cooke gave an impersonation of the ideal sailor similar to Chevalier's portrayal of the coster—John Douglass was more true to nature. Cooke's view of the seafaring class was a poetical one, but Douglass depicted the sailor as he found him, with his sea habits, his 'bacca box, and rollicking manner complete.

From The *Era* of December 13th, 1857, I take the following extract: 'Since the days of the elder Wallack (not James, but his father), and the famous Miller, the stage has not possessed so glorious a representative of the rough, and ready tar, the ideal heart of oak, as John Douglass. In spectacular display, and scenery his stage stands on a level with the best appointed in London.'

The Times of 27 August 1858 [when John was playing at Drury Lane] throws an interesting light on the subject.

John Douglass as Ben The Boatswain, with heart beating like the ocean—upsets all that comes before him—overcoming all opposition. None is a match for Ben. His hornpipe

18.   John Thomas Douglass, *The Era Almanac* (London, 1893), pp. 76–79.
19.   The *Era*, (8 February 1874).

is literally entrancing. The audience on Monday felt it to be something unequaled. The applauded to the echo. The enthusiasm was extreme–it was as it were, a maddening delight.[20]

The *Era* copied the remarks printed in *The Times* and added:

Ask Mr. T. P. Cooke (who by-the-bye was in a private box until the finish); of Mr. Douglass's claims as a stage sailor, and you will find him acknowledge the Shoreditch manager as his superior. 'Douglass,' says he, 'is at the top of the ladder.' In their respective ways these two great nautical artists are equal. The sailor of John Douglass is of a rougher order, with a big sea-heart in his bosom—beating like the ocean—as deep, as turbulent, as grand. His first burst upon the stage as Ben is astounding. He upsets all that comes before him—overturns all opposition. None is a match for Ben. His hornepipe commencing the second act is literally entrancing. The audience applauded to the echo for the wearied performer, had indeed to repeat it. Then again his fight—wild prolonged ingious, energetic and intricate, whosoever would enjoy a thorough kindling up of the minimal spirits, let him go and witness John Douglass in Ben the Boatswain.[21]

Albert Douglass, a nephew born in 1862, grew up in the Standard Theatre. His childhood memories of his uncle John come from the period between 1867 and 1874, when the Standard was at its height.

My own recollections of John Sr., are somewhat dim for I was only a tiny toddler running about the theatre, although I well remember visiting, him and his bed-ridden wife at Castle Villa Dalston. When they first resided there, dear old Joe Cave [the banjo player] was on the staff—and 'polished up the handle of the big front door.'

John was exceedingly kind. Whenever he saw me, there was always a kindly pat on the head, and a small silver coin to buy sweets—so naturally our meetings were frequent. I stage managed that.[22]

This was a glimpse of the man upon which the future of the Standard Theatre would depend.

Gibson, the owner of the property, must have begun to tire of his investment. The up-and-down financial situation, the costs of the 1845 and 1848 renovations, and the departure of Johnson and Lee, all contributed to his desire to find a new lessee. John Douglass came along at just the right time to capitalize on a number of positive indications.

The reputation of the house was a good one, industrialization accompanied by population growth, cheap labor, the railroad, and the wealth of the empire had begun to stimulate the economy. So much was this the case that in 1848 Prince Albert suggested

20. Albert Douglass, *Memories of Mummers and the Old Standard Theatre* (London, 1924), pp. 11–13.
21. The *Era*, (28 September 1858).
22. Douglass, *Memories of Mummers*, p. 18.

Fig. 21. The Central Court of the Crystal Palace at the Great Exposition of 1851.
From A.S.J.

that a great exposition be undertaken. Originally planned for the summer of 1850, The Great Exhibition of the Industry of All Nations was to bring together the arts, crafts, products and, ideas of the British Empire, and its friends, for educational, moral, and economic reasons. Chaos in the planning delayed the opening until the next year (figs. 21 and 22). How aware

Gibson, or Douglass might have been, of the potential benefit this world fair could have for the Standard is unclear. In any case John Douglass became the licensee on the 29th of September, 1848. By October 22nd of the next year, Gibson offered the building for sale.

Douglass took his profit from the 1848–1849 season, his savings, and his relative's savings, as loans, and

Fig. 22 . The Central Court of the Crystal Palace at the Great Exposition of 1851. *From A.S.J.*

purchased the property. Perhaps the eventual sale had been part of the agreement with Gibson when he took the license. The *Era* announced the completion of the sale on 6 January 1850. In his first two years in the theatre, Douglass produced a series of nautical dramas, with himself as the protagonist. The normal fare of melodramas, pantos, and guest performers filled out the program. An American named De Bar was reviewed as "hearty, and physical," in his production of Anna Cora Mowatt's *Fashion* (which was called *Life in New York* for this 1848 performance). An unusual presentation of the same season was Byron's seldom performed *Manfred*,

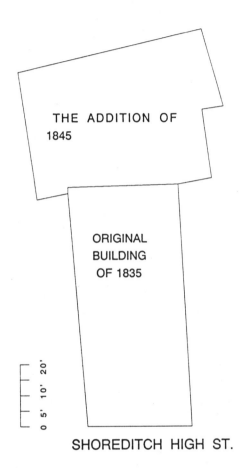

THE ADDITION OF 1845

ORIGINAL
BUILDING
OF 1835

20'

10'

5'

0

SHOREDITCH HIGH ST.

Fig. 23. The Ground plan for the Standard theatre in 1835, and for the renovation of 1845. *From A.S.J.*

starring Henry Denvil. In the spring of 1849, Freer performed Hamlet, and Shylock, while "Bravo" Hicks presented his popular melodramatic characters in a six week run.

In January of 1849, a curtain-raiser by the minor dramatist, T. P. Taylor(18??–18??) called *The Waits* was appended to the Christmas pantomime. This was a "two handkerchief drama," in which the pitiful orphan "Little" Joe turns out to be the heir to vast estates. This short play was to become a fixture of the Christmas season at the Standard the way dramatizations of Dickens's *Christmas Carol* have in the twentieth century. In May the Jewish actor David Stolberg pleased the audience in a production of *Sarah: The Jewess*. The heroine was played by Mrs. Robert Honner. She was to become a leading performer of the Standard company, and a great favorite with the audiences.

The year 1849 was not a comfortable year for East-Enders. There was a cholera epidemic, and so many died that they had to be buried in the old dumping ground of 1666 that had come to be called Holywell Mount. The Standard was closed for the summer during the worst of the cholera. Re-opening in September, the repertoire once again combined nautical plays, melodrama, Denvil as Manfred and Hamlet, and the panto. After Christmas, dog dramas, and T. E. Lyon as Macbeth, and Pizarro, were featured. However the big success was a new play by Tom Taylor (1817–1880) based on *The Vicar of Wakefield*. It ran for the considerable length of three weeks, then on and off for the rest of the spring.

This was the first of the long runs that were to become a standard technique of operation in many theatres in the mid-century. The last two productions of the spring of 1850 were *Richard III*, and *William Tell* before Douglass closed his small theatre building for the last time on June 11th.

In Household Words, 3 April 1850, Charles Dickens described the last days of this house:

> ...huge ham sandwiches, piled on trays like deals in a timber yard, were handed about for sale to the hungry; and there was no stint of oranges, cakes, brandy-balls, or similar refreshments.

Dickens continued the description, distressed by girls who he described as, "grown into bold women before they had ceased to be children."

But the presence of women and children in the audience indicated the civilized nature of the theatre. Douglass had solid foundations upon which to build: reputation, population, easy transportation, and above all the comming Great Exposition looked to be a crowd-bringer. This led to his daring decision to tear down his theatre, greatly reconstructed only five years previously, and take a chance on building a house of huge size to accommodate the fairgoers.

Fig. 24. Redington's New Drop Scene of the Standard Theatre, a toy theatre version of the act drop, about 1854. *From the London Museum.*

Fig. 25. James R. Anderson and Charlotte Vandenhoff in *Ingomar the Barbarian*, Drury Lane, 1851. This play is Maria Lovell's translation of Fredrich Halm's *Der Sohn der Wildnis's*, Wien, 1843. *From A.S.J.*

3

THE FOUNDATIONS 1850-1853

The Standard was about to become the theatre with the highest capacity auditorium in Britain. During the summer of 1850 the old stage, with its circus ring, was torn down. The original 1835 auditorium was gutted, leaving only the two-floor high shell. The ground floor of this structure, that fronted on Shoreditch High Street, was converted into lobby, service rooms, box offices, saloons, coat rooms, and passages. The upper level became a scene painting room, at least at first. In later years this area became the wardrobe, and costume shop; still later, it was converted to a meeting hall, called Bishopsgate Hall (cap. 800); then a rollerskating rink; during that fad; and finally in the twentieth century a billiard parlor (fig. 23).

To the rear in the large yard, more or less crossing the T of the lobby structure, an entirely new auditorium with an estimated capacity of four thousand was constructed. This figure was raised to five thousand plus when the theatre was actually opened. By September of 1850 the Standard had two thousand seats more than the Theatre Royal Drury Lane, or The Royal Opera House Covent Garden (fig. 41). The toy theatre printer, Redington, produced an act-drop plate of the Standard's curtain between 1850 and 1876. It is likely the design represents the drop for the new building of 1850–1854, because of its style (fig. 24).

The season of 1850–1851 was notable for many matters. William Charles Macready (1793–1873) took his farewell to the stage in February. Maria Lacy Lovell's adaptation of *Ingomar the Barbarian* was produced at Drury Lane in June (fig. 25).[24] This play was to prove one of the three or four

---

24. Baron Eligius Franz Joseph Von Muench-Bellinghausen (Friedrich Halm to his friends) wrote the original play *Der Sohn Der Wildniss* that was produced in Wien in 1843.

enduring serious dramas of the century. Also in February, James Anderson rushed into performance *Azael the Prodigal*, one of Edward Fitzball's commissioned pieces. This terrific spectacle was by Scribe, with music by Auber. It had been the success of Paris in 1850. Fitzball, never one to sit still, wrote two other versions of the same, and they opened at the Queen's March 11th, and Astley's November 3rd. At Drury Lane, Anderson wrote his own role of Azael, and John Vandenhoff wrote his part of Reuben. This may explain the differences between the three versions.[25]

An editorial explains much of this theatrical activity:

> The extraordinary success of all the theatres since Christmas [1850] has come now to be esteemed a fact of some moment. It speaks, at any rate, of the prosperity of the people at the present time, and perhaps indicates the re-production of dramatic taste among all classes. No doubt the example of Her Majesty and the Windsor theatricals have much to do with the revival of a love for stage performance. . . . Another reason is the present year is already looked upon as a kind of holiday year, and the May Exhibition has even in its bond of promise exercised a strong influence on the imagination of the masses.[26]

Fig. 26. The front entrance to the Standard Theatre in 1851. *From the Rose Lipman Library, Hackney.*

Booth, in his book on melodrama, sheds light on the nature of the

---

25.   The *Illustrated London News*, (1 March 1851).
26.   The *Illustrated London News*, (1 February 1851). In 1848 Queen Victoria had appointed Charles Kean to supervise theatricals at Windsor Palace. She also took a bold step, in support of the theatre in general, when she engaged a special box at his Princess's Theatre.

Fig. 27. The Christmas Pantomime *Hoddy Toddy All Head and No Body; or, Harlequin and the Fairy of the Magic Pippin*, by John Douglass, December 1851. *From the Guildhall Library.*

audience at this time which explains the tenor of this article.

It must be remembered that the period 1800–1870 was one of genuinely popular theatre. . . . The people occupied pit and gallery at the Patent Theatre, and more sophisticated audiences did not return to the theatre until about the 1860's, and 1870's.[27]

Douglass's new house was open, and taking advantage of the excitement being generated by the yet-to-open exposition. One of the many guide books printed for the crowds illustrated the entrance facade of the Standard, and described the inside.

Not far from the Britannia—in Shoreditch, exactly opposite the offices of the Eastern County Railway is the National Standard Theatre, a well managed place of dramatic entertainment, under the direction of Mr. John Douglass. This theatre has ten different prices of admission—the highest being two shillings six pence to the private boxes, and the lowest—three pence to the gallery. The chief attraction at this establishment, is a curious and gorgeous curtain, composed of sixteen plates of silvered glass, the largest ever made, in which nigh 5000 persons can see themselves reflected nightly (fig. 26).

The productions Douglass mounted in his new house were the kind to which an out-of-town; exhibition crowd would be most receptive. The looking-glass curtain idea was not new to London audiences. One had been hung at the Coburg (Royal Victoria) in 1822.[28] Another had been shown at the Marylebone in June of 1839. Douglass obtained sixteen panes of mirror. He then had choreographed a ballet called *The Snow Witch, a Legend of the Enchanted Island* (21 April 1851). In one scene, a multitude of gas lights was reflected from the mirror as white clad dancers swirled about the stage.

This ballet ran five weeks, and was followed by a musical spectacle called *The Water King, or, the Torrent of the Black Valley*. Featured was a cataract of real water in a mysterious valley reminiscent of the bullet-casting scene in *Der Frieschutz*. *Idrian [Adrien] the Bold*, the next feature, utilized the same waterfall. Melodramas and nautical plays were intermixed with these spectacles until July 21 when *The Trials and Triumphs of Temperance* was brought out to lend a moral tone to the repertoire. Later in the summer Coney, and his dog heroes, became the third attraction each evening. One particular act was contrived to take advantage of the special nature of the crowd. Mr. James, a quick-change artist, personated five different character types, who visited the Crystal Palace, in his *A Day at the Fair*.

The Great Exposition officially closed in September of 1851. But the holiday atmosphere continued, and the theatres

27. Michael R. Booth, *English Melodrama*, p. 56, n. 9.
28. Raymond Mander and Joe Mitchenson, *A Picture History of the British Theatre*, p. 79.

Fig. 28. The Christmas Pantomime *Harlequin and the Golden Alphabet; or, the Fairy Queen, One-Eyed King, and the Enchanted Milkmaid*, by John Douglass, December 1852. *From the Guildhall Library.*

brought out more spectacular productions for the throngs that streamed to the city. Douglass produced *Chin-Cho-Ali; or, the Charmed Pirate and the Magic Bracelet*. In October the *Era* called the Standard, "The largest and most elegant theatre in London."

At this point Douglass returned to his normal production pattern. Melodrama was represented by *Mazeppa*, followed by two weeks of nautical dramas. E. T. Lyon presented *The Lady of Lyons* for twelve performances. Then after his benefit, Douglass closed the theatre in mid-December for the mounting of the panto.

His profits before the Christmas pantomime had been enormous. In this period the London theatres often found that the only productions that made money were the pantos. Therefore they depended on these Christmas season shows to provide the capital for the next twelve months of operation. A Christmas failure usually brought an Easter bankruptcy. For Douglass even the 1850–1851 panto was a gold mine. He must have been able to retire any debt remaining on the new structure, fill the scene docks with new settings, and, above all, begin to attract a better class of guest stars.

His profit also permitted him to plan very lavish spectacles for his pantomimes. Each of these was "created" by Douglass himself. Created is a better word than written because these shows depended on pageantry, dance, mechanical, and magic tricks, and musical numbers. His first panto at the Standard in 1848 had been modestly titled *The Model Pantomime of 1848; or, Harlequin King Coppernose and the Fairy of the Golden Temple*. The second year's production was *Harlequin and the Magic Teapot; or, Chi-Ki, Ski-Hi, King of the Golden Pagodas*. The first in the new big theatre was *Harlequin Buttercups and Daisies; or, Great A, Little A, Bouncing B, the Cat's in the Cupboard and She Can't See*. Into the new big house, the audiences crowded. The panto ran ten lucrative weeks. The next two years were even better, with *Hoddy Toddy All Head and No Body; or, Harlequin and The Magic Pippin* (fig.27), and *Harlequin and the Golden Alphabet; or, the Fairy Queen, One-Eyed King, and the Enchanted Milkmaid* (fig.28).

Douglass was justly proud of his extravagant, yet successful, productions. He had unique pictorial playbills printed that showed the most striking scenes. The one for *Hoddy Toddy* pictures the maypole ballet, and the blue-fire-filled grand transformation scene. It was set in a hall of columns backed by the papier-mâché headed figures of the fairy tale opening scene. The one for The *Enchanted Milkmaid* depicts Mother Goose coming from a star-trap-like trick book, clown balancing his dog on one foot, and the hall of Amazons, backed by a firework-filled apotheosis of Britania.

The six-week panto seasons of 1852 and 1853 brought in each season about one hundred and twenty thousand paying customers. Douglass kept his prices modest, and everyone could afford to attend. In fact, his prices were lower than Gibson's in 1835. The average charge was six pence for gallery, pit, and upper circle, and a shilling for the boxes. The box office "take" averaged about £125 per performance and about £4500 per season. This is the equivalent of $22,400 in nineteenth century American dollars. Half of this would have gone for salaries, costumes and settings, but it is obvious that an eleven thousand dollar profit produced considerable financial security. It was from this solid base that Douglass began the second phase of his management, as described in the next chapter.

It is possible to contrast Douglass's success with notable failures in the West End houses. James Anderson's biography stated that at Drury Lane the nightly expenses before any profit were £170. This meant that the mandatory costs at Drury Lane would have been £6120 for the six-week panto season. Then the cost of the costumes, new settings, and other special production items had to be added. It cost three to four times more to produce at the smaller Drury Lane than at the Standard.

Douglass also approached the problem of hiring performers in a way that helped keep the costs low. His theatre's program consisted of family entertainment. He believed in family groups for his acting stable. In his first thirteen years of operation, the Douglasses, the Honners, the Lewises, the Gates, the Dolphins, the Lickfolds, the Rayners, the Nevilles, and the Terrys, all worked regularly. These family clusters consisted of husbands, wives, sisters, brothers, children, grandchildren, uncles, aunts, and so on. Of course, even in such a group, there were not enough to handle special character types like harlequin, or the big casts of the panto. Douglass filled these roles with a host of other actors. Many of the more than three hundred names in the programs from 1848 to 1860, who were outside the family groups listed above, were obscure typecast performers. These people moved from one suburban theatre to another. Some specialized in ethnic roles; others were dancers, or singers. There were aged types, rustics, and heavies. Only a few

Fig. 29. Mrs. Robert Honner (Marcia Macarthy), (1808–1870). *From the Rose Lipman Library, Hackney.*

Fig. 30. Mrs Robert Honner (Marcia Macarthy), (1808–1870). From the *Rose Lipman Library, Hackney.*

1848 through the sixties. Mrs. John Gates and Mrs. Alfred Rayner were available for the mature roles. The leading men for the serious drama, and Shakespeare, have been mentioned before: Freer, Lyon, and T.C. King.

In the melodramas, George Pennett, who was physically deformed, played villains from 1853 to 1860. The principal men's parts were taken by Robert Honner, H. Bird, John Dolphin, John Gates, E. B. Gaston, Henry Lewis, John Mordaunt, Alfred Rayner, and J. B. Johnstone. The latter was also the resident playwright. The nautical characters, and other bizarre types, were taken by Douglass himself, or by Rayner, Bigwood, or Gaston.

Between 1848 and 1860, this was a more or less stable group. Each season, beginning in September, they

of these were seen at the Standard more than one season. Douglass was endeavoring to mix fresh faces with his regulars and established favorites.

The regulars took the leads and major supporting roles according to their special lines. When guest artists came, like Mr. and Mrs. James William Wallack, the stock company actors moved down a notch, from leads to supports, and on down the line.

For serious women's roles, Mrs. Honner was the normal choice from 1848 to 1860. However, in the late fifties she gave up the younger characters to Adelaide Downing, Miss Crossman, Miss Stewart, and eventually the famous Alice Marriott. Eliza Terry (Mrs. Henry Lewis) was the chubby bouncing comedienne from

Fig. 31. Robert Honner (18091852), as Jack Sheppard. *From the Rose Lipman Library, Hackney.*

R.Honner as Peter Wilkins

Miss E. Honner

London. Pub. by A.PARK. 47 Leonard St. Finsbury.

Fig. 32 . Mrs. Robert Honner (Marcia Macarthy), (1808–1870) as Peter Wilkins, and Miss E. Honner (a sister-in-law or a daughter?) as a sprite in a Napoleonic spectacle, a toy theatre plate. *From the London Museum.*

performed a series of short dramas, farces, and comediettas, every evening, before and after the featured play. In addition, they took roles in the major piece, and supported the guest stars. Several members of the stock company became noted stars, and would be asked to guest at West End houses in their special lines. Douglass himself appeared at Drury Lane quite a few times. Of the women, Mrs. Honner was the most widely known. Her name was Marcia Macarthy (ca.1812–1870). She was born in Killen, Ireland. After an apprenticeship in small theatres in southern Ireland, she got a position in London, at the Pavilion Theatre. She moved to the Coburg (Royal Victoria) where she met her future husband, Robert Honner. After this she appeared at the Surrey. By 1838 the Honners had become the proprietors of Sadler's Wells. In 1837 she had made a very successful debut at Drury Lane as Julia in Sheridan Knowles' *The Hunchback*. Up to 1845, she was again at the Surrey, then the City of London with her husband.

Fig. 33. Robert Honner (1809–1852), as Jack Sheppard. *From the British Library.*

She is supposed to have been the actress who created the leading role of Sarah in John Knowles' *The Jewess*. This part endeared her to the Jewish audiences in the East End theatres.

Robert William Honner (1809–1852) was born in London. In 1817 he was apprenticed to Le Clercq, the ballet master at the Sans Pareil (Adelphi) Theatre. For the next years, he performed in a multitude of theatres, while learning stage management. By 1833 he had become the stage manager at Sadler's Wells; then in 1835, the acting manager at the Surrey. The Honners, as lessees of the Sadler's Wells in 1838, did not prove successful; and they were lucky to get out before they went bankrupt.

After giving up their project, Honner became the director at the City of London, where he remained until Johnson and Lee took over in 1847. At this point the Honners moved up the street to the friendly confines of Douglass's Standard. From then on Mrs. Honner undertook most of the female leads; and Robert Honner was the stage manager until his death in 1852, at the age of forty-three.

After his death Mrs. Honner continued in the company as the principal dramatic actress until 1860, when she was forty-eight. Like a number of performers who worked in the larger theatres; she began to have voice problems. Her tones had always been powerful, and rich: indeed, her principal asset as a leading lady of melodrama. Physically, she was petite, with a figure that permitted her to play boys. In the late fifties, she married Frederick

Fig.34. Robert Honner (1809–1852), as the King of the Burning Mountain, in a panto, tinsel print. *From the London Museum.*

Morton, who had made his London debut in 1848. They continued at the Standard. But, as the years passed the typefonts used to set her name on the playbills became smaller as she moved down to supporting roles. Finally in 1860, they joined the Sadler's Wells company. It was there that she took her farewell benefits in 1864 and 1865. She did not attend the 1865 performance because of poor health, described as "a partial paralysis of the voice." She had been a great favorite; and admirers, including the friends from the Standard, turned out in great numbers (fig. 29).

The male counterpart of Mrs. Honner was Thomas Eaton Lyon (1812–1879). He was born in Woolton near Liverpool. His debut was in the summer of 1832 in Ormskirk. He toured the northern

Fig. 36. Thomas Eaton Lyon (1812–1869), as Grimaud in *The Red Cap*. *From The Theatrical Times.*

circuits: York, Liverpool, Hull, etc. His success as Eleazer in *The Jewess* brought him to the attention of London managers. Because of an appearance at the Adelphi in September of 1836 Lyon was able to work steadily. He was particularly popular at the City of London from 1844 to 1847. He moved to the Standard with the Honners and gradually took over the leads from Freer, as the latter's drinking problem made him less and less dependable.

When the somber James William Wallack was brought to the Haymarket

Fig. 35. Mrs. Robert Honner as the boy Felix in *The French Revolution*. *From the Theatrical Times.*

in 1852 to counter the popularity of Charles Kean at the Princess's, Lyon came in from the Standard to act the major supporting roles (fig. 36).

Another of the young leading men of this period at the Standard was T. C. King (1825–1893). He was born in Cheltenham in 1825. His debut was at the Theatre Royal, Birmingham. He also toured the northern circuits. So many of the performers at the Standard, and other London theatres, worked out their apprenticeships in the houses of York, Leeds, and Hull, that the north must have been considered the proving ground for young actors. King made his London debut at the

Fig. 37. Edward Wright (1813–1859), The London Journal. *From the Rose Lipman Library, Hackney.*

Princess's under Charles Kean's direction in 1852. But his name was linked with the Standard as early as 1849. His most interesting performances will be mentioned in a later chapter in tandem with Alice Marriott.

Typical of the specialty performer, in the Standard's stock company, was Edward Wright (ca.1805–1859) "The London Journal." Born in London, he began his theatrical career as an amateur at the Margate Theatre in September of 1832. He came to the St. James's Theatre in 1837. Then he was at the Adelphi for a number of years. His success there brought him to the attention of the Queen, and he was invited to perform at Windsor Castle. After the Standard's resident Irish comedian Tom Lee died, Wright became a member of the company from 1852 to 1859 (fig. 37).

During his first five seasons John Douglass made progress in raising the tone of the dramas presented to the Shoreditch audience. From the beginning there were more than ten nights of Shakespeare per year, presented by the stock company. This was augmented in 1852 by the three-week classical season of the Wallacks. New scripts began to take on importance. In 1848–1849 there were three; by 1852, there were seven. Entertainment of a moral, or corrective tone, became a popular fixture at the Standard. Typical titles include: *The Drunkard the Gambler and the Beggar; or, the Soldier's Bride* by John T. Haines (February 1848); *Punishment in Six Stages* (February 1849); *The Trials* and *Triumphs of Temperance* (July 1851); *The Betting Boy's Career, from His Home to the Hulks* (August 1852); and the first foreign dramatization of a part of Stowe's *Uncle Tom's Cabin* in September of 1852 (fig. 38).

Musical extravaganzas, novelty acts, ballet, and panto were filled with technical embellishments. The cataract of real water, and the mirror curtain were but two of these. Morgan's electric arc light was featured as part of the equipment in Mme. Wharton's tableau posers (*poses plastique*). The posers came to the Standard each season for a number of years. They were a troupe of men, women, and horses, the humans in various states of undress. These whitened figures were discovered in frozen poses bathed in searing light. The groupings usually represented well-known works of fine

Fig. 38. W. Webb's plate for a toy theatre presentation of *Uncle Tom's Cabin*, Plate 9 the characters: George and Eliza Harris, Simon Legree, Uncle Tom, Dick Willis, Sambo, and baby Harry Harris. Produced at the Standard Theatre in Shoreditch in September of 1852. *From A.S.J.*

art, such as the "Greek Slave" by Gourier, as seen at the Crystal Palace; or, "The Rape of the Sabines." This is a very early date for the use of an electric arc light. In fact, Charles Kean was just in the process of finding ways to use the gas lime-light spot in legitimate dramas; and this was considered to be on the advanced edge of theatrical technology. In the very hot summer of 1852, Douglass introduced his "monster" ventilator to soothe the audience. He advertised it as the only such device in any London theatre.

The Christmas pantomimes normally ran six weeks, but for the first time dramas began to have long runs as well. *The Vicar of Wakefield* ran six weeks, and then was revived from time to time.[29] An English version of the French hit *The Courier, or the Assassins of Paris* ran for fifty nights. It was the first production of a play that became known as *The Lyons Mail*. This version may have been adapted by Benjamin Webster. *Uncle Tom's Cabin* proved popular enough to run at least forty-eight nights. This was probably the first production of this story outside the United States of America. It was a short version because there were always two other plays, or acts on the bill with it. Mrs. Stowe's book had been published as a serialized feature in *The National Era*. These installments were collected into a novel that was issued in March of 1852. The book was released in London in May. George Aiken's best known dramatization was not seen until 27 September 1852, in Troy, New York. The Standard's of September 11 was the a few days earlier. Of the ten new scripts produced at the Standard in 1852–1853, Dibdin-Pitt provided one, J. B Johnstone two or more, and John Douglass wrote a nautical drama himself. The *Uncle Tom's Cabin* story seems to have been the type of moral drama that appealed to Johnstone. On the other hand, Douglass might have tried his hand at the adaptation.

Because of the instant popularity of all the versions, the toy theatre printer, Webb, rushed out a set of plates for the play. There were eight of characters, thirteen of settings, four of wings, and one of set pieces. Since the Standard's production was the first in London, Webb's plates possibly depict this production (fig.38).[30]

Douglass was also interested in music. He presented a three-week opera season in June, and July of 1852. Mr. Isaacson, leader of the pit band, put together a pick-up company of singers for this first attempt. In order to remind audiences of the new ventilation system, he regularly led the band in his "Novel Ventilating Polka." The Ohio Ethiopian Serenaders were also engaged. They were six men, and women, in blackface. Accompanied by

---

29. There was a considerable squabble in the press between Tom Taylor and J. Stirling Coyne as to who had precedence in the rights to the dramatization of the *Vicar of Wakefield*.
30. The sensation crazed Edward Fitzball rushed three separate versions of *Uncle Tom's Cabin* on to London stages. He opened at the Olympic, September 20, the Grecian, October 25, and at Drury Lane, December 27.

the banjo, they performed American songs. Their success helped establish the taste for what came to be known as "The Christy Style Minstrels." After 1852, the summer season at the Standard was predominantly light opera and minstrel shows.

The production pattern mentioned became the hallmark of Douglass's management in his splendid new theatre. It suited the audience's tastes, and made his theatre a tremendous, overnight financial success. He was now ready to try something even more daring.

4

STARS ARRIVE IN THE EAST

An excursion into theatrical failure was made by one of Douglass's competitors. Not everyone in the theatrical profession was able to capitalize on the Great Exhibition. One who was certainly expected to, but as mentioned earlier, did not, was James Robertson Anderson (1811–1895) (figs. 39 and 40). Anderson was born in Glasgow, and like many mid-century actors, gained his experience in the northern circuits. By the 1830s he had become the actor manager of the Leicester, Gloucester, and Cheltenham theatre group.

While on tour, William Charles Macready saw Anderson perform, and offered him a London engagement as Florizel in *The Winter's Tale* at Covent Garden Theatre, 30 September 1837. Anderson's popularity grew steadily. He was called on to create important roles for Madam Vestris and Charles James Mathews, and later Macready again at Covent Garden.

In January of 1842 Anderson went with Macready to Drury Lane. In May of that year he played Othello in London for the first time. His interpretation proved a great success. Plaudits in the press admired his intelligent creation, and the poetic rhythm of his rich voice. In just three years he began to have vocal problems, and was called husky, guttural, and inarticulate. But this was an occupational hazard in the smoky theatres and smoggy atmosphere of London. After some rest he recovered.

By 1849 Macready was planning to retire, and Drury Lane was in need of new management. Anderson's talent and energy made him a logical artistic successor to Macready as the leading actor in England. Anderson and John Douglass entered upon their respective operations at the same moment. The results, for each, were very different.

In his autobiography Anderson details the story of his seasons in the Royal Patent House. His perspective of the state of the nation was very different from the rosy picture painted in the newspaper article previously quoted:

Fig. 39. James R. Anderson(1811–1895) in 1846.
From An Actor's Life.

weekly from California and Australia. . . ; no excursion trains, as now, bringing to London hundreds of thousands of persons, foreign and native, to cram theatres nightly. 'All was stale, flat, and unprofitable;' and to crown my ill luck, the prop that supported the platform of my hopes was rudely kicked from under me, in the postponement of the opening of the Great Exhibition till 1851. There was the fall that finished me![31]

The details are clear. It was the tradition of the Theatre Royal, a plum to be plucked quickly and damn the long view. The sub-committee of the owners ruled supreme. They required a certain percent return on the total investment no matter the box office income, no matter anything. The basic staff of the institution was also a fixed cost. They had to be paid; generally, in spite of their artistic contributions. The effect on the lessees was that one after the other they were seduced by the promise of social status and, secretly in their hearts, big money. Then they learned the price of hubris, several of them more than once.

In 1850 the country was in a disorganized and poverty stricken state, suffering from the effects of foreign revolutions, general elections, trade strikes, and perpetual agitation amongst the people.

It will be remembered that in those days there were no ship-loads of gold arriving

31. James Anderson, *An Actor's Life*, p. 175.

Anderson, in retrospect, described the events in his book of 1888:

Mr. Chatterton closed the doors of 'old Drury' suddenly on the night of February 4th,1879. Bad business, empty treasury, heavy debts, and failure of the Christmas pantomime were the cause. . . .

Twenty-eight years ago, as manager of the same theatre, I spent £15000 in hard cash, passed through the Insolvent Court for £4000 and sacrificed £6000 more by losing my starring engagements! Mr. Chatterton started with nothing yet he has been enabled to realize £40,000 worth of debts. 'There is something in this more than natural, if philosophy could find it out.'

The same 'old Drury' has been the ruin of many a better manager. It is a fascinating and treacherous property, 'the gilded shore to a most dangerous sea'—in short a quicksand, where whoever builds his hopes of fortune is sure to sink; witness the many men, even in my time, who have disappeared in it. First of all there was Alfred Bunn, then W. J. Hammond, William Macready, Bunn again, James Anderson, Bunn once more, E. T. Smith, Harrison and Pyne, E. T. Smith again, Edmund Falconer, Falconer and Chatterton, and lastly Chatterton alone. All were utterly ruined save Macready, who very wisely left the quicksand in time to save himself.[32]

A comparison of Anderson's management with that of Douglass reveals how wise the latter's decisions were. In 1849 Anderson

went to the Drury Lane sub-committee with his proposal because, as he said, his friends put him up to it to take advantage of the Exposition.

About this time there was much excitement respecting the wonderful structure being raised in Hyde Park for the Great Exhibition of the following year, and my friends strongly urged me to take advantage of the situation by becoming manager of some London theatre. The opening of the exhibition would bring thousands of strangers to the Metropolis, who must, I was told, go to the theatres in the evening, if only to rest themselves after standing on their legs all day. Foreigners would rush to see Shakespeare well acted, especially Germans, who have such a love for the poet, and Americans, who adore the drama, they were expected to come over in crowds. Such arguments blinded my mental vision, and I fell into the trap.

Messrs. Gye and Jullien were then lessees of Drury Lane. They kept the theatre open only six months in the year for opera and promenade concerts; it had been closed during the winter months for some time. I immediately applied to them for a lease of the six winter months they did not use. . . .

The terms proposed were these: A lease of four years, with a season of six months in each year, from January to June; but I was to be put in possession of the theatre as early as December 12th, in order to give time to rehearse the Christmas pantomime, commencing December 26th, ending June 25th; the rent to be £2500 per annum, paid monthly, for the first year, and £3000 for the

32. Anderson, pp. 338–339.

following years, together with a deposit of £1500. All this I agreed to, on condition of having free use of the painting and scene-rooms, manager's room, and wardrobe, so that I could set my people to work when I chose. . . .

I engaged Mr. George Rodwell for Drury Lane, on August 10th, as musical director and composer, arranging also that he should write the opening of the pantomime, the subject to be 'The Golden Days of Good Queen Bess.'. . .

Mr. Rodwell brought me the scenario of the pantomime (September, 25th), which I thought very good, and sufficiently to begin upon. . . .

Then I found the theatre in a deplorable condition. Not a scene or dress was fit for use; even the meters and gas-pipes, the ropes and pulleys for traps and fly borders, all had to be renewed; there was not the smallest bit of crockery in the house to use in the dressing-rooms, and all the offices were in a filthy and dilapidated condition. The chairs in private boxes and stalls had all to have their arms and legs looked to. Instead of taking possession of a trim ship ready for sea, as I thought, I had signed an agreement for the lease of a rotten wreck with not a bit of canvas on board. There were sixteen scenes to be painted for the pantomime, and more than half of them had to be on new cloths. I was prepared, of course, to furnish everything new, fresh and splendid in the way of dresses and properties for the Christmas spectacle; but when I found there was not a costume in the wardrobe fit for a Shakespearian play, I felt as if I had dropped into the bottomless pit in Mammoth Cave of Kentucky.

After spending £2000, Anderson's season began on Boxing night, Wednesday the 26th of December. The play was *The Merchant of Venice*, followed by the panto.

The production was very costly, everything being new from the cellar to the flies. Two thousand pounds did not cover the outlay. Yet I was vastly pleased when W. Dunn, the treasurer, brought me a copy of the night's receipts, which reached £365 15s. 6d. Those three figures looked hopeful, and I fervently prayed that they might crop up often. But they didn't, worse luck! The three following nights, Thursday, Friday, and Saturday, tumbled down to £184, £185, and £150!. . . And, as if to put an extra spoke in my wheel, Mrs. Nisbett was taken ill, and couldn't act Rosalind in As You Like It for a fortnight after she was announced. When she did appear, Vandenhoff, who played Jacques for a few nights, had the misfortune to dislocate his shoulder, which laid him up for a week. To make the illluck perfect, I could not take his part, suffering as I was from a severe cold, hoarseness, and sore throat, that made my voice inaudible beyond a whisper. This was the result of great exertion, night and day, in getting up the pantomime, and it rendered me incapable of acting for weeks.

On January 18th, thinking my voice was a little stronger, I tried to repeat Shylock. The attempt proved a lamentable failure! I could not be heard over the orchestra, which was mortifying after all my physicking, gruelling, and blistering. I began to fear my vocal power was gone forever.

Mr. Vandenhoff, Miss Vandenhoff, and Mrs. Nisbett played together in The Hunchback to a very poor house and a very dull audience

Fig. 40. James R. Anderson (1811–1895) in the costume he used for Coriolanus, and other Greco-Roman roles. *From An Actor's Life.*

on January 21st. I could not understand why the business should have fallen off so frightfully.

On January 28th *Othello* was given, great pains being taken with the revival of the tragedy. The scenery, dresses, appointments, and acting were much better than had been witnessed for many a day. . . .

Monday, February 4th, *Fiesco* was produced for the first time, and all but damned by the scene-painters and carpenters, who had not completed their preparations for the last act. Their behaviour was shameful, and insufferable delays in setting the scenes tried the patience of the audience and entirely ruined the play.

My hoarseness was now worse than ever, and I was persuaded to allow Dr. Hastings, of Albemarle Street, a man of great reputation, to sponge my throat with a solution of caustic, which nearly choked the life out of me. I endured the operation several times with beneficial effects, but they did not last long. After a little exertion, the throat became relaxed again, and I was hoarse as ever. I produced Serjeant Talfourd's tragedy of *Ion*, March 6th, with appropriate scenery, dresses, and decorations, a strong cast, including Vandenhoff, his daughter, and myself in the principal characters, and receipts realized £45 15s! My nightly expenses during the run of the pantomime amounted to £175, and I was playing to houses that did not average £75. It required no great arithmetician to calculate my losses.

On March 11th I brought out my alteration of Beaumont and Fletcher's comedy of *The Elder Brother*, so successful in America and the provinces, with a powerful cast, and everything new and bright, to the flattering and unexampled receipts of £32 5s. 6d.! Notwithstanding the wretched house, the comedy went off gloriously.

In March, and April Anderson added several other new productions, but the announcement that the opening of the Great Exposition was to be put off for a year caused him great distress. His narrative continued:

All the London theatres now were playing to as bad business as Drury Lane, only their expenses were nothing like so heavy. Notwithstanding the great success of an extravaganza called *The Island of Jewels,* Madame Vestris and Charles Mathews were reduced to the necessity of asking their actors to accept three shillings and sixpence in the pound! The Haymarket, Adelphi, and all the other houses were losing money nightly; nevertheless, in the face of all these disasters, Charles Kean and Robert Keeley, inspired by the hope that the opening of the Great Exhibition in the following May would make their fortunes, took a lease of the Princess's theatre for several years.

It was upon this same speculation that John Douglass took the bold step of tearing his theatre down, and over the summer, building the enormous new structure. Anderson continued:

May 4th, I brought this cruel and desastrous season to a close. . . Thus ended my first season as manager of Drury Lane Theatre with a pecuniary loss of £5,500 in one-hundred nights. What took me years to ac-cumulate melted away in four months.![33]

Anderson went on tour from the begin-ning of June to December 9th of 1850. Thus he had some cash to begin his second season, although it did not cover the losses. Douglass, in the meantime, had opened his new house on October 19th.

On December 17th I began full rehearsals of the pantomime with all the people. On Christmas Eve we had a night rehearsal that lasted till three o'clock in the morning. Wearied and worn out, I fell asleep in my chair on stage, and went through all the horrors of a dream of drowning in my enterprise.

December 26th was the opening night of the second season of my management at Drury Lane. The entertainments were Shakespeare's Winter's Tale, and Fitzball's grand comic Christmas pantomime *Humpty-Dumpty; or, the First Lord Mayor of London*. The play was received with much applause, but the pantomime was not equally success-ful; it did not make the hit that *Queen Bess* did the previous year. The house was bad for Boxing Night, everything looked black and disheartening. Several dramas were tried as companions to the pantomime but nothing helped business. On Saturday January 4th: I revived Rob Roy with great splendour—auxiliary aid in singing, scenery, and supers, backed by the pantomime, and played it to receipts amounting to £110 5s. 6d.! Fifty pounds under expenses!. . .

In the confirmed certainty that my pan-tomime was a failure, and could not hold its place in the day-bill much longer, I set my wits to work to find something to take its place. Mr. John Mitchell, the bookseller, of Bond Street, who took a warm interest in my welfare, suggested the idea that I should run over the water and see the grand opera *L'Enfant Prodigue*, which was then drawing prodigious houses in Paris. He gave me letters of introduction to the manager, music publisher, and costumer. I was charmed with the opera, music and *mis-en-scene*. I bought two or three copies of the libretto, and sat up all night plotting the scenario of a drama for Drury Lane, to be called *The Prodigal Son*; made arrangements with the publisher to supply me with what I wanted of the music, and with the costumer to furnish dresses for the principal performers and sketches for the others. . . .

But the drama had yet to be written. I gave Fitzball the scenario and a copy of the libretto, and told him to go at once to his desk and turn me out something that would 'beat Bangor' or the *Bible*. I persuaded Vandenhoff to take another copy, and write up his own part of Reuben to what length he pleased. I promised to do the like thing for mine of Azael, and when done to let Fitzball have both to incorporate with his drama. Thus was the ball set rolling for *Azael*.

---

33. Anderson, pp. 163–179.

However, the box office receipts had fallen off so completely that there were never more than fifty pounds per night in receipts. Anderson was reduced to begging the company to go on half salaries. At this time the nightly fixed costs were £170.

On February 19th, after great expenditure, much anxiety, and six weeks' laborious rehearsals day and night, I produced the grand spectacular drama, called *Azael, the Prodigal Son*, with complete success. Nothing could have been more gratifying, or more suggestive of a favorable turn in my fortunes, than the verdict of public approval that night, yet the receipts realized only £92 7s. *Azael* cost a rare lot of money, and, though played for seventy nights, never realized a profit. It was acted to the most varied receipts, ranging from £180 to £46 nightly. Still it helped to keep my head above water for some months, and I was grateful.

March 28th, the Queen visited Drury Lane, to witness the grand spectacle of *The Prodigal Son*, but as I was strictly commanded to keep her visit secret from the public, I derived no benefit from the honour. Receipts, £89 15s.

Easter Monday (April 21st), I brought out The *Robbers* for the first time at Drury Lane. It was well acted, beautifully mounted, and backed by *Azael*. We played the two of them on a holiday night to £182. This was encouraging, and I continued the two pieces in the bill for a week, fondly thinking I had turned round a lucky corner. Vain hope! The houses fell off nightly, and ran down to £95,

£83, £72, £66, and £57 12s. 6d. The end crowns the work!

The Great Exhibition in Hyde Park was opened on May 1st with a grandeur and magnificence unequaled in the world! Hundreds of thousands of people swarmed like bees inside and out of the beautiful palace, yet Drury Lane remained the same old desert still. We played that night the comedy of *The Wonder*, and *Azael* to £65 5s. 6d.

I held courageously on for three weeks longer, clinging to the wreck in the idle hope that the tide would turn; but it was not to be. There I lay a splintered bark, the victim of mistaken rashness and vain ambition.

On the morning of Monday, May 19th, in addition to my many miseries and misfortunes, my poor dear wife, who had been a long, and patient sufferer, died of the disease of the lungs, at her mother's residence, Camden Town. We had 'lived and loved together through many a changing year.' [34]

June 19th, Whit-Monday, brought out a new play, translated from the German by Mrs. Lovell, called *Ingomar, the Barbarian* [fig. 25]. It was as beautifully put upon the stage as any of my former productions, and with the same result—empty benches. Charlotte Vandenhoff sustained the classical heroine with grace, poetry, and perfection of elocution, and I enjoyed a complete triumph as Ingomar. We played it fourteen nights, and after the first night, which was really good, never to more than £40 or £50 houses. My patience, hopes, and worldly means were now exhausted, and I resolved to close the theatre.

34.   Georgina Stohwasser and James Anderson were married in May of 1836, when she was twenty-three.

Fig. 41. The Standard Theatre, after it was remodeled in 1854. *From the Rose Lipman Library, Hackney.*

Tuesday, June 24th, 1851, was the last night of my management at Drury Lane. The entertainments were *Ingomar* and *The Prodigal Son,* played to a very poor house. The actors and all my people had received due notice that the theatre would close; a few days after I had resigned the theatre, the stony-hearted committee, who would allow me no breathing time, let the theatre to an American Circus Company, which realized in a few months over seven thousand pounds![35]

In this same period, Douglass at the National Standard Theatre in Shoreditch, was setting financial records for income. Despite Anderson's attention to serious drama, often well produced, the expensive to operate, run down, Drury Lane was no match for the streamlined, low priced. large, comfortable theatre in the East. Douglass kept his house open throughout the Hyde Park Exhibition; while Anderson was forced, by his financial situation, and the terms of his lease, to snatch defeat from the jaws of victory. The failure of the 1849–1850 Christmas pantomime ultimately precipitated the bankruptcy of 1851.

The nature of Douglass's operations were described in an unidentified news clipping from about the same year.

The National Standard . . .is a large and elegant theatre, capable of containing four thousand and three hundred persons, rebuilt in 1850, from designs by Mr. John Douglass, and opened October 19th, having many improvements in its interior arrangements, evidently suggested by a desire to do everything that is possible, in order to ·afford both convenience to the audience, and accommodation for the somewhat ambitious nature of the performances. What the Adelphi Theatre, from its situation, is to the Strand and the West End, this house is to Shoreditch and the East End; standing as it does in a leading thoroughfare, directly opposite the terminus of the Eastern Counties Railway, and in the midst of a dense neighborhood, it is nightly-filled to overflowing, and while the prices are such as to meet the wants of its patrons, the aim of the management would seem to be that of giving a superior style of entertainment, a course, which if resolutely persevered in, must ultimately raise this theatre in public estimation, and rebound to the permanent advantage of the proprietor. . . Doors open at a quarter past six o'clock; performances commence at a quarter before seven. Admission: private boxes, two shillings; dress circle, one shilling and sixpence; lower circle one shilling; pit stalls, eightpence; pit, sixpence; gallery, fourpence; upper gallery, threepence [fig. 41].

The circus, and the Standard made considerable profit over the summer. Anderson surely would have done the same with his beautiful production of *Azael,* because ballet and spectacle were what was selling at the other theatres.

Anderson was cut adrift, ruined financially, a widower, but still at

---

35. Anderson, pp. 179–199.

theheightofhisartisticpowers. Looking for any work, he first took provincial tours. Then he thought seriously about a suburban London engagement. This might have seemed an admission of declining artistry. The attitude of the mid-century actor toward the suburban houses is summed up by an anecdote printed in *Reynolds's Miscellany* about 1854, and attached to a view of the interior of the Standard Theatre (fig.41).

A few years since, performers of any note would have been horrified at the notion of acting in other than a West End theatre; and even until this day many there are who entertain a similar prejudice. As an instance of the boundless influence fashion often exercises upon members of the dramatic profession, we give an anecdote related of a lady who promised to become one of its chief ornaments:— The late Miss Laura Addison, a very clever and popular actress, was engaged at Sadler's Wells Theatre,—a house in high repute for the excellence of its management, the talent of its company, and the admirable manner in which every performance is placed upon the stage. [She was in the company in the seasons of 1846 through 1848]. One evening, being in the society of a puppy guardsman, he asked the young lady at which house she was performing; and on being informed, with cool impertinence affecting utter ignorance of the theatre named and its locality, quietly demanded where she changed horses on the way thither! Miss Addison was so foolishly sensitive to this imbecile sarcasm, that she retired from the theatre, in the very blush of increasing popularity.

Laura Addison's short biography in *Tallis's Drawing Room Table Book* (1851) indicates this last statement to be inaccurate. However, the prejudice described was real. Anderson confessed he believed the same way up to 1851.

Grown thoroughly weary of running up and down the country, wearing out health, strength, and theatrical ward-robe for such uncertain remuneration as I realized, I resolved on making an experimental trial of the East End of London—a bold step, but I did it with a will, having made arrangements with the managers to try my fortunes at the minor theatres. The prejudice anent such engagements in the minds of legitimate actors at this time was very great, and I had much difficulty in 'screwing my courage to the sticking place,' but I went boldly to work to carry out my plans.[36]

First he tried Sam Lane's Britannia in Hoxton. Then Johnson and Lee engaged him for six weeks at the City of London for £60 per week, and a half of a benefit. Bunn recognized Anderson's popularity continued despite his failure as a manager of Drury Lane, and therefore brought him back there to act any roles he might choose at £30 per week. Bunn went bankrupt in just three months, and Anderson was off again to the suburbs. He was at the Marylebone in April of

Fig. 42. Barry Sullivan (ca.1821–1891) as Hamlet. *From Tallis's Drawing Room Table Book.*

1852, and at the Britannia at £100 per week in May.

For the summer it was the northern provinces, then back to the City of London Theatre from October through Christmas. Anderson decided that he did not care for Johnson and Lee because of an incident related to their house dramatist (mentioned in the next chapter), so he left them, and went to the Strand for eighteen nights in that "tiny tea-cup of a playhouse." For purposes of this narrative, Anderson's next move was the important one for it converged his fortunes and those of John Douglass.

> When I had finished exhibiting myself as the 'big cucumber in a small bottle,' as Douglas Jerrold used to say to me, I drove my stylish cabriolet and high-stepping horse over to Shoreditch, having transferred my services to Mr. John Douglass' establishment, the Standard Theatre. This was one of the most brilliant and satisfactory of all my East End arrangements. . . .

> When I began this engagement, I told Mr. Douglass I would not undertake to act more than three weeks at first, but if business continued good I would go on; it continued not only good but great, and, instead of three, I played twelve weeks with him. During those seventy-two nights, I had tremendous hard work. I played Hamlet, Othello, Macbeth, Coriolanus, King John, Shylock, Lear, Richard III, Prospero, Halbert Macdonald [in *Glencoe,The Massacre of the Macdonalds* by T. N. Talfourd, 1840], Virginius, James in *King of Commons*, Claude Melnotte [in *The Lady of Lyons*], Charles in Shiller's *Robbers*, *The Elder Brother*, Ingomar, Beverley [in Edward Moore's *The Gamester*, 1753], *The Stranger*, William Tell, Petruchio, Belmour [in *Jane Shore*, by Nicholas Rowe, 1714], Delaval [in *Civilization*, by John Wilkins and Anderson himself, 1852], and Sir Edward Ardent in *A Morning Call*. Twenty-three different characters in twelve weeks! When one looks back upon such work, remembering the long and laborious rehearsals, tremendous changes of dress, the fearful trials of temper with the stupid and obstinate utility people, in addition to the strain on the physical and mental powers to be always 'up to concert pitch' under all circumstances, it is difficult to believe one has ever gone through such severe work in so short a time; but diaries and the play-bills leave no doubt. I have jotted down these twelve weeks' doings simply to show that an actor, however popular and successful he may be, does not earn his money easily. I cleared £720 by this engagement at the Standard, but I worked hard for it.[37]

37.   Anderson, pp. 213–214.

5

THE STANDARD BECOMES A MAJOR THEATRE

The seasons of 1853 through 1855 were pivotal in the development of John Douglass's new operational technique. The phenomenal success of James Anderson brought a "classical" tradition to life at the Standard. In the seventy-two nights, after 21 February 1853, Anderson starred in ten of the favorite Shakespearean dramas, including the rarely produced *Coriolanus*. In addition, he presented protagonists from other traditional English plays, and major French and German authors. A relatively new script was presented. Called *Civilization*, it was based on Voltaire's *Huron*. Anderson had caused it to be dramatized so he could play the role of Delaval. It was the incidents surrounding the premiere of this play that led him to accept the engagement at the Standard, and this led to his financial recovery.

Most of the suburban theatres had resident dramatists. Some, like J. B. Johnstone at the Standard, were also in the acting company. Others worked in relative obscurity. Their primary duties were: to adapt scripts to fit the actors in the stock company, to make quick translations of recent French, or German successes, to adapt recent short stories, and novels into theatrical productions, and to write parts of the mandatory Christmas pantos. Often they led a precarious life with faint hope of becoming major authors. Wily impresarios could easily take advantage of their work when the occasional success occurred. In his autobiography Anderson described one such incident that happened during his 1852 run at the City of London Theatre.

Johnson and Lee wished for something new, and, if possible, something that would have 'a run,' so that they might have more time to produce their Christmas pantomime. I began to put my brains in soak, and conjured up the remembrance of a partiality I once had for Voltaire's *Huron*, thinking it immensely dramatic. I had no time to devote to writing the play, but I had promised to furnish the management with the scenario of a drama, that is, I gave them the plot, scheme, conduct, and programme, together with arrangement of scenes, acts, motives, sentiments, incidents, and names of characters, with a moral and happy denouement, to be called *Civilization*. They agreed, on their part, to have this scenario clothed in good English language by their own author engaged on the establishment, Mr. John Wilkins, who accomplished his work admirably. In conjunction with him, I made several alterations in the dialogue, cutting down and writing up speeches and scenes until we got the play into a complete, and satisfactory form, produced it triumphantly, and it had 'a long run.'

The terms agreed upon between Johnson, and Lee, and myself, were that they should have the privilege of acting the play at the City Theatre free of all payment; and when it was performed anywhere else, we were to divide the author's fees between us. I was so well pleased with Mr. Wilkins for the manner in which he had done his share of the work, that I did what I considered a simple act of justice—I relinquished to him all my interest as part author in the play. I gave him a grand dinner, a handsome ring, and a written certificate to claim my share in all fees for evermore. Wilkins was a very clever, modest, industrious young fellow, with a wife and family to support out of five-and-thirty shillings a week. That was

the munificent remuneration allowed for doing all the literary work of the theatre, and producing a new drama every month in the year if required.

It appeared I had made a grand mistake. I had no right to be generous. Poor Wilkins was extremely grateful, Johnson and Lee awfully indignant. They would not admit his right to any share in fees. He was their paid author—paid to write whatever they wished. They had given him the scenario of *Civilization* to fill up; he did it, and he had his salary; what would he have more? If Mr. Anderson chose to relinquish his share of the fees, the whole became theirs as a right. They held to that right, took the share I had resigned to Wilkins, and kept the play in their own hands for ever after.

I was so annoyed with Johnson and Lee for their meanness to poor Wilkins that, notwithstanding I had made over £500 sterling by this engagement, I broke off all connection with them.[38]

"Poor" Wilkins wrote at least seventeen plays for the venal Johnson and Lee before 1862. If his salary is accurately reported by Anderson, and it was never raised, he could not have made more than £91 a year. Without a source of outside income, one must assume Wilkins's life to have been the model Dickens depicted for Bob Cratchet and his family. In *East End Entertainment* Wilson claims Wilkins died in poverty shortly after this play was produced, although the continued licensing of plays

38. Anderson, pp. 211–213.

Fig. 43. *Roast Beef and Plum Pudding; or, Harlequin Card King, and the Island of Games*, 25 December 1853. *From the Guildhall Library.*

with his name attached contradicts this.[39]

Anderson said his success at the Standard "gave me my revenge on Johnson and Lee, who lost heavily that season, and enabled me to shut up two rival tragedians brought to oppose me—Mr. Charles Pitt at the City [of London] Theatre and Mr. McKean Buchanan at the Pavilion." [40]

At the Standard, Douglass followed Anderson with his normal mix of comedy, crime drama, and personalities, such as H. Widdicomb the comic entertainer. The stock plays of the previous season, the waterfall, and Mme. Wharton all returned. In the last week of July of 1853, the building was closed, and though only two years, and nine months old, it received a thorough redecoration, and some renovations. The auditorium was enlarged, a new stage floor put in, and the proscenium was rebuilt. The chief feature changed in the house was that looking glass decorated columns, made of the remains of the mirror drop of 1851 were installed. Eight new private boxes were created for the upper class audiences that came to see Anderson. New orchestra stalls, new chandeliers, and drapes were also added. The theatre was now advertised to hold over five thousand, about six hundred more than the original arrangement (fig.41).

Anderson reopened the theatre on August 27th, and ran five weeks. This was an unusual time of year for the classics. He was using this run to tune up the plays he was planning to take on an American tour. *Ingomar*, and *King Lear* each ran a week. Then, the fifteen plays of the previous February received one or two performances before the final night, October 1st. This run was as successful as the first had been. Douglass paid Anderson £60 per week, plus a half a benefit. To support Anderson he engaged Fanny Morant of the Drury Lane Company to be the "leading lady." Anderson said she performed splendidly.

The new production of *King Lear* was influenced, no doubt, by the antiquarian techniques Charles Kean was championing at the Princess's

Fig. 44. Tom Mead (1821–1889) as Hotspur, tinsel print. *From the London Museum.*

39.   A. E. Wilson, p. 160.
40.   Anderson, p. 213.

Theatre. It was advertised to have, "correct scenery, costume, pictorial groupings, and general original effects."

Following Anderson's departure for America, Thomas Potter Cooke (1786–1864) came to the Standard for his "pre-retirement farewell." Cooke was the acknowledged dean of picturesque, and nautical characters. He performed excerpts from his repertoire that included roles from *The Pilot*, *Black Eyed Susan*, *Poor Jack,* and *My Pol and My Partner Joe*. In this last play Tippy Cooke and Mrs. Honner performed in the original roles that they had created (figs. 75, and 76). Each night of "Cooke's October," farces, short dramas, or musical numbers filled out the program.

Douglass wished to keep the ball rolling in regard to the Shakespearean success, so he brought Barry Sullivan

Fig. 45. Tom Mead (1821–1889). *From the Rose Lipman Library, Hackney.*

(ca.1821–1891) on November 5th. *Hamlet*, *Othello*, and *Macbeth* were seen in rotation with other dramas such as *Money*, *The Gamester*, *The Wife,* and *The Stranger*. Sullivan's acting was considered to be in the new calm, quiet style of Macready. His voice was described as mellow (fig. 42).

Sullivan terminated his popular run on December 3rd. The Standard was to be closed for installation of the panto, but Douglass was persuaded to present some of his nautical plays, mixed with the stock company's regular programs. This phenomenally successful year ended with yet another triumph, *Roast Beef and Plum Pudding; or, Harlequin Card King and the Island of Games*. The *Era* reported that 114,000 had attended this Christmas spectacle in the first twenty-one days of its eight week run. This was despite the fact it was one of the coldest winters on record, dropping to eight degrees below zero at one point. *Roast Beef* was a relatively normal mid-century panto. In the doggerel verses of the opening no contemporary event or person was spared. The "odious" coal tax, and the Lord Mayor's parade were lashed in turn, and the criticisms warmly applauded. The evening's most popular event was the two "great scenes *de resistance*":

A vast galleried palace, which when occupied by the army of the King of Games had a most novel and striking effect. Nearly one-hundred of the soldiers represented each a pack of cards; a billiard table, dominoes, and several other games form a body-garde each having dice for faces and dice boxes for helmets. . . the transformation scene consists of a hall of pillars and also a gallery at the back and extreme height of the stage. In the pillars are medallions where children as fairies blend in various groups. The gallery at the back is filled with fays, and, after the transformation the whole scene descends. Forward and grouped on it are almost countless number of fairies. The entire is covered with jewels, and, when lit by the prismatic fires has a very chaste, and at the same time glittering effect. These two scenes are the best Mr. Douglass has ever done.[41]

This describes the scene on the advertising poster (fig. 43). The panto proved so popular, that beginning 2 January 1854, six morning performances were added to the six evening ones.

Momentum is a powerful agent. Virtually no play or performer in the spring season had a poor house. The Barnum Children had been with the company since before Christmas. They were well received, and compared favorably with the famous Bateman Children. Fanny Reeves, a vocalist, had a warm reception in sketches, and vaudevilles. The new temperance play created such excitement that lithographs depicting *Gin and Water; or, Its Use and Abuse* (20 February 1854 ff.) were "to be had of John Douglass at the Theatre."

The basso voiced actor Tom Mead (1821–1889) was engaged for the last week of March. He portrayed Hamlet and Othello, and took the leads in *A New Way to Pay Old Debts, The Stranger* and *Pizarro* (figs. 44 and 45). Mead had an extensive repertoire of heroes, but due to his voice, his forte was really villains. His Iago and Chateau Renaud in *The Corsican Brothers* were hair-raising. He was seen in London from time to time, but the majority of his performances were in the provinces. At the Standard the press reported his houses crowded, and hundreds were turned away.

Henry Russell (1813–1890) was an added attraction in April. Russell, while working as a music teacher in New York, invented an entertainment that he toured for many years. It was entitled *Far West; or, the Emigrant's Progress.* Russell composed the music, and Dr. Charles Mackay the poetry, for this musical travelogue. The Standard's playbill described it as "Progress of the Emigrant from the old world to the new, representing upward of 4000 miles of American scenery." The painted drops represented scenes from Liverpool to the "undulating prairies of the far west of Illinois." During the display of these paintings, which incidentally were not advertised as moving panoramas, Russell sang songs and recited verse. The songs included "Life on the Ocean Wave" and "Woodman Spare that Tree." Anecdotes descriptive of American life and manners were told. This was followed, after the inter-

---

41. The *Era*, (1 January 1854).

mission, by a second act called *Negro Life in Freedom and Slavery*, during which he sang "A Ship on Fire" and "The Maniac."

The popular vocalist and actor of Irish characters, George Hodson (1822–1869) then appeared at the Standard. His vehicle was Tyrone Power's *Born to Good Luck*. About the same time the Douglass group was reduced by the death of the playwright T. E. Wilks. Madame Wharton also died sometime before June 4th. Her troupe continued to present its "edifying" tableau for a few years, but not at the Standard. Among the early summer mix of nautical plays, and musical acts was Harry Widdicomb. He was the son of the ring master at Astley's. His "line"

was the recitation of comic poems and impersonations.

Gathering new momentum, Douglass kept the theatre open for a summer season. Capitalizing on the Crimean War, he rushed a battle drama onto the boards. *The Baltic Fleet; or, Our Admiral and the Storming of Hango.* opened June 4th, and ran three weeks. The war generated much activity in London from 1853 to 1856. Sailors and soldiers on leave brought wives and sweethearts to the theatres. Increased manufacturing and shipping brought businessmen and their families each summer. This carried the theatres during what was normally a slack time of the year.

In the last week of August, James Anderson returned from his triumphant American tour and opened the autumn

Fig. 46. Webb's toy theatre plate for *Harlequin Dame Crump, and the Silver Penny; Pig Won't Get Over the Style To-night* (1854). The toy theatre title, and those in the playbills have several variants. *From George Speaight.*

season on the early date of August 28th. After twenty–four nights of his repertoire, he premiered a new sensation drama. This anti-Russian play was *Schamyl; or, the Circassian Chief and the Prophet's Son* (30 September 1854). The script was from a French play which had been produced at the Port St. Martin Theatre, as adapted by Anderson and William Markwell. The general plot of the drama was the heroic exploits of the Circassian patriot Schamyl, in his struggle with the Russian invaders. The climax was the "wonderful escape on a raft down the torrent of the Korson river." A major feature of the production was a Circassian procession requiring two hundred extras in "classically correct costume."

Schamyl is typical of the sub-form of melodrama that came to be called in the press, "sensation drama." It was the spectacular technical effects, in a scene or two, that categorized a play in this genre.

Schamyl is the ward of Prince Ivanhoff, the military Governor of Georgia. Schamyl secretly longs to shake off Russian rule. In the first act, set in the palace of Ivanhoff, the audience discovers the locals have been unusually troublesome, and one of the officers has declared a state of war exists between the Russian "protectors" and the native tribes.

Schamyl has been absent for some time. It turns out that he has organized a plot in conjunction with an American. In Act Two, the dissident tribes meet on the mountain steppes. Following the planning meeting, numerous skirmishes are punctuated with heroic acts, and "lofty ennobling sentiments." Battlements are stormed by native hordes; but in turn treachery, and Russian force reverse the fortunes of the guerrilla army. At the last moment a secret pass permits escape. The Russians are ensnared in a trap. Later in the act flood gates are loosed upon the Circassian leaders, and a torrent descends. However, a friendly raft is found, and all are saved. The final act brings forth the events of the Crimean War period. Amidst the booming artillery, and cheers of the troupes, Teflis falls before the power of the allied armies. Anderson was described as "effective," in the title role. His costume was a tall sheepskin cap, and becartridged tunic of the mountain tribes. He performed with "great vigor and impassioned fervor."[42]

After Anderson's run ended on October 27th, Douglass brought in a typical series of entertainers for the pre-Christmas potpourri of events. Most notable were dramatizations of some of Dickens's works.

The new panto opened on 24 December 1854. Fire Burn Stick; or, Harlequin Old Dame Crump and the Silver Penny had a wonderfully popular transformation scene and, for the first time at the

---

42. The *Era*, (1 October 1854).

Fig. 47. The transformation scene from *Harlequin Dame Crump* **(1854), painted by John Neville, toy theatre plate.** *From George Speaight.*

Standard, the great clown Tom Matthews. The reviewer said:

Let us imagine the ample stage shown to its utmost limits backed with clouds of silver and gold radiant with innumerable revolving stars covered with glittering drops [of crystal]. In front of this were many brightly decorated cars, filled with Fays in gold and silver tissue dresses. From every available point, as if descending from the clouds are groups of women and children all dressed in gauzes of ethereal blue and silver. The scene when lit with prismatic fires and electric light, is surprisingly beautiful. It drew forth an instantaneous call for the manager.

In the tricks of the Harlequinade the most popular transformations included the one of the forts at Sebastopol that turned into the interior of a London-cook-shop with tables and boxes lit with gas, the conquered Russians being sentenced by public accord to three

104

months imprisonment therein (figs. 46 and 47).[43]

The new year of 1855 registered even further successes for the Douglass's management. The suburban services on new railroad lines radiating from the Bishopsgate area gave potential, but more distant audience members, the chance to see a play at the Standard, and return home at an acceptable hour.

One of the Standard's bills, as a public service, listed the trains leaving at 11:30 P.M. for Stratford, Lea Bridge, Tottenham Park, Water Lane, Ponder's End, Waltham, Broadborne St., Margarets Ware, and Hartford. These stations were within twenty miles to the north and east of the theatre.

The constant turnover of the Standard's audience led Douglass to the inevitable conclusion that long run of a play was a feasible technique as opposed to the old, nightly change, approach of the repertory system. Therefore at the end of the panto season, T. E. Lyon and the stock company revived the *Vicar of Wakefield*. One news account said that Lyon performed Dr.Primrose for seventy nights. This probably included the original long runs of the 1850 season. After this revival, two major stars came to the Standard, Isabel Glyn (1823–1889) and Henry Marston (ca.1804-1883). Miss Glyn had been a pupil of Charles Kemble. She was a

striking beauty, with dark hair, and large expressive eyes (figs. 48, and 49). Her forte was splendid diction, and stage presence. Many thought she was the finest actress of the English stage, during her years with Samuel Phelps, at the Sadler's Wells Theatre between 1848 and 1857. After leaving the "Wells," she retired to teach acting, and

Fig. 48. Isabel Glyn (1823–1889) in *A Midsummer Night's Dream* at Sadler's Wells, 1849. *From A.S.J.*

---

43. The *Era*, (31 December 1854). The punishment of the Russians was apparently equated with, at the very least, death by food poisoning three times over. This panto was popular enough to be brought out as a toy theatre set by W. Webb.

giving occasional readings of Shakespearean verse.

Henry Marston was from the same mold. He also had been a major member of the Phelps Company (figs. 50 and 51). These two revived a number of unlikely plays never seen before at the Standard. They opened with three weeks of *Antony and Cleopatra* followed by *The Duchess of Malfi*. After a week off, while the stock company revived *Black Eyed Susan*, they reappeared in *Winter's Tale*, *Macbeth*, *Isabella; or the Fatal Marriage*, *The Hunchback*, and *Henry VIII*. In all, their amazing successes ran for sixty-six nights before the end of May. Before June 7th Douglass's audiences were treated to *The Bridal*, *Venice Preserved*, *Much Ado About Nothing*, *Taming of the Shrew*, *The Merchant of Venice*, *Macbeth*, *The Hunchback*, and *The School for*

Fig. 50. Henry Marston (ca.1804–1883). *From the London Museum.*

Scandal. A notable feature of the Glyn-Marston run was that for the first time at the Standard, babies in arms were not permitted in the auditorium. This reflects on the attentiveness and sensitivity to the poetry the new audiences were demanding.

The long runs of the winter, and spring of 1855, gave John Douglass time to reflect on his fantastic success. It must have been clear to him that while his stock company could flesh out the requisite roles surrounding the guest stars, they no longer could satisfy the changing tastes of audience. Fewer and fewer weeks each season were devoted to the old repertory system. The classical revivals were being produced in a more complete way, and were taking more time in the evening's program. Therefore, even the short

Fig. 49. Isabel Glyn (1823–1889). *From the Rose Lipman Library, Hackney.*

dramas, and farces that normally accompanied the Shakespeare, were gradually removed from the bill.

The actor William Creswick, one of the future performers at the Standard, was particularly commended for the restoration of the text that audiences, and critics were demanding. At the Standard *Antony and Cleopatra* or *The Duchess of Malfi* would fill the evening except for one short curtain raiser. Another factor was the more three dimensional nature of the scenery. The intervals between scenes was taking longer for the scene changes.

Douglass could not always depend on major guest stars' availability when he had an open week. This was especially true during the summer. Therefore, he hit upon the idea of importing whole companies and productions from other London Theatres. First came the Adelphi Company with Edward Wright, and Benjamin Webster, in six weeks of their most recent successes. Then the repertory company brought out their familiar melodramas, and a new *Oliver Twist* to fill the slack weeks in August.

James Anderson returned 8 September 1855, for his third engagement. On the 23rd he was joined by the American actress, Mrs. J. W. Wallack, as his leading lady. This run included new productions of *The Slave*, *Gisippus*, and *Romeo and Juliet*, as well as the plays seen in 1854.

Anderson had a contract to perform at Drury Lane, but Douglass persuaded him to alternate nights between the two theatres. To fill the gaps, Douglass engaged the English and Italian Opera

Fig. 51. Henry Marston (ca.1804–1883). *From the Players.*

Company. Because the management was not sure what would be presented by press time each afternoon, the ads could not list the exact shows. The opera company probably did *Lucia di Lammermoor*, *The Bohemian Girl*, *Der Freischutz*, *La Sonnambula,* and *Faust and Marguerite*. One brilliant night, November 30th, Anderson revived the rarely seen *Alexander the Great*, by Nathaniel Lee, followed by *La Sonnambula*. On December 14th, Douglass had the Theatre "illuminated" for the one hundredth night of Anderson's run, and on the occasion of his benefit.

Other benefit nights for the company members were presented in the next week. Then a real novelty was introduced. The interesting Edith Heraud was engaged to play Juliet to Mrs. Honner's Romeo on December

20th. More about Edith Heraud will be described in Chapter 6.[44]

After Douglass's own benefit on the 21st the theatre was closed to mount the new panto. *A Merry Christmas and a Happy New Year; or Harlequin King Candle and Queen Rushlight; or, Princess Prettydear of Taperland* brought wonders to the holiday audiences on 26 December 1855.

The new craft of stage lighting had grown steadily since the arrival of controllable gas equipment in the 1830s. Charles Kean had used the lime-light with considerable effect in his production of *Henry VIII* at the Princess's Theatre. Electric arc lighting had been seen at the Standard and other theatres in the early 1850's, in the *Poses Plastique*, and the panto of 1854. The Standard's technical staff had become proficient in the use of this new technology.

Of all the gas artists Mr. John Douglass is about the most successful. Gas seems the agent to 'marshal' him the way which he should go. He worships it. Within the theatre, without the theatre—gas reigns, stars dramatic and operatic, appearing at this theatre are emblazoned to the world with gas. In pantomime productions Mr. Douglass has been most happy with his gas scenes. The Fleet Well, by night, at his bidding becomes an arcade brilliantly lit with gas. He can throw light anywhere. . . The public have already had from him some most beautiful gas scenes, but, to our opinion, none so beautifully, so tastefully arranged as in the new pantomime of *A Merry Christmas . . . .* The plot is of the usual character of all pantomime openings. Two young and virtuous lovers are pursued by those the very reverse. Such lovers are Prince Taper and Princess Prettydear. Prince Taper is the son to King Candle whilst King Extinguisher— Candle's bitter enemy—is the parent of Prettydear; the parents of course oppose the match. The lovers are protected by Queen Crystaline, who finally when both are in the Demon Coal Hole, appears and changes the dreary abode into the great scene of the evening, the Hall of Prisms, which is one entire blaze of gas jets carried in borders of horseshoe form, from the stage up to the extreme height, each border diminishing and thereby giving the notion of an immense depth, at the extreme end of which are numbers of gas stars and pillars, and one large revolving gas star in motion before them. All the space of the wings, not occupied with gas, is thickly studded with jewels thereby reflecting the gas lights in countless numbers. In various groups are children as fairies, dressed in white and silver gauze. This when lit with coloured fires, presents an appearance of indescribable beauty, and was the signal for one entire call for Mr. Douglass. . . . The pantomime passed off most pleasuringly, and not withstanding

44.   In the description of Thomas Douglass's work with gas lighting in *Memories of Mummers*, an account infers that gas-lit signs with the star's name picked out in flames was displayed on the facade of the theatre above the entrance.

Fig. 52. *A Merry Christmas and a Happy New Year; or, Harlequin King Candle, and the Princess Prettydear of Taper Land*, 26 December 1855. *From the Rose Lipman Library, Hackney.*

it plays three hours, it never once flagged (fig.52).[45]

The changes in John Douglass's managerial techniques reflect what was happening in many of the better theatres in the mid-century. Resident repertory companies producing mixed evenings of melodramas, farces, and novelty acts, were replaced by guest stars in revivals of the classics. The novelty acts went to the music halls. The importance of the resident repertory company was gradually reduced.

Few different plays were seen in an evening as the complete texts of the dramas were restored. Rehearsals in the Charles Kean tradition raised the quality of the productions. Long runs of major successes reveal that the habit of local audiences attending the same theatre every night was giving way to audiences of different individuals from more diverse places. Entire companies with their dramas or operas were brought in for short touring seasons at the Standard's lower prices. It was as if the Standard was a major theatre in a distant capitol, rather than a mile or less from the West-end house of origin.

As the years went on, this technique proved a boon to many stars and companies because they could treat the nearby Standard as a tryout house for productions they were about to take on tour to Australia, America, or the provinces. Douglass's audiences were not unlike those they would encounter in the more distant places. Yet the Standard was close enough to home to permit technical adjustments in sets, or recovery of forgotten equipment, props, or costumes. This then was the situation at the beginning of 1856. The operating techniques were set, and the Standard was a genuinely important and influential theatre.

45.   The *Era*, (30 December 1855).

Fig . 53. Sims Reeves (1818-1900) in 1858. *From Sims Reeves by Charles E. Pearce.*

6

EVENTS AND PERSONALITIES 1856–1860

During the next period the Standard was not only the largest, but it was also considered among the top two or three in London for quality. John Douglass now concentrated on management and playwrighting. His nautical roles were seen on his benefit nights, but the old melodramas were rarely performed. In February of 1856, a story from the *London Journal* was dramatized. Called *Masks and Faces*, it had considerable prosperity through the middle of March. This may have been a revision of Tom Taylor's 1852 script, or a new version by Douglass.

After this play closed, Isabel Glyn and Henry Marston returned. To their popular successes they added *King John*, *Jane Shore*, *The Gamester*, and *Evadne*. This took the season up to the second week of May when Douglass finished with a few music hall novelties.

The summer began with a significant new act. Professor John Henry Anderson (1814–1874), the Wizard of the North, was the greatest magician of his time. In addition to his magic illusions, he was something of an actor. Therefore, during his engagements, he usually performed in Scots characters, such as Rob Roy. However, it was for his illusions that he was most appreciated.

Typical of these were transformations of all sorts of small objects, half crowns, bank notes, hats, and wedding rings, into bonbons, plum puddings, and liqueurs of every denomination. Canaries appeared from the pages of a volume of the *Life of Napoleon*. On the more mechanical side, he exhibited a chair from which it was impossible to rise, a bar that was impossible to lay down, and a child endowed with strength enough to withstand the pulling power of twenty-seven strong men. Other illusions included the destruction of bonnets and hand-kerchiefs, after mangling and hacking them beyond apparent possibility of restoration, which were promptly returned whole to their owners. An empty crystal container was hung above the audience, and in a word it filled with marked coins borrowed from among the crowd.

A large thin book was displayed, and in an instant it yielded up an absolute poultry show, a quantity of luggage fit for a trip to the Antipodes, and a little girl who sang "Bonnie Dundee," to prove she was not merely a compressed compound of white muslin, and rubber.

Anderson was widely travelled throughout Britain and America. In 1860 he sent a long, detailed letter to the *Era* (July 8 and 15) about his adventures in California. This is one of the most entertaining descriptions of American life, and manners outside of Mark Twain. Anderson describes the American passion for minstrel shows; and he attempts to render American names, into English; for example: Yosemite becomes "Yousumnies."

At the Standard, Anderson held forth for six weeks until July 5th. On his last night he performed Rob Roy and "Sweet" William in *Black Eyed Susan*. In the latter, John Douglass played the comical Jacob Twig, instead of his normal sailorly role.

The next important new performer to come to the Standard opened the Autumn 1856 season. Sims Reeves (1818–1900) was one of those few superior tenors who appear every couple of generations. His reputation was enormous, and his artistry is remembered as extraordinary.

Douglass, heartened by East End audiences' reception of the English and Italian Opera Company his pit conductor had put together for the summer of 1855, set out to bring in the best he could obtain. He was able to persuade Sims Reeves and his wife to star with the "house" opera company. *Guy Mannering* by Sir Henry R. Bishop was the opening piece.

Reeves proved to be one of the most enduringly popular guest stars. With his wife, he appeared regularly for decades at the Standard. His most popular operas were: *Guy Mannering*, *The Beggar's Opera* by Gay, *The Waterman* by Charles Dibdin, *The Bohemian Girl* by Balfe, *Love in a Village* by Bickerstaff, and other French, and Italian works, all in English (figs. 53–56).

Reeves had a relatively frail constitution. The pollution-filled smogs of the industrialized English cities, described in Dickens and Conan Doyle, raised havoc with his voice. Large gas lit theatres, with their dusty stages, did not help either. He was often indisposed, which caused impresarios and managers no end of trouble with last-minute cancellations.[46]

One legend that circulated was that two matrons were discussing culture. The first said to the second, "My dear, last night we went to hear

---

46.   Douglass, *Memories of Mummers*, p. 16.

Fig. 54. Sims Reeves (1818–1900) as Fra Diavolo. *From Sims Reeves by Charles E. Pearce.*

Fig. 55. Emma Lucombe (Mrs. Sims Reeves). *From Sims Reeves by Charles E. Pearce*.

Sims Reeves in concert, and would you believe it—he actually showed up!"

Because of the extra expense of producing opera, Douglass normally doubled the prices. This did not deter the faithful, and the five thousand seats were sold out for virtually every performance.

On September 29th James Anderson again returned to the Standard. His co-star was Agnes Elsworthy (1825–1879). Together they brought out a new production of the 1842 script *The Patrician's Daughter*, by J. W. Marston. Anderson said the house was crowded to suffocation. They followed this hit with a week of the familiar classics. Then came the most important play of the season, the premiere of Anderson's own drama *Cloud and Sunshine; or, Love's Revenge!* It opened on 19 October 1856. In this Louis XIV costume drama the leading actor gets to play twin brothers in the tour-de-force tradition of *The Corsican Brothers*.[47]

The *Era* commented on the management of the Standard in regard to this production:

Under the present management a host of talent has from time to time appeared upon the boards of this theatre; and no sooner than one popular favorite retired than another is engaged. Experience, that surest of all tests has taught the manager that first rate talent will attract first rate audiences, and that whatever the cast secured, the speculation will prove remunerative—the extent of success being limited only by the capabilities of the building to accommodate the masses who are so ready to acknowledge and appreciate true talent. It is but a short time since Douglass secured the services of Mr. and Mrs. Sims Reeves. Of course, those eminent artists received such remuneration as their high position and unquestioned abilities entitled them to expect. To a more timid person than Mr. Douglass the venture might seem a hazardous one; the contrary, however, proved to be the case; the beautiful singing of the accomplished pair was at once recognized by the populace of Shoreditch, who flocked to the theatre in thousands, and the liberality of the manager was rewarded by a return commensurate with the magnitude of the enterprise. Whilst the system of starring is thus carried on, it is not accompanied by the vicious principle which we too often find associated with it—we mean that of engaging one star, whilst the remainder of the company is utterly contemptible, and beneath notice.

It would be unjust to lay any such charge against a manager whose general company includes such names as those of Mrs. Honner, Miss Adelaide Cooke, Miss Eliza Terry; with Messrs. James, Johnstone, Gaston, Dudley, Moreton and others. . . .[48]

---

47. Other dual role plays have always been popular for actors. Among them are *The Lyons Mail*, *The Prisoner of Zenda*, *Ring Around the Moon*, *House on the Bridge of Notre Dame*, *Tale of Two Cities*, *Prince and the Pauper*, *Cloud and Sunshine*, and for the ladies, *East Lynne* and *Green Bushes*.

48. A similar but expanded statement praising all aspects of Douglass's management since the new licensing act permitted the expansion of theatre in general, was printed in the *Era*, (13 December 1857).

On Thursday, under the unassuming title of *Cloud and Sunshine* was produced for the first time, a new romantic play in four acts, the authorship of which rumour attributes to Mr. Anderson himself. . . In the Capital of France in the days of Louis XIV there resided a Scots lady of high birth, great wealth, and rare attractions, Diana, the Duchess of Nairn. She was attended by a numerous retinue, but her sole adviser and only real friend appears to have been her steward, David Leslie, an old retainer of the family, who had saved the life of the lady's father at the battle of Willicrankie in 1689, and whose attachment to his mistress amounted to something like devotion. This man watches with a jealous eye over the honour of the Duchess, and is the principal means of saving her from the machinations alike of false friends, open enemies, and subtle foes. The fatal beauty of the Duchess gains for her a host of admirers, the majority of whom are the gay hangers-on of the court. . . But there is one whose passion for the lady is not feigned. This is the young Chevalier Edgar DuNois who loves the lady to distraction.

Rejected, the young Chevalier falls into melancholy and perishes by his own hand at the end of the first act. The gallants of the court, angered by the supposed pride of the Duchess, having caused the death of the young man, contrive a conspiracy to humble her. In this echo of the *Lady of Lyons*, the plotters select Henri DuNois, the twin brother of Edgar. He is convinced by the courtiers that she had caused the death of his brother. With the help of this cavil he succeeds in causing the Duchess to fall in love with him,

then denounces her as a heartless coquette in front of a host of courtiers. Eventually it is made clear to Henri that the Duchess was innocent, and after many complications, 'the clouds that have obscured the fortunes of Henri and Diana are cleared by their ultimate union which gilds the end of the play with sunshine.' The play was superbly mounted and the brilliancy of some of the scenes would put to shame the pretensions of many a [West End] establishment.[49]

James Anderson received plaudits for the script, and for his intelligent acting of the twin brothers. "Miss Elsworthy . . . played with equal ability in the height of her scorn and depth of her affection." The stock company actors were equally praised for their support.

Douglass followed Anderson's triumph with the East London debut of the American actors Mr. and Mrs. Keeley. Their most often performed play was W.E. Suter's dramatization of Mrs. Stowe's anti-slavery story *Dred; or, the Great Dismal Swamp*. The Keeleys were followed by Isabel Glyn in her favorite roles, until December 5th. Then, for the first time Douglass gave his technical staff a break by closing down for seventeen days to permit the mounting of the glorious new Christmas pantomime, *Hickedy Pickedy My Black Hen; or, Harlequin King Winter and Queen Spring* (24 December 1856). The press said Douglass far outstripped his previous efforts in this

49.   The *Era*, (22 October 1856).

new panto.

The scenes in the opening, upon which the production will take a position are the Grand Hall of Icicles, the Fairy World of Flowers, and the Golden Realms of Summer. When Douglass was called before the curtain because of the splendor of the scenes, he brought forth the artist to share in the applause. This was young Charles S. James, son of the manager of the Queen's Theatre.

The reviews went on to describe the Hall of Icicles: "where wonderful effect was produced by illuminating glass drops. . . ."[50]

The panto ran until February 18th, to be followed by P.T. Barnum's General Tom Thumb, the American midget. In March Samuel Phelps (1804–1878) came to the Standard for the first time. He brought his leading lady Emma Atkinson the

Fig. 56. Simes Reeves (1818–1900) and Catherine Hayes in *Lucia Di Lammermoor*, in 1846. *From Sims Reeves by Charles E. Pearce.*

mile and a half from their Sadler's Wells Theatre. For eight weeks they produced a fine series of the classics. The most notable plays not seen at the Standard before were, *Richelieu, William Tell, Werner,* and *The Fatal Dowry.* One melodrama offered as an afterpiece several times, was Edward Stirling's 1837 *Carline; or,* *the Female Brigand.* This old script permitted Mrs. Honner's star to shine once again, for her devoted East End fans. In fact, she assumed seven different characters in this dark play of female revenge. In it Carline attempts to serve retribution upon the libertine Count Vincentio; but she dies at the

50.   The *Era*, (31 December 1856).

end, having been stabbed by her own henchmen by mistake for the Count.

From time to time, since 1850, Douglass had permitted members of his company who were interested in ballet to perform their own choreography. Chief among the dancers were Richard Flexmore(1824–1860), and Mme. Auriol (fig.57). Francesca Auriol often played Columbine in the pantos, and both worked in dance roles in various London theatres. Among the pieces they danced were *The Dancing Scotchman* (October 1854), *The*

Fig. 57. Francesca Auriole as Columbine, tinsel print. *From the London Museum.*

Menorella (November1854), *Valentine and Orson* (February1855), *Divertissement* (July 1855), *The Dumb Savoyard and his Monkey* (May 1857), *L'Amour de Folie*, (August 1857), *Cobbler and Tailor* (August 1857), *My Fetch* (October, 1858), and *The Pearl of Spain* (August 1859). Spanish Dancers were also an attraction in March 1857, and November 1858.

This cannot be said to be a case of pushing the higher forms of dance-arts. But at least Douglass was open to presenting the dance form as a separate type of performance that stood on its own merits. After 1859 the dances disappear from the playbills. Perhaps after Flexmore's death, the dancers found more fertile fields in the corps de ballet of the opera houses, and eventually at the Alhambra.

After Phelps, Professor Anderson performed his magic in June and July.[51] His run ended on July 25th with several plays in the last few days. In addition to *Rob Roy*, and *Black Eyed Susan*, he had added to his repertoire *Pizarro*, and *The Lone Chateau*.

After Anderson closed, Isabel Glyn came for three weeks, then Sims Reeves for three, then Anderson again for eleven. This took the season up to the Christmas panto. At the end of Miss Glyn's series, the theatre had received a quick redecoration. The interior was painted a pale pink below, and azure blue above, with scrolls of gold and

---

51.   The *Era* recorded the head count at the Standard's box office for his first week beginning June 15th, Monday
       through Thursday as: 4031, 4241, 3903, 5071 for a total of 17,246 for the first four nights.

white. The columns supporting the boxes were lined with more mirrors, and a fancy new luster was hung in the center of the auditorium.

The Christmas panto of 1857 was *Georgy Porgey Puddin and Pie, Kissed the Girls Till He Made Them Cry; or, Harlequin Old Daddy Long Legs*. The review mentions that Douglass had originated the custom of performing the panto twice a day for as long as the extra performances brought in full houses. The transformation scene was, as usual, extraordinarily inventive.

. . .a clever spider's web is slowly drawn away, the scene behind becoming more strongly visible until the web had vanished.

The setting behind was of crystal palaces and a colossal temple of gems, and jewels. At each side stood temples with revolving columns covered with brilliant foil and gilding. At the rear was a huge pavilion with a cupola dome. This also had revolving columns. From the center of each temple rose a jeweled framework supporting women clad in feathery-looking costumes of a sliver tissue. The whole was illuminated with colored fires.

In *East End Entertainment*, Wilson mentioned the *Illustrated London News* review, describing the use of electric light in this 1857 panto. He said, "This was the earliest reference to my knowledge, for the use of electricity on the stage." Of course, Mme. Wharton had used projected light from electric arcs since at least 1851; and Douglass had used it in pantos since 1854. These early battery-powered instruments were for short-lived effects, and were much less reliable than the gas lime lights.

After the panto, in March, a new personality visited the Standard. Charles Dillon (1819–1881) had worked as John Douglass's stage manager, at the City of London Theatre, in 1832, when he was fourteen. He made his London acting debut at Sadler's Wells in 1856 as Belphegor in the play of the same name. This was a translation

Fig. 58. Charles Dillon (1819–1881) as Belphegor. *From the Rose Lipman Library, Hackney.*

of Marc Fournier, and D'Ennery's play *Paillasse*. The theme is that an itinerant mountebank could have a heart, and passions as high as those of a king. In his youth, John Coleman saw Dillon at the time when he was married to Clara Conquest of the Grecian Theatre family. Coleman described Dillon as:

> . . .an abnormally ugly young man with a huge cavernous mouth, protruding, and

irregular teeth, a corrugated nose, snake-like glittering eyes, a head of long lank black hair, growing very low down on a broad but receding forehead, over the brows of which two great bumps projected. But when he had been on the stage five minutes I lost sight of his plebian appearance in my admiration of his ability. He moved with ease, grace, and distinction. . . his sword play was magnificent, his pathos and passion were alike, admirable (fig. 58).[52]

Dillon made a career of this one role, and came back to the Standard from time to time.

After the Easter concerts, offered by Douglass each season, Samuel Phelps, Isabel Glyn, and Henry Marston returned in *The Winter's Tale*. The playbill states: "The piece has been mounted with every attention to the accessories, and many of those magnificent efforts which Mr. Kean produced at the Princess's are repeated here in a style scarcely less complete."

The Duchess of Malfi was alternated with the above, and an afterpiece called *The Seven Castles of the Passions* was presented on each bill. This play was Edward Stirling's adaptation of a French, moral extravaganza, "with gorgeous scenery and appointments."

This mixture of Sadler's Wells Stars, and the Standard's company brought out several more dramas not seen at the theatre before: *Man of the World*, *The Iron Chest*, *The Mountaineers*, and

Fig. 59. Celine Celeste (1814–1882) as the Arab Boy, in the *French Spy*, at the Standard Theatre. *From the Rose Lipman Library, Hackney.*

52. Frances Fleetwood, *Conquest* (London, 1953), p.188.

Pompeii; or, the Doomed City. The season ended on 12 June 1858.

John Douglass was at the zenith of his reputation for excellent management. Because of this, it was announced that he had been asked to manage the new Pavilion Theatre when it was finished. At this same time the Adelphi Company moved to the Standard, as they were to do each June for years to come. In this trial-run Mme. Celeste was presented in her most representative role as Miami in *Green Bushes* by J. B. Buckstone. (figs. 59–61).

Celine Celeste (1814–1882) was born in Paris, and trained at the Music Academy. In 1829 she appeared in the United States of America, and there married a Mr.Elliott. She came to England, and performed in Liverpool in 1830, and London by 1837. By 1844 she had established a fine reputation. She and Benjamin Webster joined forces to manage the Adelphi Theatre. In her early years she played characters involving a kind of dance pantomime, or mute action. Miami is an example of this, at least in the beginning of the play. She is a wild woman of the American wilderness, half-French, half-Indian. After much passion, and other complication, she shoots an Irishman who attacks her and then leaps from a precipice into a raging river to escape capture. Surviving the torrent, she is rescued by a party of French soldiers who take her to Europe. There she is recognized as the lost granddaughter of a wealthy family. The poignant scenes are those where her naive woodsy ways are contrasted with the haute monde of the Parisian salon. Eventually Miami makes amends to the wife and child of her attacker.

Mme. Celeste began as a dancer, but her English diction improved to the point that she could perform regular dramas. Her accent was considered charming, and she was at the height of her popularity in the 1850s.

For the autumn season of 1858 the Standard was redecorated. A new grand central gas-chandelier was installed. A new "Parisian" saloon was added for the upper boxes, and everything was painted anew. The season was much like the previous ones with James Anderson, Sims Reeves, and the Adelphi Company filling the dates before the panto.

The Pavilion Theatre opened on October 30th. This must have distracted Douglass because for the first time the Christmas Pantomime

Fig. 60. Celine Celeste (1814–1882) in 1831. *From the Enthoven Collection.*

Fig. 61. Celine Celeste (1814–1882), as Miami in *Green Bushes*, **1845.** *From the Illustrated London News.*

was written by an outside author, F. G. Cheatham.

It was *Queen Ann's Farthing and the Three Kingdoms of Copper, Silver, and Gold; or, Harlequin Old King Counterfeit and the Good Fairy of the Magic Mint.*

After the panto closed on February 26th, a group of American actors starred in a series of classic revivals.

McKean Buchanan (1823–1872), Mrs. W. C. Forbes, and Agnes Kemble worked with the stock company. Plays seen in this series included *Virginius*, *William Tell*, *The Bridal*, and *The Tempest*. They were followed by Barney Williams(1824–1876) and Maria Pray Williams(1826–1881) who were billed as the "original Irish boy and the Yankee girl." All-around performers, they sang, danced, and acted in plays, all of an Irish complexion (fig.62).

Two really memorable events took place in the spring of 1859. On April 20th John Douglass rented the Standard to J. B. Gough who founded the Blue Ribbon Temperance Army there. The theatre was used for the lectures and pledge-signing ceremonies.

The second event was a production of Madame Adelaide Ristori's *Medea* in English, with Edith Heraud in the lead (fig.63). The Italian play was a poetic version of Euripides's original. It was translated into English by her father, John A. Heraud (1801–1887). She had appeared in amateur performances in her youth, then made her professional debut as Juliet at the Richmond Theatre with the Marstons. In London she was first seen as Julia in *The*

GREAT NATIONAL STANDARD THEATRE,
SHOREDITCH.

Mʳ & Mʳˢ BARNEY WILLIAMS.
THE ORIGINAL
IRISH BOY & YANKEE GAL.

Fig. 62 Barney Williams (1824-1876), and Maria Pray Williams (1826-1881), the Original Irish Lad, and Yankee Girl. *From the Rose Lipman Library, Hackney.*

Hunchback. Her most unusual role of Medea was first produced at Sadler's Wells in 1854. In 1855 she starred in another of her father's dramas, *A Wife or No Wife*. Then, at the Marylebone in 1856 she played Hortensia in *The Merchant's Daughter of Tulon*. Her run of twelve nights at the Standard, as Medea, was considered unprecedented for such an esoteric drama.

In addition to her grace, refinement, and beauty, her voice was her chief asset. It was considered sweet and distinct. She seldom spoke above the conversational volume, yet her elocution and pronunciation permitted the poetry to be heard easily throughout the huge house. Because of

Fig. 63. Edith Heraud (-1899). *From the Rose Lipman Library, Hackney.*

her success at the Standard she was invited to give a reading of *Antigone* at the Crystal Palace. It was witnessed by thousands, and remembered for years to come. She returned to the Standard briefly in 1864; but because of her personal wealth and social position she retired after a relatively short career. Later she read educational lectures. One on Tennyson, that she gave in 1873, was considered so fine that it was published. Shortly before her death, in 1898, she edited her father's memoirs.

In July of 1859 the Standard was again improved by the addition of a pit and stall saloon to compliment the one built the year before for the boxes. The summer attractions were: the magician, Professor Michael Hart, and Mr. Harwood, and his trained horse "Beda." But the hippodrama's popularity was on the wane; *Claude Duval*, and *Dick Turpin* seemed very old-fashioned. The Christy Minstrels had a better box office in mid August, to be followed by "Bravo" Hicks, then Sims Reeves.

The first new attraction of the season came on October 2nd when Joseph Proctor (1816–1897) brought his New York company before the Shoreditch audience, in their hit *Nick of the Woods; or, the Jibbernoisy*. The "Jibbernoisy," as the character was called, was performed by Miss Medina. The script was fashioned from a novel by Dr. Bird. It was popular enough to run for thirteen days. Then, Proctor performed in the familiar classics for another two weeks.

After some typical standard revivals by the stock company, Sims Reeves's sister-in-law Fanny, who was known for her role of Apollo in the burlesque *Midas*, brought a full company of singers for a December opera season. Scattered among the musical favorites were two new works: *Il Trovatore*, and *Mauritana*.

The Theatre was closed on December 20th to permit the mounting of the new panto, *Harlequin Earth Air Fire and Water; or, Mistress Mary Quite Contrary and the Black Buccaneer; or, Mary Mary Quite Contrary How Does Your Garden Grow*. The transformation scene, the chief feature, was for the first time operated by Floyd's patent steam lifting apparatus. This engine was fitted up in the yard next to the theatre to windup the ropes that raised figures, and scenery in the spectacular, unfolding, revolving, scenic climax.

Douglass was trying to amalgamate the operations of the Standard and the new Pavilion theatres. But after all, one person can do just so much! The Pavilion's panto, also by Douglass, was *Mary Mary Quite Contrary, How Does Your Garden Grow? or, Harlequin Silver Bells Cockle Shells and Primroses All in a Row*, both opening the same night, 26 December 1859.

Something of the dangers of the profession this same year was revealed in conjunction with an inquest into the death of the pantomimist and costume assistant at the Standard, M. Byrd. It was stated by his brother, in a newspaper, article, that he had been injured shortly after boxing day by jumping through a trap, while in the character of Pantaloon, and the stage hands failed to catch him. John Douglass indignantly answered this in a letter to the *Era* on February 14th. He stated that Byrd had been in poor health for a long time, and that he believed it was because of the white (lead) makeup Byrd always used despite "many repeated warnings to its dangerous, poisonous nature."

This event was merely a punctuation to what proved to be the first truly unsatisfying season since the year before the Great Exposition of 1850. Musicals, novelties, and American actors did not represent the level of quality that Anderson, Phelps, and Glyn had. Business was off, but what was cause and effect? Aesthetic taste was in transition. Social and political affairs were in turmoil. Douglass spread himself too thinly, running back and forth between the two large, and somewhat distant, theatres. A general malaise spread over the theatrical profession, and deepened in the next several years.

MESSRS. BIGWOOD AND REYNOLDS.
A pair of Britannia's Veterans.

Fig. 64. George B. Bigwood (1829–1913), and Reynolds, comedians and character actors. *From Entr'acte Annual.*

7

MISS MARRIOTT, AND THE END OF AN ERA

In 1860, John Douglass's sons became old enough to take on some of the burdens of the family enterprise. In mid-January of 1860, the *Era* mentions that sixteen year old Richard Douglass, who had been trained by William Beverley, had provided his father with two fine settings for the recent panto.

As business things went, the Christmas spectaculars of 1859 and 1860 had been artistically satisfactory; but a general decline in attendance was being noticed at the box office.

The winter-spring season had a weak beginning. A new melodrama by John Mordaunt, based on a story in *Reynold's Miscellany*, called *Holly Bush Hall; or, a Track in the Snow,* ran for a few weeks. Pell Bones, the original minstrel-man "bones" player came with his company. A week after the minstrels, Tom Taylor's new drama *The Seasons* was opened. Then came William Travers's *Dinora*, a play with the same story as the opera at Covent Garden; but it had proved a dull beginning through mid-April.

Other portents appeared. On April 10th, a fire began in the scenery at the Pavilion Theatre. Panic was barely averted as the drapes, and a border flamed up. John Douglass made olympic record time for the mile down crowded Commercial Road to Stepney, where he arrived in time to calm the audience. The strain of the double management began to tell, even though he had his brother (the jovial Samuel) and his sons to assume some duties.

At this point, Alice Marriott (1824–1900), a fine actress, was brought into the operation. The acting company was still much the same as it had been for a decade. Mrs. Honner played strong women; Eliza Terry, and Mrs. Alfred Rayner, respectively, took young and mature women's parts. Alfred Rayner, John Mordaunt, Chalton, and H. Lewis took the dramatic roles for men. The low comedian was George B. Bigwood (1829–1913) (fig. 64). Alice Marriott was born in London. She made her debut at Drury Lane in 1854, in the role of Bianca in *Fazio, the Italian Wife.* After a time in the Drury Lane company, she moved to the Lyceum. On 10 April 1860 she was brought into the stock company at the Standard, again as Bianca. Charles Dillon was engaged to play Fazio. Douglass was trying to strengthen the company. Along with a traditional repertoire, the two new-comers were seen in their specialties of Bianca and Belphegor (figs. 65 and 66).

James Anderson then returned to the house on May 14th, in a series of Shakespearean standards. He also mounted new productions of Schiller's *The Robbers* and *The Merchant of Venice.* Anderson stayed three weeks, though the business was poor. His analysis of this was that, in the spring, beginning in the 1860's, the Epsom Races "always thinned my East End patrons." In addition to Derby Day on May 23rd, the Grand National Volunteer Rifle Association held its first meeting on Wimbledon Common, on the third of June. Queen Victoria, and a half a million of her subjects attended, thus emptying all the theatres. Anderson said, "this left the actors out in the cold, and made John Douglass hitch up his tarry trousers, and take extra rum."[53]

To counteract the problem Douglass moved the older performers to the Pavilion where their acting style better suited the local tastes, while at the same time young performers were brought in to support Miss Marriott at the Standard. Mrs. Honner began to alternate between the two groups, while Miss Marriott assumed the leads. Anderson considered the new company weaker than normal, except for Miss Marriott, and Alfred Rayner.

It was during this decade the Lauri family of dancers, and musicians began to appear on the playbills. One of the girls was to marry Arthur Douglass, John's younger son, and right-hand man. She performed in the music halls for many years as the "electric star." Arthur, who was something of an inventor, built a revolving, battery illuminated star affixed to a crown that she wore in her act. "This great novelty caused considerable excitement."[54]

Miss Marriott was at the height of her powers and willing to undertake the most diverse possible roles. She played Hamlet; and Romeo, as well as Juliet, during this first summer at the Standard. Douglass could see in her energy, and devotion a person of major ability, who could go beyond mere center stage. On 2 August 1860, it was announced to the press, that she had been made directress of the Standard Theatre. As part of this position, she was empowered to create her own

---

53. Anderson, p. 254.
54. Douglass, *Memories of Mummers*, p. 26.

Fig. 65 Alice Marriott (1824–1900). *From the Enthoven Collection.*

company of actors. Douglass then transferred most of his old stock company to the Pavilion. Mrs. Honner seems to have chosen not to go; it was at this time she went to Sadlers Wells.

The first plays Miss Marriott selected were her own vehicles. *Hamlet*, *Romeo and Juliet*, *A Tale of Two Cities*, *Evadne*, *Rob Roy*, *Esmerelda* (*The Hunchback of Notre Dame*), *Richelieu*, *The Lady of Lyons*, *The Wife*, *The Gamester*, *Richard III*, *Money*, *The Stranger*, and *School for Scandal*. She was in earnest, and did not stint in choosing the most popular classics. Barry Sullivan became her leading man, and they performed these works through October 1st when one of the new plays they had prepared opened.

Fig. 66. Alice Marriott (1824–1900).
From the Enthoven Collection.

The Daughter of the People; or, Ambition's Wreck, described in the reviews as a combination of *Joan of Arc*, and *A Tale of Two Cities*, managed only a two-week run. The second play was also short-lived, but of some interest because of the opportunity for bravo performance it gave the directress. *Cartouche; or, the French Housebreaker* was a translation of a popular French play. In it, Miss Marriott, as the male protagonist, played a character "demanding immense physical exertion—almost super-human indeed—and yet she was equal to it. . . .Her voice and figure are admirably suited to the character." In the scene where Cartouche's young bride dies on their wedding day, from a shot intended for the hero, she was especially effective. "Her intense but manly grief," then sudden flight bearing Cartouche's bride's body tested her powers to the utmost. Despite these good reviews the play only lasted three weeks.

During this run, several nights were turned over to Joseph Proctor and his American company. They presented John Howard Payne's *Damon and Pythias*. With Proctor was a young actor, A. B. Bierce of Kentucky, described as "a smart comedian."

The last premiere of the autumn was *Strathmore*, a tragic romance by Westland Marston. Despite a complex plot, which gave the actors a fair amount of difficulty in keeping the audience in mind of what was happening, the play was given decent notices, and had good houses. In typical fashion the theatre was then closed to mount the Christmas pantomime.

John Douglass returned and, assisted by John Mordaunt, staged Francis Cheatham's *Gulliver's Travels to the Giant and Dwarf Kingdoms of Brobdingnag and Lilliput; or, Harlequin and the Fairy Queen of the Regions of Imagination*. Chief among the sensations of this extravaganza were one hundred of the smallest children Douglass could commandeer from the theatrical families of his acquaintance. He also hired the tallest men he could for the giants. From the scene shop John Wright provided more revolving golden temples filled with dazzling lights, and fairies dressed in silver tissue. There was, as well, a moving panorama, the first use of this device at the Standard.

At the end of the panto in late February Charles Mathews the younger presented several of his entertain-

Fig. 67. Charles James Mathews (1808–1878) and Lizzie Davenport (Mrs. Mathews), (-1899) in their *At Home*. *From A.S.J.*

ments. Featured were: *The Adventures of a Billet Deux*; *A Game of Speculation*; *Cool as a Cucumber*; *Used Up*; *Little Toddlekins*; *Married for Money*; *His Excellency*; and *Patter vs. Clatter* (figs.67 and 68). This was followed by the first performance at the Standard of Phillips's Adelphi drama *The Dead Heart*, with Miss Mariott and Benjamin Webster.

During this spring John Douglass's elder son, John Thomas, had made his professional debut as a playwright. His incipient works were short farces, and adaptations of French melodramatic successes. A few were presented at the Pavilion. If they showed promise, they would be added for several nights at the Standard. The first one of these had the prophetic title of *First Impressions*

Fig. 68 Charles James Mathews (1808-1878), and Lizzie Davenport (Mrs. Mathews), (-1899) in their *At Home*. *From A.S.J.*

Everything. The melodramas of the season included the lurid: *The Mulatto of Mexico; or, the Pirates of the Savannah*, followed shortly by *The House on the Bridge of Notre Dame*, from the French original by Theodore Barrière and Henri de Kock. In another version of this story, popular at the Lyceum, Mme. Celeste was able to play two roles (à la *The Corsican Brothers*) (fig. 69).

Despite the activity, there was now some real financial strain because of declining audiences at both of Douglass's theatres. He took his first benefit since 1855 to generate some cash. All his stars, old and new, who could be assembled, filled in for the evening. This may also have represented something of a retirement from acting. The feature was Douglass's own creation *Jolly Jack; or, the Rosicias of the Fleet*, in which he played seven characters.

The Standard was then closed for the week before Easter to do some redecoration. Douglass believed he had an answer to the problem of poor houses waiting in his wings. Mr. and Mrs. Charles Kean had established a deserved reputation for their splendid revivals of Shakespeare at the

Fig. 69. *The House on the Bridge of Notre Dame*, 1861, at the Lyceum Theatre. *From the Illustrated London News*.

Princess's Theatre (1851–1859). Their forte was historical authenticity, with realistic staging and ensemble acting. This was an important step toward naturalism in the theatre. The Keans also developed the concept of the stage director, raising the position to one of major artistic prominence. Their use of stage lighting was ahead of the technology of the time, and their managerial techniques set the highest standards. The Duke of Saxe-Meiningen saw their productions, and many of his influential ideas were based on the Keans' techniques. In the quality of management and attention to detail the Keans and Douglass had much in common. It is natural that when they became available he should try to bring them to Shoreditch.

The company was strong. The opening play was Lovell's *The Wife's Secret*. This was alternated with Kean's vehicle *Louis XI*. The audience greatly applauded both. In the first week, the houses were filled despite the tripling of the prices. Then business fell off rapidly. On the last playbills, gaps were left where the prices should have been, so they could be filled in by hand at the last minute, according to what seemed possible for each night's performance. Despite every effort, in the end, the Keans productions lost some money. Perhaps they were not as effective as guests as they were in the friendly surroundings of their own company, and theatre.

An interesting anecdote about Kean's *Louis XI*, one of his favorite characters, was repeated by James Anderson. The Keans were in Paris at the same time Anderson was, in 1854. All were there to visit children who were at school. They met at the school by accident, and the conversation naturally turned to French plays. Kean asked Anderson if he had been to anything worthwhile:

> I told him I had been to a good many, but had seen nothing worthy of admiration save a marvelous representation of Louis XI by M. Perrin. 'Good God!' cried Charles, 'Louis Onze? Why I am going to play the part myself. Boucicault is doing the tragedy for me, and it is to be produced at the Princess's.' 'Oh,' I said, 'it is not the tragedy, but a melodrama, in which Perrin's representation of the hipocritical, crafty old Louis is admirable.' 'I say, Delly,' said Charles (he couldn't say Nelly), 'we must see that play.' I have no doubt he did see it, and more than once I should say. On my return from the States the following year, I went to see Charles Kean in Louis XI. For a while I really believed I was looking again on M. Perrin. The makeup, dress, gestures, gait, business, even to the manipulation of the leaden images in his cap, were all faithfully copied from Perrin. Although Louis XI was the same historical hero in both plays, treatment of the character was very different, as was also the plot, and cast of dramatis personae. Kean spoke blank verse, Perrin prose. I question

if the Frenchman could have acted Boucicault's version as well as the Englishman, for Charles Kean's Louis XI was a masterly performance from beginning to end.[55]

It is of no surprise that Anderson did not mention to the Keans that he had also been impressed with *Schamyl the Circasian*, which he promptly brought out himself when he returned to London, in 1854.

Anderson and Marriott presented their normal repertoire into May of 1861. Then Douglass announced that Miss Marriott had reassumed the position of directress. In her curtain speech to the audience she said:

> Mr. Douglass, after a number of years of increasing managerial toil and labor, having resolved on retiring a while from the scene of his many triumphs, to enjoy a little quiet repose in the bosom of his family has been induced to let me the theatre for twelve months.[56]

She was following in the tradition of managership of a number of talented women of the theatre, such as Madame Vestris, Madame Celeste, and Sarah Lane. But due to the convoluted British laws about property, married women, who, in fact, were artistic leaders, were often prevented from doing things in their own name. Therefore, when the lease was signed, it was in her

husband's, name: E. F. Edgar. He then became a minor performer, and manager of affairs for his wife. Their control of the house ran from May 1861 to May 1864. Not, according to James Anderson, a good time to assume any theatrical management.

> Theatricals in London at this time were at the lowest ebb. The Haymarket, Lyceum, and the Princess's could hardly keep their heads above water. The Adelphi, Olympic, Strand, Standard and Astley's were all under it. The legitimate drama was crushed dead in the metropolis; and here I lay, after thirty years study and labor in its service, buried in its ruins.[57]

Miss Marriott set out, with terrific energy, to find guests who would generate paying houses. The first was William Creswick (1813–1888). He was popular, and returned a number of times in future years. Then came Charles Pitt (1819–1866) and John Drew (1828–1862). Miss Marriott produced her own new scripts with characters that gave her full reign to use her strength and musical voice: *The Flower Girl*; *Ambition; or, the Tomb, the Throne and the Scaffold*, and The *Gipsy Girl of Granada*. By some mysterious, or not so mysterious, agency, young John T. Douglass's translation of a Barrière and Plouvier melodrama entitled *Twelve O'Clock; or,*

55.   Anderson, p. 225.
56.   The *Era*, (26 May 1861).
57.   Anderson, p. 261.

Fig. 70. *Jeanie Deans; or, the Sisters of St. Leonards*, by C. H. Hazlewood. This play is based on Sir Walter Scott's *Heart of Midlothian*, 20 September 1862. *From the Rose Lipman Library, Hackney.*

The Midnight Angel was accorded eleven performances.

Though the Court was in deep mourning for the death of Albert, the Prince Consort, at Christmas of 1861, he had not been popular with many of the people. It probably comes as no surprise that the Standard's Christmas pantomime *The Sleeping Beauty in the Wood; or, Harlequin Prince Pretty and the Seven Fairy Godmothers* was performed to "great crowds." Young John T. Douglass apparently wrote at least part of this production.

But after eight-week run of the successful pantomime, it was downhill again. Phelps came, as did other guests up to May 17th. Then the melodramas of the previous autumn, along with some Irish comedies, were performed to sparse houses. However, something finally loomed on the horizon that had real potential.

In September of 1862 the most significant event of Miss Marriott's management took place. C. H. Hazlewood's new play, tailored for the starring actress, *Jeanie Deans; or, the Sisters of St. Leonards*, opened on the 20th. It created such a sensation that houses were crowded for the entire autumn season, and sold out for the first time in four years. The play is based on Sir Walter Scott's 1818 novel *The Heart of Midlothian*. This ushered in the passion for dramatizations of Scott's books. It was a perfect vehicle for the powerful acting of Alice Marriott

Typical of the action filled incidents was the fight on the bridge (fig.70). This was reminiscent of similar incidents in *Pizarro*, and *Peep O'Day*. Another scene, ever popular with the English, and American theatregoer, was that of a courtroom filled with electric moments (fig.71). The acting of the role of the picturesque Madge Wildfire, and the comical Scots character, John Dumbiedikes, added much to the enormous success of the production. The playbill in typical fashion virtually reconstructs the first act in sentence fragments of the sort Jingle speaks in *Pickwick Papers*:

INFANTICIDE! St. Leonard's Craig, between Edinburgh and the mountain called "Arthurs seat." Farm of David Deans—old man allowed to drive his sheep into the meadow—"can a mother's heart inherit the breast of a Gypsy thief." Ruben's proposal for the hand of Jeanie—meeting of Effie and her betrayer—THE CONCEALED BIRTH!—The riots—"You shall be lawfully mine yet." Jeanie Deans learns the secret for the first time. The informer. "It would kill my poor father."—Stanton and Reuben—the threat—"Do a good action, if you would serve me and Effie Deans; tell her that one she has seen before to-night wishes to see her for a moment"—the proposal; the meeting with a stranger—A brave sister's resolve—Her departure for the Craigs. Salisbury Craigs (by moonlight)

with the murderer's stone, appearance of the outlaw. His attempt on Jeanie's life—"You can save your sister and you won't." The maniac's warning!—The ruffian jailer—Jeanie's subterfuge. A road near the common, Madge Wildfire and the Magistrate!!! David Deans' Farm, by moonlight. The surprise—"sorrow has fallen upon our house."—Arrest of the Lilly of St.Leonard's for Infanticide—"Father Sister save me" TABLEAU.

And so the curtain fell on the first of four breathtaking acts, filled with picturesque characters, mysterious strangers, and Margery Murdockson the Gypsy witch, with her daughter Madge Wildfire, the wandering Maniac!

This significant success ran until the Christmas panto, and was revived on and off for the next seasons as well. Alice Marriott, after giving up as manager in 1863, moved to Sadler's Wells. Although her husband, E. F. Edgar remained behind at the Standard, until his contract with John Douglass ran out in May of 1864.

After six years at Sadler's Wells, she toured America. Later she was known for her portrayal of one of the witches in Irving's *Macbeth* at the Lyceum. She was also remembered for her rendition of Lady Isabel in *East Lynne*. But her habitual role was Jeanie Deans, which she constantly toured in provincial productions up to the 1890s.

H. Chance Newton in *Crime and the Drama* described his theatrical uncle W. W. Lacy, as touring with Miss Marriott for years, playing one of the minor villains, Tom Tyburn. He was the originator of the character at the Standard. In the first act the character tried to bar Jeanie's progress, and is pushed off a wooden bridge over the chasm. "In this episode my very acrobatic pantomimic uncle did a back-fall from far up in the flies down... down far below the depths of the stage, where he was caught by a convenient mattress. A marvelous feat!" (fig. 70).

In December, the panto by Francis Cheatham, was *Cherry and Fair Star; or, the Dancing Waters, the Singing Apple and the Little Green Talking Bird*. It ran to mid-February 1863. Following it was William Creswick in favorite Shakespearean roles, and then J. H. Tully's English Opera Company. Several of their presentations had not been at the Standard before: *Martha, Satanella, Fra Diavolo, Rose of Castille, Norma, Robinhood,* and *La Traviata*.

After six weeks of the operas, various guests, and mixed bills were announced until June 30th. Then, Miss Marriott produced another of her surprises when she assumed the male role of Jack Hayward in *The Return of a Ticket of Leave*, a new script first licensed for the Standard Theatre. This, and Tom Taylor's famous version produced at the Olympic in May, were both based on a French original. Their character, Hawkshaw, became the model for the stage detective forever

Fig. 71. *Jeanie Deans; or, the Sisters of St. Leonards,* by C. H. Hazlewood. This play is based on Sir Walter Scott's *Heart of Midlothian,* 20 September 1862. *From the Rose Lipman Library, Hackney.*

Fig. 72. *Never too Late to Mend*, **at the Princess's Theatre.** *From the Illustrated Times.*

after, although in Taylor's version he is something of a bungler, in comparison with Holmes.

By the 13th of September 1863 Miss Marriott was no longer listed as directress. During her period of control the productions at the Standard had slipped back into the old-fashioned melodramatic type. Most of them provided powerful and athletic characters for the directress herself. Except for Phelps and Creswick, the guest companies and stars had a distinctly provincial tone. Anderson's aforementioned analysis explained this as a general decline in taste, and a turn away from the classics.

Edgar's short-lived operation of the Standard was less distinguished yet. William Creswick was brought into play in *Ambition; or, the Tomb, the Throne and the Scaffold*. This romantic drama was one of Creswick's favorites. He played Ethelwald Earl of Derby in this tale loosely based on the marriage of Henry VIII, and Catherine Howard. As

Ethelwald he is supposed to become the headsman for Catherine, whom, of course, he secretly loves.

Following a dull autumn was an equally dull panto by W. E. Suter entitled, *The Prince and the Lion King; or, Harlequin the Invisible Cap, and the Fairy Queen that Turned into a Frog*. The normally lucrative Christmas tradition did not prove a crowd pleaser. The *Era* reported on January 24th that the panto had been much changed to try to fix it up; but it closed a month earlier than normal. Several new operas appeared during the dismal winter season: *Ernanni*, *The Crown of Diamonds*, *The Barber of Seville*, and *Lucrezia Borgia*.

After this the Standard closed for the first spring in the history of the house. Edgar's lease ran out, and Douglass assumed command in late May. As has been demonstrated through the centuries, art does not flourish during major war periods. It is certainly true of the 1862–1865 years.

Douglass reopened the building with Charles Reade's *Never to Late to Mend* (fig. 72). This was followed by production by a provincial company in a play that has become famous as the archetype of the lurid crime drama, *The String of Pearls; or, Sweeney Todd the Barber of Fleet Street*. George Dibdin-Pitt was apparently the first to dramatize this story. His play appeared at the Britannia Theatre in 1847. The author is not identified for the Standard's presentation. It lasted two weeks until the end of May (fig. 73). The second play on the bill was another of

Fig. 73. Sweeny Todd the, "demon" barber, dumps a victim with his trick chair. *From A.S.J.*

young John T. Douglass's efforts, *Mark Winslow; a Story of the Cornish Coast*. The beginning of June featured the entertainments of Mr. and Mrs. Howard Paul (fig.74).

In 1854 Isabella Featherstone (1833–1879), a promising singer, joined forces with Howard Paul (1830–1905). The Pauls devised an entertainment called "a patchwork of fun, frolic, song and impersonation." Later Isabella returned to stage productions and was popular in Gilbert and Sullivan. Her last appearance was in *The Sorcerer* in 1877. Following the Pauls, Douglass filled the summer with the Christy Minstrels.

There were a few notable theatrical events in the Spring of 1864. The wonderful actor T. P. Cooke died at the age of seventy-eight (figs.75 and 76). The *Era* gave an extensive biography listing his major achievements. The roles he created were typical of the picturesque characters of Romantic drama. Most representative were Long Tom Coffin, in *The Pilot*, and the monster in *Frankenstein*. In 1826 Cooke took the monster to Paris, where he played at the Port St. Martin for eighty successful nights. In 1829 he created William the Sailor in Jerrold's *Black Eyed Susan*, and in 1835, Harry Halyard in Haines' *My Poll and My Partner Joe*. When Cooke retired in 1860 he had numbered up his principal personations as follows:

William -------------------------	785 times.
Long Tom Coffin-----------------	562
The Monster --------------------	365
Harry Halyard -------------------	269
Roderick Dhu -------------------	250
Aubrey(*Dog of Montargis*)----	250
Luke the Laborer ---------------	181
Vanderdeken ---------------------	165
Joe Hatchway(*Union Jack*)----	140
Red Rover ----------------------	120

Another of the performers of the older school also retired at this time. Marcia Macarthy (Mrs. Honner), who had served the original Douglass Stock company so loyally, took her farewell benefit, as mentioned before, 6 June 1864 at Sadler's Wells. She had been Cooke's leading lady in many a nautical play before 1848.

In the twelve years she performed at the Standard, she played at least seventy different roles. They ranged from small boys, Little Joey in *The Waits*, to Cordelia in *King Lear*. She played each of the heroines in *Ingomar*, *Fazio*, *Virginius*, *Romeo and Juliet*, *Carline*, *The Gamester*, *The Stranger*, *Uncle Tom's Cabin* (Eliza), *Lady of Lyons*, *The Vicar of Wakefield*, *The Robbers*, *Katherine and Petruchio*, and all the major ladies of the nautical dramas. She played a multitude of supporting roles and strong women in the curtain-raisers. She performed every evening the theatre operated, even if only in the afterpieces to an opera, or guest company's Shakespeare. In the later years she did get summer vacation while the Christy Minstrels performed. Also at the end of the year, if the panto was a success, she did not have to perform, although in 1858 and 1859, *The Waits* was an afterpiece to the panto. She was given a star's clear benefit in years from 1854 to 1860. Her last major role was playing Juliet to Miss Marriott's Romeo. She left the Standard when Miss Marriott became the directress, and went to Sadler's Wells where she continued in her line. But, the strain of the somewhat noisy, powerful characters of melodrama, performed in huge theatres, with smoggy environments, took its toll. On 20 June 1865, a year after her retirement, when her last benefit was held at Sadler's Wells, it was in her absence. She was embarrassed to appear in public because her voice had failed.

In summary, in the spring of 1864, the *Era* reported fewer theatres were open than in many years. It was the end of an age that had seen the Standard rise to preeminence. A regular playgoer at the Standard, between 1850 and 1862 could expect to see the better plays of

Fig. 74. Howard Paul (1830–1905), and Isabella Featherstone (1833–1879) (Mrs. Paul) in their duologue, *Dog and Cat*. *From the Rose Lipman Library, Hackney.*

Fig. 75. Thomas Potter "Tippy" Cooke (1788–1864) as Union Jack, tinsel print. *From the London Museum.*

New plays, based on contemporary literature, were premiered at Douglass's house. The *Vicar of Wakefield*, *Uncle Tom's Cabin*, *Jeanie Deans*, *Oliver Twist*, *Masks and Faces*, *The Lyons Mail*, and *Schamyl* serve as examples.

American actors were given London productions, as were the major novelty entertainers, George Wilde and Fanny Williams, The Mathewses, The Howard Pauls, Professor Anderson, Pell Bones, and George W. "Poney" Moore, and his Christy Minstrels. The Adelphi Company, with Ben Webster and Mme. Celeste, always came to Shoreditch for some weeks, in their special, high-quality melodramas.

the old melodrama, contemporary new plays of wide interest, and the best stars in revivals of the classics. Major serious dramas, not seen for decades, if not centuries, were revived: *Alexander the Great*, *Medea*, and *The Elder Brother*. Virtually all the plays of Shakespeare were produced by the best performers of the English language stage, in diverse interpretations, and with serious attention to technical, and scenic excellence. Opera in English, with major stars, was regularly seen. It was, for the most part, only at the Standard that the new and important Italian and French operas were presented in English.

Fig. 76. Thomas Potter "Tippy" Cooke (1788–1864) as "Sweet" William the sailor, tinsel print. *From the London Museum.*

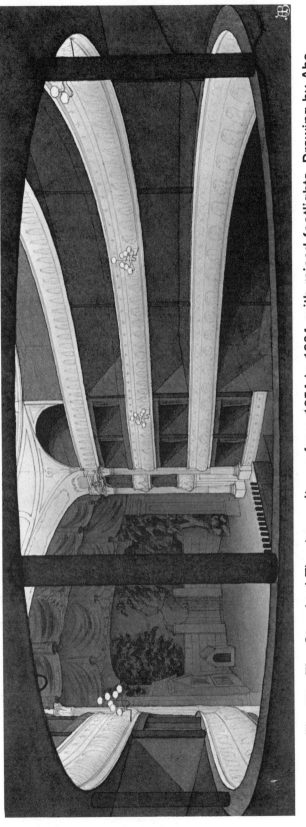

Fig. 77. The Standard Theatre as it was from 1854 to 1864, with raised footlights. Drawing by Abe Boycott. *From the Harvard Theatre Collection.*

Fig. 78 The Standard Theatre after the renovation, showing the sunken footlights, 24 September 1884. Premier of *The Market Cross*. From the *Illustrated News of the World*.

The Standard Theatre was always commended for its order, cleanliness and tasteful productions. Douglass kept his prices low, but was most liberal with his salaries, even down to the most minor performers and technicians. Therefore as an honorable, and moral business man he was usually looked upon as a paragon. Although, there was nearly a lawsuit because of a problem about paying his stars at the time of the Kean's failure. At Easter he presented concerts of serious music. At other times of the, year moral dramas intended to be patriotic or corrective in nature were presented, with antislavery, and protemperance as the predominant themes. In fact, The Blue Ribbon Temperance Army was founded on the Stage of the Standard in 1859.

The Standard's Christmas pantomime was normally a success, given the highest marks in the press as one of the ones "not to be missed." The moving panorama, and the new stagecraft of lighting was featured in Standard productions, and the electric arc was presented as a method of lighting as early as 1848. Vast numbers of audience were brought into this high-quality theatrical environment, helping to raise new standards of artistic appreciation in the swelling middle classes of London.

8

RECOVERY, THEN DESTRUCTION 1864-1866

The Standard was closed in August, and most of September of 1864. John Douglass took this opportunity to extensively remodel and redecorate for the first time in a number of years (figs. 77 and 78). Throughout September the progress of this was followed in the press. Entrances to the different sections of the auditorium were opened on different street corners. This was to spread the crowds more widely before and after performances. The box, and stall patrons entered from Shoreditch, the original entrance; the pit from George Street, to the south (now Fairchilde street); and the gallery from Holywell Lane, to the north.

The dress circle was given individually numbered red velvet chairs. The whole auditorium was lightened by white with gold trim. The stall and box patrons passed through the shell of the 1835 auditorium that was now a domed vestibule and outer lobby. It was decorated with marble. A new double flight of stone stairs led upward, illuminated by glass chandeliers. There were now twenty-two boxes. The whole was lit with gas. Branch fixtures were placed in the boxes, passage ways, and around the walls; while in the center was a spectacular, crystal, grand central burner. The main drape was crimson silk velvet, with gold trim, and gold tassels. The orchestra stalls had cushioned seats. The capacity remained in the vicinity of five thousand.

John Gates, of the Lyceum and Princess's Theatres, painted the act drop. New settings were painted by William Gowrie, John Neville, and others. This probably included young Richard Douglass. The architect was Mr. Lucas.

The new proscenium was described like the one at Covent Garden; the dress circle was like that at Drury Lane. The old, gloomy, solid divisions between the boxes were removed, with slim pillars taking their place. This allowed light to penetrate and, people to see each other.[58]

Another new feature was that the footlights that had projected above the stage floor, as in the other London theatres, were now sunken into an inclined trough at the front edge of the stage. The *Sunday Times* remarked that all the theatres should adopt this technique. The final change was that the boxes and doors normally found in the proscenium, a practice dating to the 1660s, were finally removed.

The commodious new building was opened with John Thomas Douglass's new romantic drama, *The Market Cross*, 24 September 1864.

The plot was: Don Miguel de Castro, was mysteriously bereft of an infant daughter, who was then exposed to perish on the Pyrenees by her kidnappers. Of course, she was saved by some peasants. Some years afterward De Castro has become suspicious of his second wife, Donna Agila. He forces a duel upon an English physician, Edward Cleveland, who he has been told, betrayed his trust with his wife. The duel is fought in a picturesque night scene; the duelists having sword in one hand, and bull's-eye lantern in the other. Actually De Castro's wife is faithless, as he suspected, but Cleveland is not the man. Donna Agila is also the original agent in the kidnapping. After some years, the child Inez is recognized; and eventually restored to her father. Then the malignant stepmother seeks to destroy the now grown young woman, by concealing an infernal, explosive, poison perfume machine in a casket. Her plan is foiled by a good-humored lawyer's clerk, who manipulates the package with the casket in such a way that Donna Agila is "hoist with her own petar," inhales the puff of gas, and perishes miserably. The play was well received, with good notices for Minnie Davis as the grown Inez, and Brittain Wright as the comic lawyer's clerk (figs. 78 and 79).

Not content with just one new play, twenty-two year old John T. was determined to make a considerable mark. To that end, another original play was added to the first during the second week of the season. It was a burlesque of *The Forty Thieves*, written in the punning style of the Christmas pantomimes. Some American Civil War influence was noticed in this show, when a parody of the patriotic southern song, "Stonewall Jackson," was rendered with comic words, under the title of "Brickwall Johnson." The great sensation of the production was a ballet with the dancers distributed all over a mountain set that occupied a vast area of the stage. Members of the stock company again got good notices, with Davis and Wright being singled out.

In November the *Era* called the Standard " The Eastern Drury Lane," for the first time in print. The theatre was to be called this regularly for

58. The *Era*, (25 September 1864).

Fig. 79. The Standard Theatre. Premier of *The Market Cross*, 24 September 1864, with the picturesque duel by lantern light. *From the Rose Lipman Library, Hackney.*

decades, although it was more of a compliment to Drury Lane than to the Douglass's house. The article went on to say, ". . . at the present moment actors earn more money in a night at the Standard than they can in a week at any theatre in the West End . . . ."

The considerable success of John T. Douglass's two new plays was quickly followed by T. H. Glenny (1821–1881) and Edith Heraud in a two week classical season, and then the new panto. *Dame Durden and Her Five Serving Maids; or, Harlequin Robert and Richard Were Two Pretty Men*, opened to extravagant praise. It ran eleven weeks to the second week in March, thus indicating the shows in the newly renovated theatre were crowd pleasers, despite the low state of theatre in general. The technical aspects of the panto were particularly popular:

Some of the scenes are of a most beautiful character, and we may especially instance that in which the ballet takes place, the mistletoe glade, and the transformation tableaux, the palace of revolving prismatic worlds, and colossal temple of animation. The latter is a scene of almost wondrous brilliancy, and Herr Kozenour's new patent steam shaft has been brought into requisition

Fig. 80. *Robert Macaire* **at the Lyceum in 1885.** *From the Illustrated Times.*

to raise the figures necessary for completing the gorgeous picture.[59]

This steam shaft was of the sort being used to raise elevators in mines and factories. It consisted of a piston that was forced down a cylinder, thus providing movement that was translated into lifting power by pullies, and ropes. Later in the century, safer water pressure hydraulic engines of the same, design replaced the rather dangerous steam apparatus. Edwin Booth's Theatre in New York used such hydraulic lifts for scene changing.

It was announced that one hundred stage hands were necessary to produce the scene changes; and that the transformation scene of a magnificent temple covered with one hundred living figures mounted on revolving globes, was raised all together, by means of the fifty horspower steam shaft.

The fortunes of the Standard appeared on the rise. Another new script was rushed to the stage by John T. Douglass. *The Assassins of the Roadside* was a translation of *Auberge des Adrets*, normally called *Robert Macaire* (fig. 80).

The new settings for this popular, but relatively old-fashioned crime drama, were the primary elements of notice. The three sets, exterior of the Inn, with a view of the road, and distant vineries was by William Gowrie; the interior of the Inn, with galleries, rooms, and

Fig. 81. William Creswick (1814–1888) as Cassius, tinsel print. *From A.S.J.*

staircases was by John Neville; and the yard where the final conflagration of the Inn ended the spectacle was by both designers. This play's five-week success, bolstered by the fire scene, led to a series of other plays. *Lady Audley's Secret*, which has a similar building on fire, *The Italian Wife*, *The Lone Chateau*, and *Ashore and Afloat*, followed one after the other. Technical effects (the sensation scene) continued to bring in the audiences. In one of these, a cataract of real water appeared

59. The *Era*, (1 January 1865).

Fig. 82. William Creswick (1814–1888). *From Tallis's Drawing Room Table Book.*

in the workings of an underground mine.

John T. Douglass's next new script was a burlesque of *The Brigand*. An Italian landscape with a translucent sun setting behind distant mountains, painted by Richard Douglass, was praised.

Various classics followed until mid-May, then, Professor Anderson, the magician, and the Christy Minstrels, divided the summer by halves. This summer of 1865 was when Charles L. Dodgson (Lewis Carroll) published

Alice in Wonderland, a literary version of a Christmas panto. Perhaps in his twenties he saw the Standard's 1853 production of *Roast Beef*, with its packs of cards that came to life.

The Standard had a very profitable season for the first time in five years. It looked as if the investment in the renovations had paid off. On 18 September 1865, the Autumn season began. Richard Douglass was now painting scenery full time in his father's theatre.

When William Creswick, and the rising young actress, Sarah Thorne (1837–1899) opened a series of classics in October, Richard provided all new settings for *The Bridal*, *Othello*, and *Henry IV Part 1*. Creswick was at the height of his popularity in this decade. His success at the Standard as opposed to the rapid decline, of James Anderson, indicates the more conversational and quiet style of Creswick was becoming the taste, at least for the poetry of the classics (figs. 81 and 82).

Albert Douglass was the nine-year old call-boy at the Standard in 1875, and he described his memories of Creswick in 1924:

This excellent actor of the old school was always a welcome visitor to the Standard, where he frequently appeared, giving ample proof that 'one man in his time plays many parts.' He was extremely careful and painstaking, taking his work very seriously, but not overburdened with humor. His favourite roles were Macbeth, Hamlet, King Lear, and Othello. Emulating Booth and many other Shakespearean stars, he played Othello and Iago on alternate nights. On one

Fig. 83. The North London Railway arches from the opposite side of the tracks from the Standard Theatre. Right to left, the bridge over Great Eastern St.; first arch, paint and rope storage; second arch, carpenter shop; third arch, furniture and prop storage. *From A.S.J.*

occasion forgetting which character he was portraying, he emerged from his dressing room only to find 'two Othellos in the field,' the other being George Hamilton. Hurried explanations followed, and the curtain was kept down for some time, a fact the audience were not slow to resent.

One night when Creswick was playing in that gloomy play *The Stranger* he was handicapped by severe hoarseness, and one of the gods in stentorian tones requested him to 'speak up.' Creswick, advancing to the footlights immediately replied 'I would if I had your voice.' What the management said to

him for breaking such a strict rule of the contract is unprintable.

I distinctly remember one performance of *Macbeth* when Creswick was furious. In the scene where the witches are discovered dancing around the cauldron, there was only one actor available to enact the three apparitions, who rise from the cauldron to warn Macbeth. The first speaks thus:—'Macbeth! Macbeth! Macbeth! beware Macduff; Beware the Thane of Fife. Dismiss me:—Enough.'

The second apparition should appear almost immediately, but there was a delay, and one could plainly hear the scuffling down the 'grave trap,' whilst the actor was hastily

156

effecting a change of appearance. When he eventually appeared, Creswick who stood with his back to the audience, muttered beneath his breath: 'Why didn't you come up before?' Then recognizing the same man seemed lost in amazement.

Another unnecessary interval occurred before the embryo Fregoli appeared as the third apparition (a child), and when Creswick observed that once more it was the same man, he hissed 'My God—you again—why don't you play the whole damn piece yourself?'[60]

Sarah Thorne, Creswick's leading lady in these productions, was for some years very popular in "strong" women's roles. When she retired from acting she

Fig. 84. The interior of the furniture and prop room. *From A.S.J.*

became the manager of the Theatre Royal Margate where her excellent training of the young actors in her stock company led to a number of notable careers.

The Standard's audience found in these two performers the kind of excitement that James Anderson, Samuel Phelps, and Isabel Glyn had generated in the 1850's. With this new team Douglass produced eleven classic revivals before the panto opened on 26 December 1865. *Pat-A-Cake, Pat-A-Cake Baker's Man; or, Harlequin Bah, Bah, Black Sheep*, was popular, and ran nine weeks. As in the year before the patent steam shaft was used to raise the elements in the transformation scene.

The year 1865 was when the North London Railway completed its elevated brick arch trackage past the stage right side of the Standard Theatre. Several of the large arches of the viaduct faced into the theatre yard. These were put to good use by the technical staff (figs. 83 and 84).

> . . . it must be remembered that in the eighteen seventies it was one of the largest in the kingdom, with almost unlimited resources. Nothing was hired, every scene being made and painted, all props modeled and manufactured, and every costume designed and executed on the premises. From the enormous stock of scenery the management were capable of putting on almost any Shakespearean play or well-known opera at

60. Douglass, *Memories of Mummers*, p. 55.

a day's notice, correct in detail too, whether the scenes necessary were Danish, Roman, German, early English, or any other locale the play demanded.

The huge scene-dock extended right into the railway arches rented from the North London Railway, one arch being used for storing scenery, the other being transformed into a commodious property-room, where thirty or forty 'big heads' could be moulded and dried round a large brick fireplace in one corner, whilst a full-sized railway engine was in process of construction in the other. In this room could be found any prop from a sedan chair to a pair of handcuffs. Think of ye modern touring managers who often have to hire a couple of armchairs![61]

After the panto closed 24 February 1866, Creswick and Thorne provided a different group of revivals. Among them was a highly acclaimed *King John*. Richard Douglass painted the scenery, and the show ran solidly for three weeks.

Following this extraordinary success, Avonia Jones (1836–1867), (Mrs. G. V. Brooke), came with the first

Fig. 85. *East Lynne,* **the death of Little Willie.** *From A.S.J.*

61. Douglass, *Memories of Mummers,* pp. 43–44.

presentation, at the Standard of *East Lynne*. By 1885 this play had been produced one hundred and ninety times in this theatre; it was by far the most popular new play of the 1870s (figs.85 and 86).

The summer was a familiar pattern, with the Great Maccabe, a ventriloquist, in June, and the Christy Minstrels for seven weeks afterward.

The autumn 1866 season began with James Anderson for the first time in five years In a play he wrote himself, based on Sir Walter Scott's *Quentin Durward*, Anderson portrayed Louis XI of France. Titled, *The Three Great Worthies* this play owed something to the 1854 French experience that had produced

Schamyl, and Kean's Louis XI character. The scenery by Richard Douglass was called "capital." But, there were problems with the production:

I made the great mistake in thinking the piece would suit the taste of my East End Patrons, who, accustomed to see me in nothing but dashing heroes, could not understand my now assuming the character of the crafty, superstitious old man. . . the play besides being weak in itself, was butchered in performance. We did not begin until twenty minutes after the time, which caused a great riot in the house; then there was a delay of nearly a half-an-hour between every act. The scenery by that clever and rising painter Richard Douglass, was admirable, but the

Fig. 86. *East Lynne*, **at the Surrey Theatre in 1866.** *From, the Illustrated Times*

time the sets took up would have damned a better play. The dresses properties and utility people were all that could be wished, but the actors were execrable, especially the creature who played Oliver Daim [Brittain Wright] who outraged all propriety by playing tricks like a circus clown in the ring. . . we ran twelve nights without money or applause. (figs. 87,88, and 89).[62]

Fig. 88. Brittain Wright (1837–1877). *From the Rose Lipman Library, Hackney.*

This major failure might have foreshadowed a dismal autumn season, if it were not for the new burlesque John T. Douglass rushed in to fill the gap. *Der Freichutz; or, the Bride, the Bullet, and the Bobby,* opened October 20th. The newspaper review that made the night deadline for the first morning edition of the paper, found the show enjoyable and comical. But it didn't matter, as the

Fig. 87. Brittain Wright (1837–1877), the low commedian at the Standard Theatre after G. B. Bigwood went to the Britannia. *From Memories of Mummers.*

62. Anderson, p. 280.

Fig. 89. Brittain Wright (1837–1877).
From the Rose Lipman Library, Hackney.

Illustrated Sporting News Reported:

One of the leading characteristics of the burlesque was the 'Incantation scene,' which was treated in a highly sensational style, and it is conjectured some of the inflammable materials employed in its production had effected a concealed lodgment amongst the scenery or in some fissures of the boards, and lay smouldering until after the closing of the house, which took place about midnight, everything at that time appearing to be in perfect safety, a thorough inspection by the carpenter of the 'magazine floors' used in the production of the scenic effects failing to detect the slightest traces of fire. This examination was also supplemented at three o'clock by Mr. Thomas Douglass (brother of the lessee) who resided in the theatre, . . . the first alarm of fire was raised at ten minutes past six o'clock . . . within a very brief period after the outcry had been raised, Captain Shaw and a strong body of Fire Brigades were on the scene of the disaster, while engine after engine came in hot haste, until something like twenty surrounded the ill-fated building; but for nearly three-quarters of a hour their presence was utterly useless from the usual absence of a supply of water in the mains on Sunday.[63]

According to the news accounts a large tank of water in the flies used for waterfall effects, and as a standpipe for interior fire hoses was already out of reach in the flames. It soon crashed to the floor as its supports burned through. It had little effect as it splashed to the stage. Once the city water supply was turned on, the engines seemed to make some headway. Then the fire won, and it was too late. At 7:05 the roof fell in. By 9:00 A.M. the building was thoroughly gutted. Captain Shaw and the Brigade were able to prevent the fire from spreading to the homes in Shoreditch High Street, and Holywell lane. Mr. Armitage, the inspector of Theatres, and Dyer, the foreman of the

Independent Gas Company, were able to turn off the gas supply mains, and thereby averted explosions.

The papers reported the loss at £25,000. The wardrobe alone was worth £600, and the center crystal chandelier in the auditorium, a duplicate of the one at Covent Garden, had cost 300 guineas. The lobby that fronted on Shoreditch was saved. It was all that was left of the original 1835 theatre. John Douglass was insured to the extent of £9,500. It was estimated that two hundred people were thrown out of work. Most of the actors lost hard-to-replace items of their personal props, and costumes. Some members of the orchestra had left their precious instruments and music in the pit. All the records, playscripts, and music belonging to the theatre, and to the Douglass family were burned.

Another account of the fire described the version of the events from an interview with Thomas Douglass, the chief of staff, lighting technician, and night watchman.

He had observed the borders were blazing when he was able to get to the stage through the smoke. This indicated the fireworks or gas lights had started some end of a drop smoldering. The account went on to say that: Captain Shaw was in a terrible fury because the parsimonious East London Water Company habitually didn't run their pumps enough to generate pressure on Sunday, merely to save a bit of money on coal. Captain Shaw told John Douglass that there would not have

Fig. 90. The ruins of the Standard Theatre, burned 21 October 1866. *From A.S.J.*

been half as much damage if, "a supply of water could have been got" (figs. 90 and 91).

Two weeks before the catastrophe, when Anderson's play failed, he had returned to his old standards *Macbeth*, *Hamlet*, *Ingomar*, and *The Lady of Lyons*. But business was so indifferent that he lost heart altogether, and had asked John Douglass to cancel the rest of the engagement. Douglass willingly did this, and got his son's burlesque onto the boards to replace Anderson. The hurried preparations for this may have led to the fire. In any case Anderson did escape just in time:

On my last night after playing in two pieces for my benefit, I was quite tired and quite used up and too feeble to assist in packing up my wardrobe, which was lying all about my dressing room after four weeks of use. My servant George, who was a very superior, thoughtful fellow, reasoned with me on the propriety of doing it at once, and not leaving it till Monday. He poured out a tumbler of claret for me, rushed out of the theatre, secured a couple of four-wheel growlers,

Fig. 91. The ruins of the Standard Theatre, burned 21 October 1866, with the members of the Douglass family on the rubble. John Douglass is rear left, still looking like his nautical role. *From Memories of Mummers.*

helped me pack my traps, and in two hours after I was fast asleep in bed. That boy George was my Guardian Angel. His persistence in laughing at my laziness saved me the loss of my valuable stage dresses, armour, swords, and dressing cases.[64]

---

64. Anderson, pp. 281–282.

Fig. 92. The National Standard Theatre as it was from 18 December 1887, with a country cottage stage setting by Richard Douglass, drawing by Abe Boycott. *From the Harvard Theatre Collection* .

9

THE NATIONAL STANDARD THEATRE 1867-1871

John Douglass understood the audience's tastes in 1851. he was able to take advantage of every circumstance. His formulae worked for twenty years, particularly the idea that when business was slack for an extended period, he would take the opportunity to close down, and remodel the building.

By 1867 there were real changes in theatre and in Shoreditch that he did not understand. The nearby neighborhood was in a social, financial, and physical decline. The institution of theatre was about to evolve a new aesthetic that would require a different kind of drama, a new stagecraft, and a new audience-actor relationship within the auditorium. Naturalism would require intimacy.

Douglass's approach depended on large scale spectacular production, and masses of audience. If he had known what was to come, it would have been better for him to invest his insurance money, or take over some

smaller West End theatre. His reputation was at its highest. He surely could have done this. Such was not in his nature.

He had little contact with avant-garde critics, or dramatists. His style of production was more like that of the evolving musical forms, light opera, burlesques, Gilbert and Sullivan. "Big" melodrama, Pantomime, opera, and super scenic productions of Shakespeare were happy in the big theatres; it was this kind of building that John Douglass choose to build in 1867.

The result of the fire was the cast of the burlesque of *Der Freischutz*, thirteen actors, and a corps of dancers of forty, plus the flymen, cellarmen, stagemen, carpenters, property men, modelers, dressers, gasmen, bill-posters, cleaners, money-takers, checktakers, supers, lime-lights, the band, workwomen, tailors, officers, store keepers, door keepers, watchmen—two hundred people—

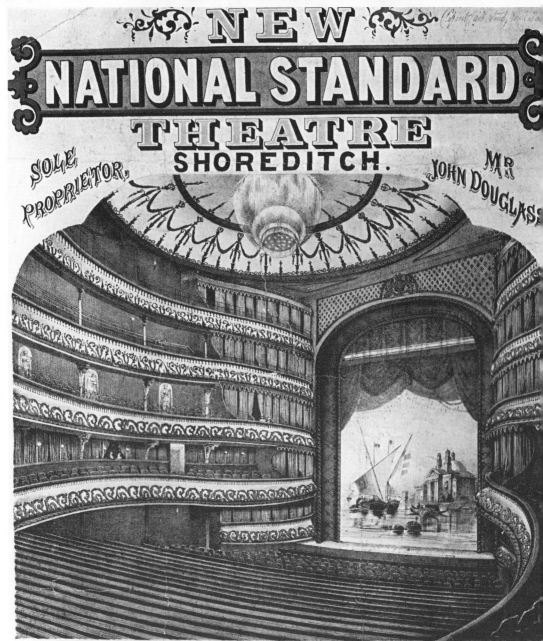

Fig. 93. The National Standard Theatre Shoreditch, opened 18 December, 1867. The Venetian Canal Act Drop is by William Telbin. The colors on this hand tinted poster are: tier-front white with gold trim; drapes and back walls amber; orchestra and stall seats crimson; ceiling above the gas sun-burner, French blue with gold trim; proscenium gold with blue trim above the arch. *From the Victoria and Albert Museum.*

were out of work. Worst of all, the planned Christmas pantomime would not take place. Relief efforts were begun at once. John Douglass refused any help for himself, and said he would pay all the women of the company from his own pocket. The local businessmen met at the Primrose Tavern in Bishopsgate street, and raised some funds. Nelson Lee, from the City of London Theatre, didn't mention money but said he, and Mr. Wright would call on the managers of other theatres to try to find employment for the Standard's people.

By 9 November 1866, Douglass had talked Lee into renting the City of London. A modest production of *King Rene's Daughter* was mounted, with Sarah Thorn in the lead. The house was crowded with the Standard's most loyal patrons. Then, some stock scenery was obtained, costumes borrowed; and to the astonishment of the press, *Der Freischutz* was added to the bill. The shows managed a run of several weeks, then other plays replaced the opening ones, including *Lady Audley's Secret*, *Barnaby Rudge*, and several comedies. The Standard's company remained until March when the theatre reverted to Nelson Lee's management.

In the meantime the rubble of the old Standard was cleared to the dump. On December 22nd the Allied Grand Circus rented the cleared ground for three weeks.

After the new year Douglass set about in ernest to design his new theatre. He served as his own architect, and began the construction by tracing the points of the plan right on the ground with a stick.[65] The cornerstone was set 3 July 1867. It took five and a half months for the workmen to complete the new structure. The site was L shaped. The stage and auditorium leg was 149 feet long by 90 feet wide. It ran north and south as had the old structure. The depth of the stage was sixty-one feet. The fly gallery was ninety-four feet from the stage floor. The square proscenium was fourty-two feet on a side. The gold trimmed auditorium was fifty-six feet across at the widest part of the horseshoe. There were four tiers, and ninety private boxes. The dress circle was described as like the one at the Adelphi. The act drop, a Venetian canal scene, framed at the top by the painting of a crimson velvet drape, was painted by the renowned William Telbin. The old groove system for side wings and shutters was replaced by extensive fly gallery equipment to hang the newer drop, leg drop, border and cut drop scenery. The main curtain was crimson velvet, as was the upholstery of the seating (figs. 92–94). In his books Albert Douglass described the technical details of the new theatre:

> The proscenium was forty-two feet and the stage sixty-five feet deep. The scene dock was quite a hundred feet in length, and there

65. The *Era*, (8 February 1874).

were two large railway arches used as scenery stores in addition. There was a huge property room where everything from a gridiron to a railway engine was manufactured: a commodious stable for the accommodation of about sixty horses or ponies; a very large carpenter's shop; and a painting room where scenery could be painted on the premises. And there are many modern West End theatres—each of which could be rebuilt within the four walls of the extensive wardrobe, which was afterward transformed into a miniature theatre, or hall capable of seating over a thousand persons. In this wardrobe hundreds of dresses, including historical costumes of every period, were stored. Any well known Shakespearean play could be supplied with appropriate costumes, complete in every detail, at twelve hours' notice. The same expeditiousness would be observed with regard to the stock scenery. It mattered not if the throne room for *Hamlet* was required, or a tapestry chamber for the palace of *Henry VIII,* the architecture would be correct; also the armour, copied from models in the Tower of London, or museums in Denmark, would be authentic. So, perhaps I may be pardoned for being just a little contemptuous of the manner in which Shakespearean plays are sometimes presented nowadays, when the ramparts of the castle, a street in Verona, Juliet's Garden, or the Forest of Arden, are all represented by the same depressing black velvet curtains.[66]

In the wardrobe room for about two months before the pantomime was produced—forty women would be seated comfortably round a rostrum (I cannot call it a table) working with might and main on various costumes. Round the walls were built about two-hundred cupboards the top shelf of which each requiring a twelve rung ladder to reach. One would contain perhaps every gentleman's costume necessary for *Hamlet,* the next all the ladies' dresses for *Othello,* in fact from this room one could obtain any costume from a Roman toga to a pantomime donkey's skin. To give the reader an idea of the vast dimensions of this wardrobe room I might add that later it was transformed into a skating rink.[67]

The new house opened 17 December 1867, with a concert. This permitted one night of shakedown with an audience present but no staging requirements. The next night Rose Hersee opened at the Standard for the first time, singing Amina in *La Sonnambula.* This was the first of scores of operatic productions in which she was to appear at this theatre (figs 95 and 96). The review described the opening as filled to capacity but not crowded due to the spaciousness of the building. Not everything was working. The "immense chandelier," was not illuminated. Its three thousand gas-jet splendor did not appear until another night.

In these days of universal electric lighting it is probably difficult to visualize an enormous

66. Douglass, *Footlight Reflections,* pp. 98–99.
67. Douglass, *Memories of Mummers,* p. 45.

Fig. 94. The National Standard Theatre Shoreditch, opened 18 December 1867. The Venetian Canal Act Drop is by William Telbin. *From the Builder.*

theatre lit entirely by gas, yet every evening about an hour before the doors were opened, three or four men would patrol the theatre, lighting hundreds of gas jets one by one. All along the ground floor of the orchestra stalls, pit stalls, and pit; round the four large tiers, dress circle, upper circle, upper boxes and gallery; in the dressing rooms, numbering between thirty and forty; in the various offices in the front of the house; in the lounge, and pit bar—each gas jet had to be lighted separately. Even in the long corridors there were domed alcoves containing statues representing Grecian goddesses, and other mythological figures—each one holding aloft a gas globe. In the carpenter's shop; in the property room; along the scene dock; and in the wardrobe, numerous gas-globes with small primitive taps were the sole means of illumination. The footlights were gas, also the battens, both controlled by pilot lights, but it was necessary for a man to light the latter à la the ancient street lamp-lighter, only his rod, instead of being five-feet long, was about thirty-five feet high, and fitted together on the principle of a fishing rod, or, a chimney-sweep's broom. The lighting from the flies would have hardly satisfied the artistic souls of Robert Courtneidge or Basil Dean, as it merely consisted of battens surrounded by a circular arrangement of red, white and blue linen, which revolved around the wired [guarded], lighted batten, and could be manipulated so as to throw the desired

Fig. 95. Rose Hersee. *From the Enthoven Collection.*

and being a firm believer in 'Safety First,' started a firework factory.

The main light of the auditorium was supplied by a huge gas chandelier suspended high up on the roof—even above the gallery tier. Many early Victorian chandeliers, with their octagonal or semi-circular glasses and shimmering dangling lustres of assorted sizes, are still in existence, but it is difficult to give an adequate description of the giant chandelier in question, which must have weighed many tons. The top iron ring was quite forty feet in circumference, the bottom ring being about twenty feet. The glasses fastened together in long chains with copper wire (a tedious process) were festooned from ring to ring—gradually tapering off to the

colour on to the stage. These primitive contraptions were called mediums, and in conjunction with an assortment of gaudy coloured glasses for the limelight boxes, completed the equipment for twilight, sunset, dawn, or any other effect required. The oxygen and hydrogen necessary for the limelight was manufactured on the premises and kept in specially constructed rubber sacks. Accidents were frequent, and I well remember the chief of the limelight department, who having lost his right arm, his left foot, and one eye in various explosions, reluctantly came to the conclusion that his occupation was a trifle risky, so he resigned,

Fig. 96. Rose Hersee. *From the Enthoven Collection.*

smallest ring at the bottom; the whole design being rounded off with circular rows of scintillating lustres.

The annual cleaning of a structure of such magnitude was a herculean task that could only be undertaken during the few days prior to the pantomime production, for with this solitary exception, the theatre was never closed. In those days there was no infamous Entertainment Tax to make summer vacation in many cases almost compulsory.

On one occasion, long before the annual renovation was due, one of the ropes from which the chandelier was suspended must have rotted, and this had evidently put too severe a strain upon the other supporting cables, for on one memorable Sunday night, when sleeping in the rooms adjoining the theatre, we were suddenly roused by hearing a tremendous crash. The North London Railway runs behind the theatre, and the first impression was that an engine had crashed through the wall and had fallen on the stage. Alarmed and somewhat apprehensive, we rushed into the theatre—and what a sight we beheld! The enormous chandelier had fallen from the roof into the pit-stalls below, and wedged between the splintered seats, it lay shattered and twisted, while the floor was strewn with thousands of prismatic glasses smashed into countless fragments. Had such a catastrophe occurred when the audience had assembled, the death roll would have been too terrible to contemplate. That such a calamity happened on a Sunday night was truly providential. Then began the almost superhuman efforts of the staff in trying to repair the chandelier, and haul it up before the performing on Monday night. Fortunately, Messrs. De Fries, the well-known Houndsditch firm responsible for most of the London illuminations during Queen Victoria's Jubilee, King Edward's Coronation, and other historical celebrations, came to our assistance, sending every available mechanic, and thanks to their incessant labours and wonderful efficiency, the chandelier, although still in an incomplete state, was finally hoisted into position a few minutes before the public was admitted. Of course every precaution was taken to prevent the recurrence of such a disaster, and so it remained a fixture until the following Christmas, when, during the customary closure for the pantomime rehearsals, the chandelier was lowered once more to be overhauled and undergo its annual cleaning. Imagine the scene! Christmas Eve! In the auditorium the huge chandelier slowly descends to the pit-stalls. It is then surrounded by numerous zinc-lined mangers, or miniature horse troughs, which are constantly replenished with fresh water. Dozens of boxes, barrels, crates, and cases packed with bran and sawdust for cleansing purposes, are ready at hand. Thousands of various sized cut glasses (known to children as spy-glasses) and innumerable elongated lustres reflecting myriads of rainbow rays from their scintillating facets, are being washed, cleaned, re-wired, and re-fastened on to their respective rings. Men, women, boys, and girls are pressed into the service if they prove to be willing workers, for there is no room for drones in this hive of industry. [68]

68.   Douglass, *Footlight Reflections*, pp. 104–106.

The building was fully illuminated by the time *Oranges and Lemons Said the Bells of St. Clements; or, Harlequin and the Fairy of the New Year* opened on 26 December 1867. With this opening John Douglass's sons began to be the major force in its operation. Twenty-five-year-old John Thomas became the resident dramatist and stage director; twenty-three year old Samuel Richard became the major scenic artist. Richard, as he preferred to be called, dropped his first name, Samuel. Young Arthur Douglass became the theatre's jack of all trades. John Senior's brother Thomas remained the treasurer, lighting designer and head of staff. In *Memories of Mummers* Albert Douglass gave brief biographies of his theatrical relatives:

A great character was Thomas, and as a worker unequaled; the first in the theatre every morning and the last out at night—never trusting the keys to anyone. He was treasurer, head of the staff, and having been formerly a builder and gas engineer, supervised all the alterations and repairs in the huge theatre, and took personal charge of the 'switchboard,' [gas table] at every performance for over thirty years, never missing a night, with the exception of an annual week's holiday in the summer, which he took under protest and never enjoyed.

Of course the theatre illumination was secured solely by gas, and the modern electrician can have no conception of the vast amount of labour necessary to work the lighting effects, which were not exactly up to Basil Dean's standard. The enormous center chandelier, and the stage battens had pilot lights, but every other light on the stage, in the dressing rooms, and in the auditorium had to be lighted separately. . . .

Thomas was responsible for all the gas effects in the Christmas annuals, and so elaborate were they, that it meant many months of labour. For instance the valley of Jewels, in Sinbad the Sailor [December, 1881], fairies would advance to the front of the stage each carrying a white wand surmounted by a perfectly formed capital letter. These wands (really gas tubing) were plunged into sockets [called water joints]—and made to spell a word, such as RUBIES, when a crowd of pretty girls clad entirely in red would enter. Then EMERALDS, which heralded a bevy of green garbed damsels, then TOPAZ, followed by various other jewels.

Fig. 97. Thomas Mace Douglass (1823–1906), or James Willing (1838–1915)? *From the Rose Lipman Library, Hackney.*

Fig. 98. John Thomas Douglass (1842–1917). *From the Rose Lipman Library, Hackney.*

It would be comparatively easy to gain such an effect with electricity—but in those days it meant miles of gas piping beneath the stage, a thousand holes punched in every letter, with care to ensure each tiny gas jet being equal in size, a patent tap containing a roll of paper percussion caps (similar to those used today in toy revolvers) to ignite the gas, and the whole prop covered with non-inflammable leaves to prevent the letter being distinguished before being illuminated.

Thomas not only worked sixteen hours every weekday, snatching his meals when possible, but also on Sunday, when all accounts were made up during the day, and the theatre was always let in the evening for religious meetings. A total abstainer, a non-smoker, and possessing a happy disposition, Thomas was beloved by all the artistes,

many going to him with their troubles, feeling sure of sympathy and good advice. His Shakespearean quotations on every conceivable occasion would have gladdened the heart of my dear old friend H. Chance Newton. If an actor after referring to 'his millions' on stage came off to request a loan of five shillings, Thomas would quote from the advice of Polonius—'Neither a borrower nor lender be,' but the actor received the 'sub' safely. Once noting a bad house, the leading actress late—and an important prop missing, he muttered 'one woe doth tread upon another's heels—so fast they follow.'

He referred to a stage wait as 'the puppets' dallying,' and to a stage aspirant who called with her face palpably rouged, and hair redolent of henna, as 'Excellently done—if God did it all.'

[John Thomas Douglass was:] undoubtedly the leading spirit of the Standard Theatre—being responsible for the staging of all the plays, and author of many of the most successful dramas. . . . He was a man of remarkable energy, and possessed a wonderful capacity for work. He knew exactly what was required and had a special faculty for getting it. I never remember him being tired, even after working fifteen hours daily, in fact he was thoroughly miserable when away from the theatre. The realistic scenes he put on the vast stage of the Standard drew all London. In the presentation of pantomime he stood unrivaled, being his own author, designer, modeler, and producer. To see John at his best was to watch him rehearsing one of his Christmas annuals. Having fixed his cast of principals, he would select the girls for the ballets and processions. About five-hundred applicants would assemble on the stage anxiously awaiting his decision. Girls engaged in previous pantomimes having first claim—the rest would be surveyed critically, and eventually a hundred and ten chosen (the odd ten for understudies) and it was sad to note the disappointment plainly written on the faces of the unsuccessful candidates.

A system of fines was instituted, but at the conclusion of the run (generally from twelve to fourteen weeks in those days) all the money collected was equally divided amongst the girls, and as most of the fines were inflicted for talking, naturally the amount was considerable. Prizes were given to the girls who kept their costumes in the best condition.

As the rehearsals progressed John became more excited and irritable, and by the time Boxing Day arrived he had generally lost his temper, his voice, and his hat, for when things were exceptionally unsatisfactory, he would snatch off the last named (always a silk one) dash it to the ground, and conclude his entertainment by jumping on it. This 'hat trick' was strongly condemned by the family and all his friends (excepting the local Lincoln and Bennett). Yet there were occasions when his patience was exemplary. One can imagine the gigantic task of producing a colossal pantomime of twenty scenes, and the tact required in handling the crowd, but I have seen John accomplish it with more ease than many modern producers stage a comedy with a cast of eight people. [See figs. 98, 175 and 179-182.]

Richard Douglass had been a student of William Beverly: Although closely associated with all the productions at the Standard, Richard paid little attention to the business side of the management, devoting himself entirely to designing, and painting the scenery, and what a magnificent artist Richard was—his landscapes and still water scenes being exceptionally beautiful. He took his work very seriously, and his first finished set for the pantomime would be painted by June—six months before required—and by November all eighteen or nineteen sets, including the transformation scene, and harlequinade would be painted, set and stored. Richard never painted figures, holding the view that this intricate art

Fig. 99. Amy Sedgwick (1830–1897).
From the Enthoven Collection.

should be entrusted to an expert. For many years his great friend Mr. Mordecai, R. A. (the now famous portrait painter) always came to his assistance, and this unfailing kindness was fully appreciated.

In these days when a beautiful scene seldom gains applause, it is worthy of note that in the days of which I write the scenic artist was repeatedly called before the footlights, not only on the first night, but at every subsequent performance during the run of a play or pantomime.

Most scenic artists excel in some particular branch of their art, such as architecture, foliage, or perhaps an aptitude for oriental scenes, though occasionally a genius (like Stafford Hall) will be an artist capable of treating all subjects with equal skill. Richard's forte was still water. I recall the first night of a drama when a cloth representing a stretch of the Thames at Henley descended; it was

Fig. 100. Amy Sedgwick (1830–1897).
From the Enthoven Collection.

merely a front cloth with neither wings nor borders, yet the audience sat spellbound by its wondrous soft colouring. It was just as if one were looking through a magnifying glass at a delicate water-colour exhibited at the Royal Academy. The scene opened with a comedian addressing an up-river girl, but the dialogue was ignored, for the sheer beauty of the scene aroused the audience to such enthusiasm that they stopped the play and called for Richard so insistently that the actors were compelled to retire whilst the scenic artist bowed his acknowledgments to the delighted throng [figs. 130 and 196–197].

This is the only instance I ever remember of a scene painter taking a call for a front cloth. Richard with his soft voice and disarming smile was not excitable like John T., but it must be borne in mind he had not so much anxiety, for once having supervised the setting of the scenery his duties ceased [figs.175 and 182].

In later years Richard's services were in great demand all over the country, and no doubt many will remember his large outdoor canvasses of Windsor Castle and other well known spots, painted annually for the Earl's Court Exhibition, and pronounced by the press marvels of scenic display. [See figs.189–195.] He married Miss Stella Brereton, a charming actress who has retired from the stage.

Arthur Douglass, a man of many parts, was Arthur. His position at the Standard was Acting-Manager [casting director], but nothing came amiss to him. When Richard was hard pressed in the painting room, Arthur would don overalls and help paint scenery. If the orchestra needed augmenting for a musical play, or the leader happened to be unavoidably absent, Arthur would play the first violin, or the second if necessary. Arthur invented many revolving electric advertising signs (exploited by the firm of James Willing), which were primitive compared to those on view at present in Piccadilly Circus, but were very novel and effective at the time.

He was also the composer of that celebrated comic song, 'Ask a Policeman,' probably no great achievement, but the music has lived, for even to-day the entry of a funny policeman is heralded by the orchestra playing the familiar strain of 'If you want to know the time—ask a policeman;' although the droll Harry Pleon was more subtle, for when he entered in his im-personation of a member of the force on night duty, the band softly played 'Sing me to sleep.'[69]

The 1867–1868 Christmas panto was successful, running until February 20th. After that the popular actress Amy Sedgwick (1835–1897) came as a guest star for the first time (figs. 99 and 100). She was followed by H. N. Warner and Henry Marston in two weeks of the classics. Meyer Lutz's opera company presented *Faust*, followed by seven other operas over three weeks. Isabel Glyn then joined Marston, in a kind of old-timers reunion, that included John Douglass as Ben the Boatswain, Professor Anderson," The Wizard of the North," and others who kept the house filled until June.

The great hit, however, was the Adelphi Company with all their scenery, and effects, in their terrific play, *No Thoroughfare* (27 June 1868) (fig.101). This drama by Wilkie Collins and Charles Dickens, was from their story in *All the Year Around*. The production featured Ben Webster, and Teresa Furtado (fig. 102). At the Adelphi the cast included Carlotta Leclercq, and a youthful Charles Albert Fechter, as the villain.

No Thoroughfare takes its name from a courtyard in London that diverged from a winding street connecting Tower Street with the Middlesex shore of the Thames. In this cul-de-sac stood Wilding and Co. Wine Merchants that made it no thoroughfare for vehicles, or pedestrians. This theme reoccurs throughout in the dead ends encountered in the investigations to find a lost heir.

Twenty-five years before, Miss Wilding had abandoned a child at a foundling home. Years later she returned to reclaim the child. A sympathetic nurse had secretly told her the name the home had given the child, and she assumed she had reclaimed her own child. Later after Miss Wilding's death, by coinci-dence, her now grown, supposed son and heir, had hired a housekeeper. Of course, she was the very nurse. Eventually, she remembers the young man's case Also she remembers that a first baby, who had been given the name, had been adopted, and taken to Switzerland; Wilding was the second child to have been given the same name. He was not the rightful heir.

69.   Douglass, *Memories of Mummers*, p. 26.

Wilding reveals his predicament to a new partner, George Vendale. About this time an unctuous person, Jules Obenreizer, is introduced. He is a Swiss, also in the wine business—the London representative of a Swiss company. In his household is matronly Madam Dor, and his beautiful young niece Marguerite, whom is also his ward. George Vendale had met this trio several years before while traveling on the continent.

After some attempts to trace the heir, Wilding makes his will stating the business should go to the true heir if he is found in two years after his death. Otherwise, it would revert to the foundling home. The lost heir preys on Wilding's mind. His health rapidly fails, and he dies at the end of Act I.

In Act II, Vendale proposes to Marguerite. At the same time he discovers there has been an embezzlement of £500 intended to pay a Swiss wine supplier. The Swiss Company needs the forged receipt to apprehend the thief in their company. Vendale sets off to Switzerland with the receipt. Obenreizer finds a sudden excuse to accompany him.

Fig. 101. The Adelphi Theatre Company in *No Thoroughfare*, 26 December 1867. The story and the play by Charles Dickens, and Wilkie Collins. Left to right: Ben Webster as Joey Ladle, Mrs. A. Lewis as Mme. Dor, H. G. Neville as George Vendale, Charles Albert Fechter as Jules Obenreizer, Carlotta Leclercq as Marguerite, Mr. Billington as Wilding, and Mr. Belmore as Bintry. *From A.S.J.*

Act III finds the two on the road to Switzerland. Obenreizer plots to kill Vendale, and destroy the receipt. Vendale hears some statements that lead him to suspect Obenreizer may be the lost heir. They arrive at a wayside Inn. By lucky chance Vendale escapes being murdered during the night. The next day in the snow upon the precipice of the Simplon pass Obenreizer, openly attacks; and Vendale seems to fall over the cliff. The next morning Marguerite, and Joey a loyal elderly employee of the London wine company arrive at the spot. They have hurriedly followed the two men. The Pass Patrol, with their dogs, are with the two travellers from England. The dogs find Vendale on an ice out-crop; Obenreizer had become lost in the blizzard, and he also is found in the snow near the top of the pass.

In Act IV the impression is that Vendale is dead. Some time has passed. Obenreizer has been discharged by the Swiss wine company, and has found work in a notary's office. Marguerite and Madam Dor have returned to England and refuse to communicate with him. Obenreizer discovers papers in the notary's office that prove Vendale himself is the lost heir. He is about to destroy the evidence when he is confronted by the supposed dead man, Marguerite, and their lawyer. He is forced to consent to their marriage upon threat of exposure of his murder attempt. Obenreizer plays his final card: his knowledge that Vendale was an illegitimate child. He believes this will cause Marguerite to reject the marriage. No such thing happens, and the act curtain falls on the happy couple.

In the final Act the lovers are united in marriage; and Obenreizer dies by his own hand, assuring that everyone will be free of his malignant influence.

It was about the spring of 1868 that John Douglass introduced the use of theatrical programs. The first ones, such as that for *No Thoroughfare*, are crude. The paper and print were similar to that used in playbills. These measured fifteen inches wide by ten inches high. They were folded in half. The type was in all the extremes of sizes, and contained the extravagant phrases of the old playbill style. They

Fig. 102. Teresa Furtado (1845–1877) player of Marguerite in *No Thoroughfare* at the Standard 27 June 1868. *From the Rose Lipman Library, Hackney.*

were free to the audience, and more convenient than trying to hold a playbill while watching a production.

After a summer season with Creswick, followed by the Christy Minstrels, J. B. Buckstone brought his Haymarket Company to the National Standard for the first time. *School for Scandal, She Stoops to Conquer*, and *London Assurance* were the major plays. The farce that accompanied these was the legendary *Box and Cox* with Buckstone himself as one of the lodgers.

In the autumn the Covent Garden Opera Company came with Julia Matthews (1842–1876), in Offenbach's *The Grand Duchess of Gerolstein*, another first at the Standard. Julia Matthews was one of Albert Douglass's early memories of the theatre. He was six at the time.

> This charming and delightful artiste caused quite a sensation at the Standard when she appeared in The Grand Duchess, being simply worshiped by the public. She possessed a fascinating manner, and excellent voice, and received innumerable encores for her vocal contributions, ... My personal recollections of Miss Matthews are somewhat dim, but I distinctly remember being taken into her dressing room every night during the interval, sitting on her knee, and being regaled with ices. It was solely due to her initiative that I became a child actor, for she persuaded my parents (who foolishly consented) to allow me to play a page with her. From this part I drifted to many others with dire results. Miss Matthews must have

proffered this advice without bestowing a thought to the long-suffering audience, but I think this is the only unkind deed ever recorded against Julia Matthews [fig. 103].[70]

In the autumn of 1868, Alfred Rayner, a member of the Standard's stock company, was accorded a production of his sensation drama *Danger*. In it, the villain, one Everton Mist, tries to kidnap a young wife, drown her father, then drown her as well. He plots to extort an heiress's fortune, and rob a bank. In all, the actor, Mr. Vivian, must have had a wonderful time creating his unabashed villainy.

Fig. 103. Julia Matthews (1842–1876).
From Memories of Mummers.

70. Douglass, *Memories of Mummers*, p. 59.

Fig. 104. The new Liverpool Street Railway Station in 1870, with its tower in the smog. *From A.S.J.*

The sensation scene created by Richard Douglass was the first of the real railway scenes produced in this most appropriate theatre. The new Broad Street, and the Liverpool Street Stations, were now opened (fig. 104). An endless stream of the North London Railway's commuter trains passed a few feet to the west on the stage right side of the theater. John Douglass had to prevail on the Railway Company to restrain their engine drivers from blowing off, or using the whistle when standing near the theatre. Evidently they came to an agreement because of the business they created for each other. The North London schedules were listed in the programs of 1870.

Fig. 105. The Queen's Theatre Company about 1869, Henry Irving standing right of center, showing his "good side." *From A.S.J.*

They said that special trains would be added after eleven P. M., for the convenience of the theatre's audiences.

The Close proximity of the North London Railway was not exactly an advantage, especially as the engine drivers seemed to take fiendish delight in blowing shrill blasts on the steam whistle as the trains passed the theatre.This practice not only helped to ruin local colour but destroyed the atmosphere especially if the scene happened to represent the Sahara Desert or a South Sea Island. All the engine drivers possessed an uncanny gift for scenting a pathetic incident, or a tense dramatic moment. A favorite cue for them would be Willie's dying speech in *East Lynne*, when he gurgled 'Madame Vine—why don't you speak,' or Little Eva softly murmuring to Uncle Tom 'Hark I hear the angels.' It was most distracting and disconcerting for the artists, and one can realize how difficult it would be for a distraught heroine to throw open her

Fig. 106. The Queen's Theatre Company in *Dearer than Life*, 1869. The anniversary party, standing left to right: Miss Everard, Charles Wyndham, Miss Ewell, John Clayton, and Henrietta Hodson. Seated: J. L. Toole, Lionel Brough, and Henry Irving (as Gassitt the villain). *From Memories of Mummers.*

casement window and whisper 'Nature sleeps. How still. How peaceful,' whilst the 9-20 from Camden Town was letting off steam.[71]

The railway scene in *Danger*, occurs when one of Mist's toadies is employed to throw a switch to produce the destruction of an express train. This is to be done in order to cause the death of one of the characters. Little Jem, a street boy, played by Sarah Thorne, climbs up the slippery iron ladder of the railway signal post, to turn out the light, thus indicating stop, and preserving the train. This scene takes place during a thunderstorm, the events being picked out in the lightning flashes. "Real rain was to be seen falling" in copious torrents. The railway scene, the Thames, and the Mill Pool scenes of Richard Douglass, were all commended for

71. Douglass, *Memories of Mummers*, pp. 43–44.

Fig. 107. The Queen's Theatre Company in *Dearer than Life*, in 1869. The gin drinking scene in Act III. J. L. Toole and Miss Everard as the tradesman and his wife reduced to living in a garret. *From A.S.J.*

their realistic features. The rain troughs for this effect are described below in connection with a play called *The Ruling Passion*.

Alfred Rayner (1823–1898) was a main stay of the company, and seen in support of the major stars for decades:

A fine old actor of a school that probably would not be tolerated today, Alfred Rayner chiefly scored in 'heavy' parts. Possessing a voice of thunder it was sometimes satirically said that when appearing at the Standard he was audible at the Brit. No such charge can

be brought against some of the modern West End actors.

Rayner was a kind hearted man, and many a time he took me by the hand and led me to his apartments in Nicholl Square, Hackney Road, to see his splendidly equipped model stage, the finest I ever saw, and many enthralling hours I spent with this wonderful toy.

Rayner reveled in parts like Macduff, Ingomar, and the Ghost in *Hamlet*, in fact he had a certain amount of contempt for comic relief, preferring heavy and gloomy plays, and to him *Manfred* followed by *The*

184

Stranger was a gala night. Ye gods! What a bill—from 7 o'clock till 12 o'clock. What would a modern audience think of such a program?[72]

After the 1868–1869 Christmas pantomime, *Tell Tale Tit; or, Harlequin Dickory Dickory Dock*, several new features were seen. For the first time, the famous Vokes family performed one of their semi pantomimic musical burlesques, *Kitchen Bells*. J. T. Douglass's sensation drama *For Sale* ran for four weeks; then Meyer Lutz conducted Handel's *The Messiah*, *Judas Maccabaes*, and Rossini's *Stabat Mater* during the Easter period.

Most important of all, Henry Irving, a rising young actor, was presented in H. J. Byron's *Dearer than Life* by J. L. Toole, and the Queen's Theatre Company (figs. 105–107). The play ran four weeks. It was a forerunner to the many hits Irving was to bring to the National Standard after his stardom was assured by the 1871 production of *The Bells* (figs. 120 and 121).

Dearer than Life is the story of an industrious tradesman, a kind of Willy Loman, married to a woman whose whole interest is in her weak twenty-five-year-old son. The son is led into gambling and silly speculations by a false friend. This causes him to embezzle. His loyal girl friend discovers this predicament, and tries to help, by obtaining the pitiful life savings his mother had scraped together over many years.

During a family wedding anniversary celebration, the son's employer appears. He reveals, to the father, the embezzlements. Taking his son to another room, the father urges the boy to fly from justice, then returns to admit abetting the escape (fig. 106).

The final Act takes place in a garret. The tradesman and his wife have been reduced to starvation. There are scenes of drunken invective and general misery. At last the errant son returns to make amends with money he has properly earned. The play ends with the defeat of the schemer Gassitt, played by Irving, who had caused all the trouble merely to try to get the girl into his power.

J. L. Toole carried the play by his acting of the intense grief of the father when the guilt of the son is revealed; and by the scene, in the third Act, where he portrayed the brave old man, who could endure starvation, and be cheerful under the most miserable burden. That is until, under the influence of drink, all the frustration bursts out in his denunciation of his son (fig. 107).

In May of 1869, Susan Denin an American actress, presented Augustin Daly's 1862 version of *Leah the Forsaken*. This was adapted from Mosenthal's *Deborah*. A similar play had been presented with Edith Heraud in her final engagement in 1866 (figs.

---

72. Douglass, *Memories of Mummers*, pp. 50–51. In June of 1869 Rayner played leads on a bill with *Manfred*, and *A Woman in Red* coupled.

108 and 109). Then Samuel Phelps returned to the Standard in his spectacular production of Byron's *Manfred.* William Beverly had created the settings for the 1863 Drury Lane production. Richard Douglass had been apprenticed to Beverly, and had helped on the drops for *Manfred* (fig. 110). He painted all new sets for this presentation at the standard, and they were similar to the originals. Phelps was greatly applauded during his two-week run of the play. In June, Alfred Rayner took over the role. He kept the show running another week coupled with Mme. Celeste in *The Woman in Red.* John Douglass took a rare benefit on 19 May 1869 in *Ben the Boatswain.* This was to be his last stage appearance.

The summer included: Buckstone, and the Haymarket Company; Mme. Celeste; Sims Reeves; Ben Webster, and Miss Furtado. E. A. Sothern presented his celebrated Lord Dundreary, in Taylor's *Our American Cousin.* Despite the exceptionally hot weather, the theatre was very crowded for Sothern's first appearance at the Standard. The Christy Minstrels then performed until October.

Fig. 108. *Leah* **at the Adelphi Theatre in 1863.** *From the Illustrated London News.*

The autumn season, for the first time, had no dramas or classics. Frederick Maccabe the ventriloquist, was followed by Julia Matthews in *The Grand Duchess of Gerolstein*. They were followed, in turn, by the Christmas entertainment.

It was during this autumn that Douglass decided to improve his theatrical programs. They had proved popular. Therefore, he began to provide the fancy, embossed, high-quality paper programs, sponsored by the Rimmel perfume company. The ink with which these programs were printed had a different scent added each week. They were much more elegant than the old playbill like folded sheets. The printing was organized, and the lacy elegance of them added class to the organization. Best of all, the ink did not rub off onto the hands as had that used on the playbills (fig.111).

John Douglass directed the panto for the last time in 1869. *The Story of the Bean Stalk; or, Harlequin Jack the Giant Killer and the Seven Champions* was as spectacular and popular as ever. In fact, it ran very late into the winter, not closing until 18 March 1870. A grand moving panorama, one hundred knights in armor (the armor made in Paris and costing £1000), and a grand transformation scene were featured.

A few days before the end of the run a testimonial for John Douglass was held to celebrate his years of service to the theatre. He was presented a sterling tea service, suitably engraved, and

Fig. 109. *Leah* **at the Adelphi Theatre in 1863. A number of the illustrations of this play show Leah (or Deborah) all wound-up ready to throw her curse.** *From the Illustrated Times.*

containing four hundred ounces of silver.

John Douglass withdrew into partial retirement. At the time of his death three years later, in January of 1874, it was reported he had had an accidental fall in the theatre, and had been crippled by it for several years. He was partly bedridden, which required changes in the management of the theatre.

Fig. 110. *Manfred*, by Byron, with Samuel Phelps, and Rose Leclercq at Drury Lane in 1863. Richard Douglass worked on the settings, and made similar ones for the Standard's production. *From A.S.J.*

NEW NATIONAL
STANDARD ✠ THEATRE
BISHOPSGATE.

Sole Proprietor ... ... Mr. JOHN DOUGLASS
Licensed by the Lord Chamberlain to Mr. JOHN DOUGLASS, Castle Villa
Dalston, Actual and Responsible Manager.

THE LARGEST AND MOST MAGNIFICENT THEATRE
IN THE WORLD.

Mr. DOUGLASS has the gratification to announce that he has made
arrangements with Mr. J. RUSSELL (Late Manager of the Theatres
Royal Covent Garden and Olympic, (London) for the re-production of
OFFENBACH's celebrated Operatic Extravaganza,

THE GRAND DUCHESS OF GEROLSTEIN
FOR A SHORT SEASON.

COVENT GARDEN ARTISTES !
COVENT GARDEN BAND AND CHORUS !
COVENT GARDEN COSTUMES & EFFECTS !

Miss JULIA MATHEWS Madlle. ALBERTAZZI
Mr. J. D. STOYLES Mr. AYNSLEY COOK
Mr. OLIVER SUMMERS Mr. W. H. NORTON
Mr. W. H. PAYNE Mr. HARRY PAYNE
Mr. FRED PAYNE
Madlle. ESTA and Mr. WILFORD MORGAN

On MONDAY, the 8th of November, 1869, and during the week, the
Performances with, at Seven, a New and Original Comedietta, written
by the Author of "A Royal Marriage," entitled

IN AND OUT OF SERVICE

Sergeant Tip Top (in the Military Service) Mr. F. TYARS
Thomas Stubbs ... (in the Civil Service) ... Mr. G. BURT
Herr Von Hardstein (in the Belgium Volunteer
 Service) ... } Miss A. HERBERT
Miss Letitia Prudence (in no one's service)
Susan (a Servant in the Home Service) Miss MARIE LESLIE

RIMMEL

Fig. 111. One of the first Rimmel-type programs at the National Standard
Theatre. These were introduced in 1868, and the ink was impregnated with the
scent of the week. *From A.S.J.*

10

A PERIOD OF TRANSITION 1871-1874

Long runs of guest companies, with all their scenery and effects, became the norm in the next five years. Musical burlesques and sophisticated melodrama predominated. Guest stars in the classics were seen less often. The pantomimes remained very important to the financial health of the theatre. James Anderson went to the pantos in 1869–1870; and he said that the ones at the National Standard and the Britannia were always better than either Drury Lane or Covent Garden.

After the panto closed in March of 1870, the first significant run was Douglass's burlesque of *The Forty Thieves*. It ran until Easter. Then the Drury Lane Company came for several weeks in *Formosa; or, the Railroad to Ruin*.

The author, Dion Boucicault, had supervised the production himself. It was famous for the effects of its railroad scene, with the red danger signal, and the Oxford and Cambridge boat race on the Thames.

Julia Matthews followed in a burlesque by John T. Douglass called *Guy Fawkes; or, a New Way to Blow up a King*. On this same bill was the Gaiety Theatre Company with J. L. Toole in *Uncle Dick's Darling*. Toole had played Dick Rolland in this H. J. Byron comedy for one hundred nights at the Gaiety. It was considered one of the top plays of the quarter century.

After four weeks of Gaiety comedy, Edmund Falconer's 1861 success *Peep O'Day; or, Savourneen Deelish* was revived, in a spectacular new production by the Drury Lane Company. They brought in their scenery, which included the "old quarry in the Foil Dhuv" (dark valley) (fig. 112). This is the scene where Black Mullins is about to bash Kathleen with his shovel, when the hero, in the archetypical cliff-hanging scene of theatre, swings down on a sapling in the nick of time.

June and July of 1870 were very hot in the ninety-degree range. The plays performed were modestly successful despite the heat. The Adelphi company presented a "life in the glamorous theatre play," *The Prompter's Box!*

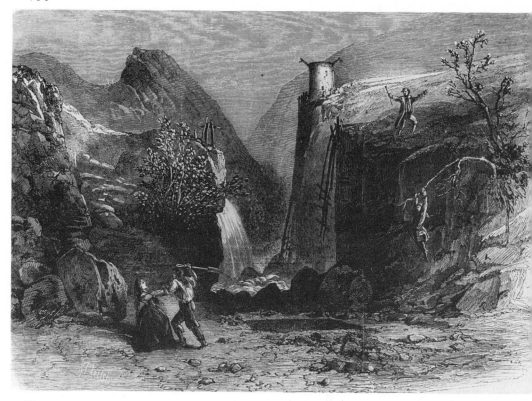

Fig. 112. The old quarry in Edmund Falconer's *Peep O'Day; or, the* **Savourneen Deelish, at the Lyceum in 1861. Black Mullins is about to bash Kathleen.** *From the Illustrated London News.*

A story of the "footlights, and the fireside." This utterly forgettable script ran three weeks. It was followed by an interesting drama titled *Put Yourself in His Place; or, Free Labour.*

In this play, a scrim was used to reveal the blacksmith's dream, an early example of expressionist technique (fig. 113). Henry Little has set up his forge in an abandoned church. The interior is illuminated by the fire, and the sparks thrown out from the anvil. While he is working, he becomes aware of supernatural influences, and sees two visions. In the first, Raby, the founder of his family, appears, like the ghost of old Hamlet; in the second, he sees the supposed marriage of his love, Grace Garden, with his rival.

In the summer of 1870, a young actress applied for a position in the company at the Standard. Amy Steinberg (1850–1920), whose real name was Alice Rachel Koning, was Belgian (fig. 114). She had been educated in Hanover, and Brussels, Though barely twenty, she could speak six languages. Her artistic training had been thorough. She had been able to obtain a role in Barry Sullivan's and

Fig. 113. The vision scene in *Free Labour; or, Put Yourself in His Place* at the Adelphi Theatre in 1870. *From the Illustrated London News.*

Samuel Phelps's revival of *King John* at Drury Lane in 1866, in which she played Prince Arthur (fig. 115).

Amy immediately caught John T. Douglass's eye. She was bright, talented, and vivacious. He hired her, and this autumn she was given several roles in his comedies and afterpieces. One of these, *A Chapter of Accidents*, was premiered 26 September 1870. It became Douglass's most successful short play, regularly being performed at the Standard, and other theatres as well.

A new and amusing farce by Mr. J. T. Douglass, entitled *A Chapter of Accidents*, was produced here on Monday night, it has played all week after the still attractive drama Little Emily. The action takes place in a well-furnished drawing-room in the house of Muswell Hill, Esq., near London. This gentleman has a daughter named Matilda, on whom Mr. Frederick St. Pauls, who is unknown but has been highly recommended, is expected to call to make an offer of his hand. An applicant for the situation of man-servant arrives, and is mistaken by the maid Kitty for Mr. Frederick St. Pauls, and is announced as such to her master, who, to the great perplexity of Henry, who has called about the place, treats him kindly and introduces him to his wife and daughter, and calls him his future son in law. While Henry is away with the ladies the real suitor calls, and in turn is dealt with as the man who wishes to be engaged as servant. He is naturally much astonished at the singular way in which he is received and dealt with, but thinking it is a joke, humours the party by pretending

Fig. 114. Amy Steinberg (Alice Rachel Koning) Mrs. John T. Douglass (1850–1920). *From the Rose Lipman Library, Hackney.*

to be such as they insist on regarding him. This continues till the arrival of Mr. Worthyman, the friend of Frederick, when everything is explained and set right. The hearty laughter which was occasioned by the representation of this lively and diverting little piece indicated that it was enjoyed by those who witnessed it. Mr Hamilton threw great energy and humour into his personation of St. Pauls, Mr. G. Burt was droll as Henry, Mr. C. Swan made a capital Mr. Muswell Hill, and Mr. F. Tyars suitably enacted the part of Mr. Worthyman. Miss Amy Steinberg as Kitty, was extremely smart and forcible; Miss Morelli efficiently sustained the part of Mrs. Muswell Hill; and Miss Ida Hertz pleasingly represented her young and interesting daughter, Matilda. The house fills well, and the applause which is elicited by the acting of the principal performers who appear in *Little Emily*, and by the beautiful scenes depicting Canterbury Cathedral, the Wreck, and the Emigrants' Departure, affords gratifying evidence that Mr. Douglass has been sagacious in getting the piece produced here, and is fortunate in being able to present it in a thoroughly efficient and satisfactory manner.[73]

These plays were performed for five weeks, until Douglass could rush to completion another production for his lady love. Oliver Goldsmith's *Vicar of Wakefield* had always been a popular play at the Standard. Douglass adapted the script with an expanded role of Miss Carolina Wilelmina Skeggs for Amy Steinberg.

Oliver Goldsmith's world-famed and charming story of *The Vicar of Wakefield*, which, as one of its author's latest biographers has truly said, 'delights the young by its adventures and the old by its wisdom,' was produced here on Monday night in the form of a four act drama. Mr. J. T. Douglass, the adapter, has cleverly accomplished the task of selecting and linking together the chief incidents in the history of Dr. Primrose and his family so as to make the piece suitable for effective representation on the stage. The dialogue is marked by the simplicity, clearness, and naturalness, which characterize the style of Goldsmith, whose words are in many scenes exactly transcribed. Ephraim Jenkinson and Baster are first presented to notice in the drama in the neighborhood of the Vicar's dwelling, and after some conversation has taken place between them, which affords glimpses of their evil propensities, the Doctor enters with his two little boys, followed by Mrs. Primrose and Sophia. The mother, to her Charles's annoyance, proceeds to talk of Olivia's chance of winning Squire Thornhill, and that young lady, who presently arrives, soon lets it appear that her mind is as full of the matter as her mamma's . . . the squire himself·appears, bringing with him his friends, the so called Lady Blarney and Miss Carolina Wilelmina Amelia Skeggs. Then follow dancing and the elopement of Olivia with the Squire. The second act opens with a lively representation of a country fair, with Jenkinson as a cardsharper and cheap Jack, and Skeggs as a

73. The *Era*, (2 October 1870).

showwoman. To this place Olivia comes . . . she is found by her father, who saves her from being ill treated by the mob, and proceeds to conduct her home. On their way to their dwelling, as is shown in the third act, it is perceived to be burning, and the Vicar hastens to his house, rushes in, and saves his two boys. To add to the troubles of the good Doctor and his family . . . he is sent to prison for debt by the squire. In the last act Burchell makes it known that he is Sir William Thornhill; has the Vicar released from prison, and makes Sophia his lady. Jenkinson produces the licence, which shows Olivia was lawfully wedded to the Squire, and the latter expresses penitence for his past misconduct, and promises to amend, Olivia is made happy . . . the worthy Vicar has good reason for saying, in the words with which his delightful autobiography closes, 'All my cares were over, my pleasure unspeakable. It now only remained that my gratitude in

Fig. 115. Shakespeare's *King John* at Drury Lane in 1866, with sixteen–year–old Amy Steinberg as Prince Arthur, center, Samuel Phelps as King John, and Barry Sullivan as Falconbridge. *From the Illustrated Times.*

Fig. 116. *The Vicar of Wakefield* at the National Standard Theatre, Act III. Vicar, Dr. Primrose; Sam Emery; Olivia Emily Pitt. *From the Illustrated London News.*

good fortune should exceed my former submission in adversity.' An able representative of Dr. Primrose was found in Mr. Sam Emery, who depicted the character of the Vicar in an artistic and exceedingly interesting manner, making him appear benevolent, humorous, simple, or elevated, as the occasion required . . . The beautiful, but vain and weak Olivia, was excellently personated by Miss Emily Pitt. Being attractive-looking, frank, and sprightly in her manner, and artless and pleasing in her speaking, she was almost a

perfect facsimile of Goldsmith's picture of the elder Miss Primrose. Miss Pitt acted with most commendable skill and good effect. She cleverly and touchingly sang 'When Lovely Woman Stoops to Folly,' which was highly appreciated and enjoyed by the assembly . . . . Miss Amy Steinberg played with great vigor and liveliness, Amelia Skeggs . . . Capital scenery has been provided by Mr. R. Douglass, Mr. Neville, and assistants. Their scenes representing the Fair and the fire are among the most elaborate and effective displays of the kind which have been witnessed.[74]

The Christmas panto of 1870–1871 was *Ride a Cock Horse to Banbury Cross; or, Harlequin and the Silver Amazons.* The spectacle scene was inspired by the Franco-Prussian War that had begun in 1870. In a setting of mountains and cataracts, one hundred ladies, called Silver Amazons, were led by Amy Steinberg as Prince Brilliant. They sang: "See the Conquering Hero Comes," "Watch on the Rhine," "The Marseillaise," and "Rule Britannia." The grand transformation scene had a flight of aerial sylphides that were projected in "a salvo into the air," by machinery operated by Herr Kozenour's patent steam shaft.

Recent events of note included the death of Charles Dickens and of Alexandre Dumas. In London, the aging Sadler's Wells Theatre was declared unsafe, and closed. At the other end of town, the wonderful Albert Hall was opened.

The international news of 1871 was the war. It provided opportunity for dramas the way the Crimean War had in 1850. The 6th of March 1871 J. T. Douglass's new play *Germans and French; or, Incidents in the War,* provided East End audiences with a living news report. In the story, Amy Steinberg portrayed Marie de Lange, a French peasant girl. The march of the French Army for the relief of Metz was illustrated by Richard Douglass's moving panorama depicting Chalons, Rheims, Espernais, Beaumont, and Sedan.

This plotless spectacle was followed by Douglass's play *For Sale.* Not an important script, it is typical of the majority of the dramas of the 1870s. The plot is about the miseries brought on his parents by a selfish, wayward son. The story provided the opportunity for Richard Douglass to design two novel scenes. The first was the exterior of a mansion by moonlight, where a snowball fight takes place. The second is a large hall in the mansion set up for an auction. The excitement of this scene was that the villain and another character each think there is a large amount of money hidden in the back of a mirror, and they try to outbid each other. The villain succeeds; but the money had been removed, thus he was foiled. The auction itself provided much excitement to the audience because, in the words of the reviewer, "it seemed so real."[75]

Amy Steinberg was now seen in almost every production: *Damon and Pythias, The Mysterious Lady*, with Julia Matthews in *The Grand Duchess of Gerolstein*, and in Andrew Halliday's dramatization of Dickens's *Old Curiosity Shop* entitled *Nell.* John Thomas Douglass and Alice Rachel

74.   The *Era*, (6 November 1870).
75.   The *Era*, (7 February 1869).

Koining (Amy Steinberg), were married on 6 June 1871.

A vogue for military things brought an unusual performer to the National Standard during the summer of 1871. W. H. Pennington performed as Richard III, Hamlet, Macbeth, and Othello (fig. 117).

At the ripe old age of ninety-one, this gallant soldier and sound actor, passed away on May 1st, 1923. On reading the account of his death, I opened my desk, and took out a book entitled, Heroism of Boyhood, which has been in my possession for about forty years. On the flyleaf was written 'To Albert Douglass, as a slight token of gratitude for services always rendered at the right moment, from his sincere friend W. H. Pennington.' The so-called services were very trivial. It needs no imagination to guess how, as a boy, I worshiped this hero of Balaclava, for he was in the famous charge of the Light Brigade, being wounded in the right leg, his mare shot under him, and probably would have lost his life, but for the good luck of a sergeant-major picking him up and placing him on a loose horse. In lady Butler's well-known picture, he is the middle figure—having given many sittings to the great artist. Needless to say Tennyson's poem, 'The Charge of the Light Brigade' delivered by one of the survivors, and in the real uniform, was always enthusiastically received by audiences.

He was frequently alluded to as Gladstone's pet tragedian, being a great favourite with that renowned statesman. Pennington was more of an elocutionist than an actor, but in those days this was expected by lovers of Shakespeare—consequently the

Fig. 117. W. H. Pennington (1832–1923), hero of Balaclava, and the charge of the Light Brigade, elocutionist, and actor of Henry V. *From Memories of Mummers.*

acting of many stars was rather stilted. Today there is a danger of artistes being so natural that they cease to be interesting especially in plays that do not call for any great expression of emotion or passion.

I can only remember Pennington being nonplussed once, and that was when playing Ingomar. Turning to his leading lady (Kate Neville), he unconsciously made a slip in the text and said 'what is thy name Parthenia?'—

and she replied with ready wit—'Thou already knowest, my lord.'[76]

During the rest of the summer there were various performers and the Christy Minstrels for eight weeks. The American actress Jeannie Gourly, performed the yankee favorite *Fanchonette, the Will-O-the-Wisp* for three weeks. Autumn was again a mixed bill, Rose Hersee in five weeks of opera, and Henry Marston and Mrs. Herman Vezin in eight classics. Their prompt book for *Macbeth* at the Standard has survived. It has light and sound cues, and two diagrams: one for the banquet scene, and one for the sleepwalking scene.[77]

By Christmas, John T. and Amy were back at work in the theatre. The pantomime was *Aladdin and the Wonderful Lamp*. The printed books of words for sixteen of the Douglass pantos survive, beginning with the 1865 show. This was when John T. became the house dramatist. Albert Douglass described an insider's view of the creation of the typical 1870s production.

> The band is loudly blaring, being repeatedly stopped by the excitable musical director in order to make corrections and additions; while on stage the final dress rehearsal of the pantomime proceeds amidst indescribable confusion. Everything goes wrong! All is chaotic! Pandemonium reigns! Yet no signs of unpreparedness are apparent at the first performance when the curtain rises on boxing night.

And what excellent pantomimes they were in those days! How they were enjoyed by the playgoing public! Many pantos ran till Easter, and although the salaries paid to modern artistes were undreamt of by the older generation of comedians, they were expected to deliver the goods. If their parts happened to be bad, there were no commiserating critics to deplore the poverty of the material provided for them. They had to find their own material, and many were very successful in that capacity. Many years ago I witnessed a Christmas annual at the P.O.W. Theatre, Liverpool, when that little house in Clayton Square was notorious for its splendid pantomimes and long runs. In the cast were four of the finest comedians that ever worked together. Fred Eastman was one—Walter Passmore another, and the combined salaries of the four amounted to £35; and with all the present-day talk of swollen salaries, and sometimes with heads to match, I have yet to see such team work equaled.

The vast stage of the old Standard, naturally demanded a large crowd, and in addition to the lengthy cast of principals, there were over a hundred girls in the chorus and ballet. From a throng of clamorous applicants, one hundred and ten would be selected . . . and no girl was known by her name. Each had a large numbered card hung around her neck, and in teaching all the necessary ballets, marches, and evolutions, the girls would be addressed by their respective numbers.

76. Douglass, *Memories of Mummers*, pp. 73–74.
77. The Lilly Library at the University of Indiana.

In those days the chorus girls vied with each other in generous curves; in fine and shapely nether limbs, and were endowed with a superabundance of bust that would probably not be considered 'good form' today [in 1926]. To them, the art of 'slimming' was unknown, and the modern attenuated flapper who prides herself on her boyish figure, would have stood little chance of being selected.

The choosing of these fair damsels was generally entrusted to two judges of whom I was one. All the girls assumed tights and paraded before our stern and critical gaze. It was our lofty mission to eliminate all who erred on the scraggly side, or those inclined to be too plump. Soulful maidens blessed with bulging ankles, or giddy matrons cursed with elephantine extremities, were speedily rejected. And a similar fate awaited any unfortunate possessor of knees resembling door-knobs. When, like Paris, I was sitting in judgment, I was the most envied youth for miles around, for in the mid-Victorian era ladies were not supposed to possess legs. Long dresses were the vogue, and no young man at that period ever dreamed that a day would dawn when it would be possible to witness the free exhibitions on view today.

The old pantomime scripts were not exactly over-burdened with wit. Their humor chiefly consisted of puns, yet often some remarkably clever ones, but punning has long been taboo. Like many other accomplishments it fell into desuetude through being overdone. Every Tom, Dick, and Harry would try to raise a cheap laugh by vilely distorting simple sentences and torturing the English language, to say nothing of their victim's ear-drums . . . . In a way it is to be deplored, for the really clever pun, when uttered by a gifted comedian, demanded a quick ear to detect it. One was never certain, even after its delivery, if intended, for it could be so neat as to often pass unnoticed. For instance: 'I had a shilling, so I put it on a horse in the last race. It was my last racehorse!' Another example: 'Many seaside resorts are low, but surely Lowestoft is the lowest oft them all!' Or to quote the burlesque line of a bold bad pirate: 'Everything I sees upon the seas I size upon!' How unforced. The punning seams quite unintentional and almost unavoidable. A punning line in spite of itself, as it were. H.J. Byron, who was a past master of this gentle art, once remarked, apropos of theatrical productions in general, that: 'A play was like a cigar. If good, everybody wanted a box, if bad, nothing on earth would make it draw.' But today there are more punters than punsters.

One of the great features of the old-fashioned pantomimes that delighted the playgoer of the past generation was the wonderful transformation scene. They were indeed triumphs of ingenuity, combined with beautiful kaleidoscopic effects. And although the skill of the scenic artist was aided by the mechanism of the stage—a mechanism almost obsolete in modern theatres—yet they were always founded on a poetical idea, such as 'The Spirit of Spring,' or 'The Birth of a Flower.' The model of a transformation scene would be prepared some months prior to production, and many anxious hours would be spent by the resident scenic artist and master carpenter in constructing its manifold beauties. A transformation scene generally began within a few feet of the floats, and with a series of cut cloths, gauzed cloths, and set pieces rising, sinking, or perhaps unfolding, to disclose fairies in every conceivable pose, it would gradually develop until the whole of the vast stage became a blaze of glittering glory, ending in a gorgeous spectacle of Fairyland, with probably the Fairy Queen, gracefully suspended on a wire, triumphantly reigning over her allegorical kingdom. The scene, which would frequently occupy ten minutes in unfolding, would be accompanied by specially written music, starting perhaps with a harp solo—then the full orchestra, at first piano, gradually swelling forth, and finally ending in a maestoso movement sounding like a paean of praise.

What the working of these intricate scenes meant to the painstaking stage manager is difficult for the public to imagine. To him fell the onerous duty of perfectly timing every cloth, every border, every set-piece, technically known as a 'rise,' or a 'sink;' each trap and each rostrum to be wheeled into its correct position. This ticklish task was performed by means of signals such as bells, flags, speaking-tube whistles, gongs and so forth, for electric bells were not invented, and one had to depend on old-fashioned wire bell-pulls. Moreover, every signal was preceded by a warning, consequently it was frequently necessary for the stage manager to give the bell cue for a scene to rise—nod to an assistant in the prompt wings who flag-signaled to the O.P. side for a rostrum to be drawn on , or off—and give the warning for a grave-trap to sink—all simultaneously. In fact, the supervising and manipulation of a transformation scene entailed more work for the stage manager than twenty modern three—act comedies. Indeed, when observing a touring stage manager, whose duties, barring a few trivial details, consist of

merely ringing up and ringing down the curtain (generally too soon or too late), getting frantically excited, is it surprising that I sometimes retire to my private office—and smile?

After the transformation came the harlequinade, which was, in fact, a continuation of the story. In a previous scene, the Fairy Queen would change the principal characters into pantomimists necessary for the Harlequinade, and in that guise they carried on till the end. In doggerel calculated to make the Sitwells writhe in agony, the Fairy Queen would chant:

> And you, sweet Cinderella
> No longer need you pine;
> I wave my wand-so change at once
> To pretty Columbine.

This metamorphosis was by no means an elaborate illusion, the character named bowing to the Fairy Queen, and making a rapid exit as the pantomimist appeared to take his or her place. Again the Fairy would wave her enchanted wand and intone another couplet of alleged poetry:

> And to be parted from your love,
> 'twould surely be a sin;
> So you, Prince Charming-now appear
> As sprightly Harlequin.

The agile Harlequin would then enter and go through a series of postures known as 'the animations.' Again the Fairy would bleat:

> From you, Baron Stoneybroke,
> I crave one final boon.
> Get hence! Avaunt! And change at once
> To lean and slippered Pantaloon.

And to a measured and staccato strain, the Pantaloon would slowly totter on. Till finally:

> And now to provide the fun
> To capture all the town-
> You-Billy Buttons- come
> Change at once to Clown.

To a rousing refrain, and with a merry 'Hullo, old'un! Here we are again!' on rolled the ever welcome Clown, and after a brief 'rally' by all concerned, the gorgeous transformation scene (see small bills) started to unfold, and the Harlequinade followed.

To the modern playgoer the posturing of Harlequin is merely a series of picturesque poses, but the mid-Victorian audiences being weaned, as it were, on pantomime, knew the true inward meaning of every attitude. They knew that fore-finger to the forehead denoted 'thought.' Right arm gracefully curved to the heart meant 'admiration.' Another striking position would signify 'flight.' Even each section of his bespangled patchwork costume had a deep significance of its own. For instance, if the Harlequin pointed to a yellow triangle, it indicated 'jealousy.'

But the exquisite art of pantomime gradually became decadent. Beaten and battered, it recoiled before the furious onslaught of slap-stick comedy, and today, it is doubtful if there is one playgoer in a thousand who knows that Harlequin is supposed to be invisible when wearing his mask, but visible from the moment it is removed.

As for the humours of the Harlequinade, in the hands of great clowns like George Lupino, Harry Payne, Whimsical Walker, J. M. Jones, Tom Lovell, and one or two others, the fun and frolic proved to be exceedingly mirth provoking. There would be about seven or eight scenes, each one honey-combed with clever gadgets and mechanical devices, all of which were very costly to construct, but when the deplorable deterioration set in, the clowns descended to speeches known in the vernacular as 'Give us your kind applause!' For instance, Joey would purloin a Union Jack, and remark to the Pantaloon, 'Old-un-ere's a Union Jack! I'm sending it to the wash.' 'Oh,' the Pantaloon would query in quavering tones, 'What for?' And the Clown, posturing, and with eyes fixed beseechingly on the gallery, would reply, 'Cos they're colours that never run!'

The husky raucous voice peculiar to Clowns is traditional, and like the shrill tones of Punch must have descended through the ages. This was rather fortunate at times, for many Joeys, not having the advantage of a public school education, discovered that an assumed voice, like charity, covered a multitude of sins. It is recorded that the only occasion on which the aspirate was correctly used, was when a clown, suffering from laryngitis, appealed to a Shakespearean actor to kindly shout the familiar phrase from the wings.

'What are the lines, laddie?' ponderously inquired the tragedian. 'Ullo, old'un! Ere we are again!' whispered the almost voiceless pantomimist. Then the clown bounded on to the stage as the legitimate actor, in deep sepulchral tones, so effective when playing

Fig. 118. *Notre Dame; or, the Gypsy Girl of Paris*, **from Dumas, by Andrew Halliday, at the Adelphi and Standard Theatres, 1871.** *From the Illustrated Times.*

the Ghost in *Hamlet*, declaimed: 'Hail, aged one! And so we meet again!'[78]

In the seventies the Harlequinade was considered to be of far more importance than the 'opening,' and usually consisted of seven or eight elaborately painted scenes honeycombed with quaint tricks, and clever mechanical devises. The 'props' too, were on a lavish scale—one trick, in which the Harlequin was placed upon a table, then severed limb by limb, and restored to life whole again, necessitated a trick table that cost over thirty pounds to manufacture on the premises. [See Chap. 12, note 110].

The pantomimists in those days were often the highest paid artistes, and the esteem in which the clown was held can easily be gauged by reading the newspapers of the period, and noting how the audience constantly clamoured for him to sing 'Hot Codlins.'

Many reasons have been given for the decadence of the Harlequinade, some tracing it to the popularity of Revue, others to public indifference to the art and history of

78. Douglass, *Footlight Reflections*, pp. 106–113.

pantomime, asserting that not one in ten thousand understand the animations of Harlequin (which is true), but the real reason I am afraid, is the humor is too primitive and does not appeal to the younger generation.

Can anybody conceive the modern blase schoolboy, tired of gramophones, weary of Wembley, board with the wireless, and fed up with the pictures, laughing at a Clown stealing sausages? The early Victorian child was not surfeited with distractions: even toys were expensive and scarce, but today one frequently sees the children of people in humble circumstances surrounded with teddy bears, miniature prams, golliwogs, and dolls in profusion.

Certain forms of humour become obsolete, for instance, take the situation in *Caste*, where D'Alroy unexpectedly returns, and Polly Eccles and Sam Gerridge mistaking him for a ghost, dive under the table trembling with fear. I have nothing but admiration and affection for this human comedy, for was it not the pioneer of the natural school of acting? But if such an incident occurred in a modern play I doubt if it would raise a smile.

Perhaps a better illustration is found in the puns that besprinkled every line of the old Gaiety burlesques, which convulsed our grandfathers with merriment. Today, punning is practically a dead art, and I fear the humour of the Harlequinade is in the same category. I may be wrong. I hope I am—for I write these lines with a tinge of sorrow, having such pleasant recollections of Harry Payne, . . . and many others.[79]

Apparently "quiet" Richard Douglass had been smitten a year or so before John and Amy were. Following the closing of the panto of 1870, the Adelphi Company came in with Andrew Halliday's *Notre Dame; or, the Gypsy Girl of Paris*. This dramatization of *The Hunchback of Notre Dame* had in its cast a pretty young actress playing Ninette, a maid. Called in the program, Estelle Brereton, her real name was Laurina Campland which on the whole seems a more lyrical, and theatrical name; but she preferred to become Stella. When *Notre Dame* moved out she remained behind in the stock company. She became Richard's wife in June of 1870. They went to Shanklin in the South of England for their honeymoon. Richard took his easel, and they spent a leasurely summer sitting in the woods, and wandering the paths. Three paintings survive all dated June 1870 (figs. 198–200). Back at work Stella played chambermaids, children, Fairy Godmothers, and the Player Queen in *Hamlet*. She was petite, and a dancer as well as actress.

T. C. King (1825–1893), who led the Adelphi Company in *Notre Dame*, used some psychological tricks to "get into" his characters.

> In 1871 when this Shakespearean actor . . . came to the Standard, I was just commencing my duties as call boy, and remember being really frightened for he was a ferocious looking man with a permanent scowl.

---

79. Douglass, *Memories of Mummers*, pp. 108–109.

To watch him lash himself into a fury before making an en trance was enough to terrify any impressionable youth. I learnt later he was a lovable man, never tired of doing kindly deeds, and helping other members of the company in every conceivable way. Like all true artists he took his work seriously, therefore was easily upset if anything went amiss on the stage.

He had an extensive repertoire, but changing the play at every performance was sometimes confusing to the staff, and one night an incident occurred which caused great hilarity in front, but grave concern behind the scenes. The play was *Macbeth* (the title role being one of King's favourite parts), and the head flyman instead of lowering a landscape cloth, unfortunately dropped a street scene formerly used in the harlequinade of the pantomime that had finished the previous week. As the lights were lowered, the prompter vainly hoped that King would not observe the mistake, but the constant titters of the audience caused the tragedian to look around, and his horror can be imagined when he beheld on one side 'Block-Barber-Hair Cut While You Wait,' and on the other 'Chop-Butcher-Prices To Suet All Pockets.' Dashing off the stage in a furious temper, he made a bee line for the prompter, as if to strangle that unfortunate individual, shook his fist and yelled 'Damn you, sir, What do you mean? This scene should be a blasted heath and you give me a blasted butcher's shop.'[80]

Fig. 119. The main entrance of the National Standard Theatre from Shoreditch High Street, with advertising for Henry Irving, August 1874. *From Memories of Mummers.*

After King came the Olympic Company in Andrew Halliday's version of *David Copperfield* called *Little Emily.* Stella Brereton played

80.   Douglass, *Memories of Mummers*, pp. 49–50.

Fig. 120. Henry Irving in *The Bells* by Leopold Lewis. The dream of the murder scene. *From A.S.J. .*

Little Emily, and in her brother-in-law's comedietta afterpiece she played an ingenue. The normal practice had been for these short plays to be changed every day or two. By the spring of 1872, as John T. Douglass provided more translations and adaptations, they were held over for weeks at a time. This may reflect a change in the makeup of the audience: less repeaters, a greater turn over of individuals.

In July the Standard's programs carried the exciting announcement:

"Mr Henry Irving and the Lyceum Company will appear Monday July 29, 1872, for a limited number of nights. Mr. Irving will appear in his famous character of Mathias in the drama of *The Bells* as performed by him 151 nights at the Lyceum Theatre this season" (figs.119–121). Irving was popular, and the production ran four weeks.

Stella Brereton continued to play in larger roles and receive good notices. Her husband provided new settings for the spectacular *Rebecca*; Andrew

Fig. 121. Henry Irving in *The Bells* by Leopold Lewis. The dream of the trial scene. *From the Illustrated Times.*

Halliday's adaptation of Scott's *Ivanhoe.*

The autumn season began with a series of the old classics. This time the star was the second continental actor to appear at the Standard, Daniel E. Bandmann (1840–1905). He and his wife, Millicent Palmer, were given excellent reviews for *Richlieu*, and *Hamlet*. Then, Stella Brereton was pressed into Mrs. Bandmann's parts, when she became ill during the second week of October.

On 11 November 1872, The English Opera Company opened Jules Benedict's *Lily of Killarney*, for the first time at the Standard. This Victorian favorite opera was based on Dion Boucicault's *Colleen Bawn*. The rest of the repertoire was the epitome of standards: *The Bohemian Girl, Il Trovatori, La Sonnambula, Maritana, Fra Diavolo,*

The Crown of Diamonds, Luccia di Lammermor, and Faust. Alice Mariott in Jeanie Deans, and the opera company ran until the panto.

Harlequin Cinderella and the Glass Slipper, provided Stella Brereton with the dual roles of The Fairy Godmother, and The Queen of the Air. Richard painted fifteen spectacular settings, including a moving panorama of a palace grounds. The pageant scene revealed two-hundred ladies illuminated by two thousand lights.

John Douglass Senior was training the family to take over entirely. Richard was now fully in charge of the painting and design departments. In fact he was accepting outside commissions to paint sets for other theatres. John Junior was the dramatist and stage director. Stella Brereton continued in her type of roles, in the stock company. Only Amy Steinberg was not fully

Fig. 122. G. W. "Pony" Moore and Frederick Burgess with the Christy Minstrels, in the *Walk Around*. From the Rose Lipman Library, Hackney.

integrated into the company. She had been with the Olympic Theatre for a season. In March of 1873 she placed an advertisement stating she was willing to accept engagements as a guest star for amateur performances of plays.

A new production of W. T. Moncrieff's 1823 oriental spectacle *The Cataract of the Ganges*, was produced at Drury Lane in early April. Richard Douglass provided all the settings. After Easter, the whole production was transferred to the Standard, with all its old fashioned hippodrama elements, in the thrilling flight of the Princess on horseback up the precipices of the great cataract of **"REAL WATER."**

The summer that followed this sensation drama included the Moore and Burgess Minstrels. Beginning in April of 1871, George Washington (Pony) Moore (1820–1909), and his partner Frederick Burgess (1825–1893), had changed the name of their St. James's Hall minstrels. They dropped the "Christy" because there were so many inferior provincial troupes calling themselves "Christy Minstrels." The word "Christy" was the name of a formulistic type of a production, rather than the name of one of the performers. Albert Douglass tells of his memories of Pony Moore:

This celebrated troupe visited the Standard . . . they were undoubtedly the best exponents of a form of humor now almost obsolete. G. W. Moore was a great martinet, and his troupe went in fear of their chief, who did not hesitate to criticize adversely (sotto voce) the performance, whilst the artistes were seated on the stage, engaged in singing a song or cracking a wheeze.

It must have been very disconcerting for a tenor, whilst warbling 'Put some green leaves on my grave,' to hear ventriloquist growls from Pony Moore sarcastically asking 'Is THAT the best you can do?' Pony's language was enough to turn a modern sergeant-major green with envy, and compel a bargee to bury his face in shame.

On one occasion a member of his company having spilt some water over the dressing room floor, whilst removing his make-up after the performance, Pony, in a few well chosen words probably picked up from a Sunday School teacher, intimated to the troupe that in future they would not be allowed to enter their dressing rooms until they had washed off their burnt cork in a pail provided for that purpose placed at the back of the stage. No marathon race could equal the rush to be first at the pail when the curtain fell.

A remarkable incident occurred on the opening night of this famous troupe's visit. When the interlocutor announced that Walter de Brenna would sing a well known ballad, a man seated in the pit shouted 'Oh! give us something new.' In an instant Pony Moore leapt to his feet, and imperiously stopping the orchestra, advanced to the footlights and proceeded to wither the poor pittite by delivering a lengthy oration. 'Could the new songs compare with the old?' he angrily enquired. He appealed to the audience and demanded fair play. 'Did not the songs their parents crooned to them, when they were tiny tots grip their hearts today?' Suppressing a sob he reminded the astonished interrupter 'that when the toiler, after his day's work was over, sought relaxation in a temple of amusement, he loved to listen to songs of a bygone

Fig. 123. The vision scene from Leopold Lewis's, *The Wandering Jew*. The setting is by Frederick Lloyds, at the Adelphi and Standard Theatres in 1872. *From the Illustrated London News.*

day. They recalled cherished memories. The old songs would live when the modern rubbish was forgotten. If ballads of yesterday brought comfort, then it was the mission of Moore and Burgess to minister to those in need of such comfort,' and much more in a similar vein.

This rhetorical response to an unexpected remark, roused the audience to such a pitch of excitement that when Pony resumed his corner seat he gained one of the biggest ovations ever heard inside the old theatre. It was indeed a great achievement. Behind the scenes all were loud in their praises of Pony's eloquence and pathos, but enthusiasm waned somewhat when it was discovered later that this extemporaneous effort had really been carefully prepared and well rehearsed—the dissatisfied patron having been 'planted' in the pit by Pony Moore himself.[81]

The arrangement of a Moore and Burgess Christy Minstrel was in three parts. The "First Part" consisted of a row of singers and comedians in burnt

81. Douglass, *Memories of Mummers*, pp. 75–76.

cork makeup. They told jokes, and sang favorite comic or pathetic ballads. Favorites of the latter were "Kiss me mother ere I die," "Gone are the days," "Fireworks on the brain," and "She sleeps beneath the daisies on the hill."

"The Second Part" consisted of comic sketches, burlesque scenes, and dances. Typical titles of the sketches include: *Ten Minutes in an Old Kentucky Court House*, *Slippery Times in Old Virginny*, *The Wig Makers*, *Lemuel's Ghost*, *The Pilgrim Fathers*, and *O-Tell-O*.

"The Third Part" consisted of comical musical, and dance numbers, followed by the whole company in the grand finale, called the "Walk Around" (fig. 122).

Fig. 124. *Harlequin Whittington and His Cat*, panto of 1873–1874, the exploding piano trick. *From A.S.J.*

Following the minstrels, William Creswick returned for his most splendid run of classical revivals. This lasted nine weeks. Stella Brereton played Princess Margaret in Creswick's favorite vehicle *Ambition*. She also played an important role in John T. Douglass's translation of a French farce. He called it, *What Will the Neighbors Say?* Again her reviews were complimentary.

In November the Adelphi Company brought their play *The Wandering Jew*. In several scenes the protagonist has supernatural experiences staged by placing tableaus behind scrim sections of the drops (fig. 123). The sets were designed by Frederick Lloyds who had worked at Charles Kean's Princess's Theatre, during the great Shakespearean period there. Lloyds was one of the first to write a textbook on Victorian stage craft (1875). It is a beautiful book with delicate engravings of Kean's production of *Midsummer Nights Dream*, and color swatches of typical scene paint pigments.

The pantomime for Christmas of 1873–1874 was *Harlequin Whittington and His Cat*. It was a particularly fine example of the form, and perhaps the last production John Douglass Senior was to see.

The pantomime . . . is distinguished by several points of novelty . . . which Mr. J. Douglass has treated in a very original manner. Dick, flying from his persecutors, is seen near the traditional stone, where the spectator may re-acquaint himself with the well known features of Higate-hill and the celebrated view of London from its summit. The bells of the churches bid the runaway 'prentice return to his cruel master. He does so, and reappears in the soap-merchant's kitchen, where he is learning the mystery of cooking. Fitzwarren summons all his servants and wishes them to send something on board his ship, the 'Pretty Polly,' the profit of each venture to belong to the sender. Everyone makes his offer. Dick, having nothing else to send, agrees, at Pussy's instigation, to send his cat, or rather to sail himself, with Pussy, to try his luck abroad. A storm overtakes the vessel, she is wrecked, but, by the intervention of the Fairy Fairweather, Dick, the cat, Captain, and crew are landed safely at Morocco. At the Palace of the Dey a grand procession of Eastern Warriors takes place.

The arrival of strangers is announced. A banquet is prepared, when the visitors are overwhelmed with rats and mice, Pussy soon clears them. The Monarch offers fabulous sums to buy the clever cat, eventually a bargain is decided upon, and Dick sets sail for home, loaded with riches. A grand double moving panorama is here introduced—the procession of the Lord Mayor's Show; its progress through the Strand, Fleet-Street, Old St. Dunstan's Church, Old St.Paul's, and arrival at the Guildhall, decorated for the reception of the Lord Mayor, Richard Whittington, destined to hold that office three times in succession. The King, hearing of the fame and sudden rise of Whittington, orders a grand pageant and war-like celebration in his honour. Emblems of Peace, Industry, and War are summoned, and the last named

chosen. The spectators are now introduced to the armoury in Guildhall, and thence transported to Cannock Chase, in Henry IV's time. The whole of the troops assembled, a warlike parade takes place, manoeuvres terminating with a costly, magnificent pageant. The festival of Fame succeeds, displaying brilliant costumes, armour, and appointments. We have next the interior of the Mansion House, occupied by the interview of the King, and the Marriage of Dick Whittington to Alice Fitzwarren. The grand trans-formation scene represents a rapid descent from sky to sea, concluding with a gorgeous and imposing tableau . . . It is obvious that the materials associated with the incidents will much conduce to the success of this costly pantomime.[82]

The army in real silver armour was described as: ". . . for brilliancy of effect is not to be paralleled." The armor was provided by Gustave Lafayette, costumer to the Parisian theatres. The lighting of the campfires of the army at Cannock Chase was supposed to be an "entirely original effect never before attempted on any stage in Europe." The spectators were astonished by the extraordinary, and sudden ap pearance, and disappearance of the lights all over the plain. This effect was probably produced by a pierced drop, backed with a white drop as a reflector, that would show through the openings representing the campfire flames when properly illuminated. Each campfire could be controlled with flaps of cloth

82. *The Illustrated London News*, (27 December 1873).

that could close off the hole when required.

The performers were roundly praised:

John Barnum as the cat, seems to be here, there, and everywhere and as the 'cat Comique,' enrolled in the police force his song and dance never fail to secure an irresistible encore. His makeup is fairly astounding and when he lights his cigar with the tip of his tail the audience literally scream with merriment .... Those members of the 'upper ten' whose boast it is that they never go east of Temple Bar, would do well to break the rule for once, and pay their respects to Dick Whittington without delay.[83]

Albert Douglass remembered the Payne family that specialized in the Harlequinade characters, and who starred in this panto:

My first recollection of this family was their special engagement at the Standard to dance an interpolated 'Can Can' in a comic opera. When they were engaged for the pantomime of Dick Whittington, playing the principal comedy parts and in the harlequinade they were a splendid troupe, in fact with the exception of the Hanlon Lees, the best pantomimists I ever saw. The father, W. H. Payne, was Pantaloon; Madam Esta, the mother, Columbine; Harry, the Clown; and Fred, the most versatile of all, the Harlequin.

Years after, when all the family had passed away with the exception of the great clown, Harry and I often chatted over old times. He was a delightful companion . . . . When playing Clown for so many pantomime seasons at Old Drury, he carefully husbanded his salary to enable him to live in modest comfort for twelve months, so being fond of country life, and a keen votary of the sport that does not demand strict veracity when describing the catch, he enjoyed himself in a quiet way until the next Christmas Annual came round. The question of 'Where do all the Clowns go in the summertime?' was frequently raised when Joey held sway. During the months their services were not in demand for pantomime, some obtained employment in the ballets, once a feature of The Alhambra and The Empire, whilst others were found in strange places. I saw one in Billingsgate Market indulging in a piscatorial pursuit, or to be precise, shoveling up 'winkles,' a delicious dish seldom served at the Ritz. On another occasion, when as a boy I took my boots to be repaired, I was surprised to find the old cobbler was a popular clown, but my astonishment was even greater, when travelling on an Elephant and Castle bus, I recognized an old Standard Joey, in the conductor who greeted me with the familiar 'Hullo! Here we are again!'[84]

Unfortunately the merriment wasn't to be permanent. John Douglass Senior had been in declining health for three years. He died 31 January 1874. Thus ended the career of the man who had built the Eastern Drury Lane, one of the finest, and financially sound theatrical

83. Quoted from an unidentified review reprinted in advertising.
84. Douglass, *Memories of Mummers*, pp. 60–62.

institutions in the world. He was not quite sixty years old. The hard life of his youth, and decades of sixteen-hour work days, had taken their toll. He was remembered as a hearty, homely person, friendly, warm, and with a generous nature. From the stars to the stagehands, he was considered among the best, most open-handed of the theatre proprietors of his time.

His personality may have been formed the way it was because as a youth, he saw how the managers of suburban theatres exploited the actors and technicians. Also some of the role he played in the nautical plays rubbed off. He and Tippy Cooke were in real life a realization of the idealized British tar: sturdy, dependable, loyal, frugal, honest to the extreme. Under their simple brusque exterior was intelligence and resourcefulness. They could be depended on to do the right thing. They were the real life William from *Black Eyed Susan*. John Douglass had other skills as well; he was an excellent folk dancer, pantomimist, and broad-swordsman.

He was buried in Abney Park Cemetery. Members of the profession turned out in the hundreds, and lined the streets that led to the site of the interment.

In John Douglass's final years of work, there were some changes in the production patterns. There was a precipitous drop in the number of nights of Shakespeare and other classics. There was a rise in the number of new scripts performed. Though these were still melodramas, they were more sophisticated than the ones of their fifties and sixties. The new plays were large, with big casts, and extensive three dimensional exterior settings. Stage-lighting effects were integrated into the performances. New equipment was being perfected. Lime lights, with colored glass mediums, proliferated in the fly galleries. They were now being used to spotlight areas of the stage for sun, moon, and fire effects, as well as being used as follow spots. Scrim effects for fade-through techniques, and supernatural visions, anticipate expressionism.

Opera, and other serious musical events became even more important than in the sixties. For Ash Wednesday, or Good Friday, or sometimes for Easter week, Handel's *Messiah*, with five hundred musicians was featured. Rossini's *Stabat Mater* was given a similar treatment. Moore and Burgess, the original and best of the minstrel companies, always performed for a month between May and November.

The patterns between 1859, and 1874 show the changes in theatre. 1859 is at the end of the first decade of Douglass management, when Tudor, Stuart, and other classics had brought respectability, and riches. James Anderson, Charles Kean, and Samuel Phelps were at the height of their success. After 1859, social and economic conditions were in turmoil. Theatre trended to musical forms, and more nineteenth century dramas, as the 1868 table indicates. The War year of 1870 is an extreme example of, perhaps, escapist tastes, and 1871 is more representative of the patterns for the first half of the 1870s.

In the period after 1868, the trend to bring whole companies, and their scenery to the Standard took some pressure off the technical staff. This let them concentrate on the pantomime, and their own home-grown premieres. The runs grew even longer, and the repertory system, with its nightly changes faded.

Type	1859	1868	1870	1871
CLASSIC	61	45	0	32
19TH	28	31	32	31
PANTO	48	54	60	60
NEWPLAY	29	43	176	58
MINSTREL	26	43	33	52
MUSICAL	24	34	0	49
VARIETY	12	18	0	12

The strength of the acting in the revivals of Shakespeare, Bulwer, and Knowles was not as significant or represented by so many stars as it had been in the 1860s. Only William Creswick seemed to carry on a superior artistic tradition in the classics. On the other hand, Mr. and Mrs. Sims Reeves, Julia Matthews, and Rose Hersee became eminently popular. The Strong companies of Webster and Celeste at the Adelphi, J. L. Toole's Queen's Theater Company, and Buckstone's Haymarket Comedians were the strength of contemporary London acting groups. Young Henry Irving was beginning his spectacular rise to dominance. These ensembles presented models of artistry that John T. Douglass, his brothers, and their wives, saw as the way of the future.

John Douglass cannot be castigated for pandering to low taste. His twenty-four seasons as proprietor had always emphasized the classics, opera, and quality contemporary productions. Yet, he has not been recognized by historians, and critics as have Macready, Charles Kean, and Samuel Phelps. The reason seems clear. He did not star as actor-proprietor in the classic plays, in his own theatre, as the others did. Douglass had to provide quality art through the performances of others. Perhaps, after he was gone, memory of his accomplishments dissipated more rapidly. On the other hand, the effect of his work was that he probably had more influence on the rise in artistic taste than any other single one of his contemporaries, purely based on numbers. More people came to his huge house than the rest of the theatres added together. Taking James Anderson as an example, more people saw his series of Shakespearean plays at the Standard than saw all the Shakespearean performances of Edmund Kean, William Charles Macready, Charles Kean, and Samuel Phelps put together. A normal six-day week during Anderson's heyday, was forty thousand admissions; Sims Reeves and Julia Matthews did as well; a good first week of January for one of the pantomimes was one hundred and twenty thousand admissions because of three performances a day.

11

HEROINES IMPERILED 1875-1880

In the years from 1850 to 1874, the operations at the National Standard Theatre presented the East End patrons the best of the mid Victorian performing arts. The relatively low costs of the operation, large volume of audience, and constant visits of guest performers permitted even the poor a chance to see the quality theatre of their time. Of the major performers, and productions of this period, only Boucicault, and his plays *Poor of New York* (1850's), *The Octoroon* (1861), *Arrah-Na-Pogue* (1864), *The Shaughraun* (1874), and one or two of his other plays had not come to the Standard.

On 29 June 1874 the innovational dramas of the Robertson's arrived in the East End. Their one-word-title plays, on the leading edge of the naturalistic theatre, had been premiered between 1866, and 1870, at the Prince of Wales Theatre. It had a six-hundred seat auditorium that suited these conversational dramas. The engagement at the Standard was undertaken with trepidation, but in their book the Bancrofts said its results were remarkable:

It was sometimes said that the Robertson comedies could only be effective in a small theatre. To refute this let me state that in the summer of [1874] we played *Caste* for a few weeks at the enormous Standard Theatre in Shoreditch. It was a risky experiment to act this delicate comedy in a theatre larger even than Drury Lane, and before an East-end audience, and we ourselves were a little in doubt as to the result; but any fears we entertained were soon dispelled, for densely packed houses nightly received the play with enthusiasm, appreciating fully its most tender scenes, and listening with rapt attention. The case was well put in a long article on this engagement in which it was said that, apart from the perfection of the play and players, the East-end theatre was a sight worth going far to see when the play was *Caste*, and the players the Prince of Wales's company. From basement to ceiling within its vast area gathered night after night interested, intelligent, enthusiastic audiences,

216

who received the play with storms of impulsive applause. It made the writer wonder whether, 'wise as we were,' we did not err in one respect—that of playing ordinarily in too small a theatre for the attractions we offered and the amazing popularity we commanded.[85]

The acoustics at the Standard must have been quite good, as A. W. Pinero stated that as a young man he sat in the rear row during this engagement, and he heard every word.[86] As to the realistic acting, no coarsening was inserted to make up for the distances in the huge house. In *Caste* for example:

Mr. J. F. Young was wonderfully made up as old Eccles and gave a very striking performance of the part. In the third act, the old sot left in charge of a 'bloated aristocrat' in the form of a baby, he occupied at least five

Fig. 125. *Ours* **by T.W. Robertson, the Prince of Wales Theatre production performed at the Standard Theatre in 1874.** *From the Illustrated London News.*

85.   Squire and Marie Bancroft, *The Bancrofts*, (New York, 1909), p. 98.
86.   *Fifty Years, Memories and Contrasts 1882-1932 by Twenty Seven Contributors to the Times,* (London: Thornton, Butterworth, 1932), p. 74.

minutes in preparing filling, and lighting his pipe, and so natural was every movement of the actor that without speaking a word he fairly riveted the attention of his audience.[87]

The play *Ours* was added in rotation with *Caste*, and others after 13 July 1874. It is the story of two young ladies who accompany their guardian Colonel Sir Alexander Shendryn to the camp of the British Army in the Crimea. The setting of their humble dwelling in the snow is considered one of the early examples of serious scenic naturalism. Every detail was carefully prepared, the simulated sparkling snow on the roof, the props, the firelight playing across the rude furniture made homey, a bit of England, with cloths, and utensils, by the girls. Then came the exciting scene with the arrival of the stranger in the snow storm, the falling snow, the girls alone, night, danger; the plucky, resourceful, young women don't cower in the corner. They pick up weapons,

Fig. 126.*Ours* by T.W. Robertson performed at the Standard Theatre in 1874, the Prince of Wales production. *From the Illustrated Times.*

87.   The *Era*, (12 July 1874).

and prepare to give a good fight if necessary.

The spring, and summer of 1874 was quite a brilliant period. Excellent productions of *East Lynne*, *The Ticket of Leave Man*, *School*, *Caste*, *Ours* followed one upon the other. Then came Henry Irving, and his Lyceum Company, with *Charles I*, and *The Bells*. His acting of the Bergermeister particularly suited the East End taste.

In the more thrilling scenes of the play and notably in the realization of the horrible dream in which the murderer arraigned before his judges re-enacts his bloody work under the spells of the Mesmerist, Mr. Irving seemed to hold his audience spell-bound, and a glance around the house revealed scores of faces bearing some impress of the terror excited. The striking tableau at the end of the first act showing the Polish Jew on his journey amid the snowstorm and followed by the greedy man, who seeks his life for his money belt seemed to arouse the spectators

Fig. 127. *Hal O'The Wynde* **by Leonard Rae (John T. Douglass), 14 September 1874.** *From the Illustrated Sporting and Dramatic News.*

to great excitement (figs.120 and 121).[88]

As John T. Douglass wrote more, and more of the plays produced at the Standard, he began to use several pen names. This was so there seemed to be a greater variety of authors. Those "in the know" understood that Leonard Rae,[89] and James Willing were merely Douglass's alter egos. On the flyleaf of a bound set of the Standard's programs for the 1881 season, John had written,

"July 1890, I hereby assert that wherever the name of James Willing appears as author of any dramatic work produced by me or under my direction, such a *nom de plume* has been used by me since 1878. And every work professing to be the literary work of James Willing has been and is the sole production of my brain, yours John Douglass." He may also have been assisted in the dramatizations by his wife. She had a facility for foreign

Fig. 128. *Amy Robsart*, **Drury Lane and National Standard Theatres in 1874.** *From the Illustrated Sporting and Dramatic News.*

88. The *Era*, (2 August 1874).
89. The *Illustrated London News*, (19 September 1874).

languages that would be useful for translations. Some years later, she did publish a script or two under her own name. There actually was a James Willing (1838–1915); John Douglass calls him his brother-in Law, which would make him Isabella Douglass's husband (see Appendix I). He was apparently in the advertising business (fig. 97 may actually be Willing rather than Thomas Douglass).

The September 1874 premiere was a relatively old-fashioned costume play *Hal O' the Wynd* adapted from Scott's *Fair Maid of Perth* (fig. 127).

The National Theatre of the East End, in emulation of its co-rival in the West, has ventured this year on a Sir Walter Scott spectacle, and on Monday produced a new drama, in four acts. . . . The text of this story is rather complicated and the circumstances attending the famous battle of the Inch have rather to be imagined than witnessed. The adaptation is by Leonard Rae—a convenient substitute for, we believe, the name of the manager; and is illustrated by some very fine scenery, the work of Richard Douglass. . . . The first of the performers, we must signalise Mr. T. Swinbourne, who, as Henry Smith, the armourer (Hal O'the Wynd), the faithful and valiant lover of Catherine Glover, the Fair Maid of Perth, sustained a long and impas-

Fig. 129 *Harlequin Robinson Crusoe and His Man Friday*, **Standard Theatre 1874. Scene by Richard Douglass.** *From A.S.J.*

sioned part with vigour and decision. We next have Mr. James Bennett as Sir John of Ramorney, who, having lost his hand in defense of David Rothsay, son of King Robert III, and not having been thanked for it, desires revenge on the ungrateful Prince, and also on Hal O' the Wynd, contrives it with his mediciner, Henbane Dwining. . . . The third celebrity was Mr. Pennington, who made a decided feature of the glover's apprentice. . . known as Eachin Mac Ian, head of the clan Quhele, which was at feud with clan Chattan. The battle between them was fought on Palm Sunday, 1396. Eachin on this occasion showed the white feather; nevertheless, he fought with Hal O' the Wynd and was slain. Mr. T. Mead, as foster-father of [Hal} acted with emotion and force. Mr. John Murray as Oliver Proudfute, who is killed through the machinations of Sir John of Ramorney, gave an example of low comedy which relieved the first act. . . [It] consisted of five capitally-painted scenes. . . there are seven in the remaining three acts-making altogether twelve painted scenes, some of which are most elaborately set. The interior of the palace and that of the church of St. John, where the ordeal takes place, [Fig.127] are both good. The view of Loch Tay and the exterior of Falkland Castle are likewise most picturesque in their arrangement and accessories. The performance is of a striking description, and of nature to command large audiences.[90]

Hard on the success of *Hal O' the Wynd*, that ran five weeks, came the Drury Lane production of *Amy Robsart*,

alluded at the beginning of the review above. Douglass was capitalizing on the interest in Scott generated by his own play. *Amy Robsart* was a dramatization of Scott's *Kenilworth*. (Fig. 128). Richard Douglass painted new scenery, and the reviews compare it favorably with that made for Drury Lane by the great William Beverly.

In December, before the panto, the classic revival season was a series of the old standby Shakespearean plays plus *The Bridal, Lady of Lyons, The Stranger*, and *Ingomar*. The guest stars were W. H. Pennington, and Dolores Drummond (1840–1926), an Australian actress. She became popular in the East End and was seen at the Standard many times.

The Christmas annual for 1874–1875 was *Robinson Crusoe and his Man Friday* (fig. 129):

> After an introduction we arrive at Crusoe's farm, and witness the squabbles of the hero and his wife. The latter has been three times a widow, and her family extends to thirty-two members. The eldest girl has two sweethearts, one of whom seeks the removal of Crusoe, and procures his arrest by a press gang. A splendid view of Wapping in the olden times follows. . . . The ship is seen to sail out of the dock, fully rigged and manned. Here is an opportunity for a nautical ballet, with illustrations of naval tactics. . . . The vessel proves to be a slaver, with Friday as a prisoner on board, whom Crusoe releases and engages as his servant. An attempt

90.   The *Era*, (19 September 1874).

Fig. 130. *Harlequin Robinson Crusoe and His Man Friday*, the moving panorama by Richard Douglass for the first scenes of the sinking of the ship in a storm at sea. The panorama shows changes of place, weather and time. *From A.S.J.*

being made to scuttle the vessel, Crusoe and Friday resist the conspirators; but the ship breaks up, and then we have the open sea, with a moving panorama representing Crusoe's journey to his landing on the unknown island [fig. 130]. . . . There is a grand Indian procession numbering more than 250 persons. . . Crusoe, asleep, has a vision of the inhabitants of the mystic isle , forming a spectacular display of wonderful brilliance. The transformation scene shows the transition from the storm to sunshine, including five distinct mechanical changes. Altogether, this pantomime is a gorgeous production.[91]

Fig. 131. Ada Cavendish (1847–1895). *From The Theatre.*

This production succeeded well into February of 1875. Several events of importance happened in this year. The Circle Line's underground railway was opened as far as Liverpool Street. Thus the Standard's audience had another easy method of access. The second event of notice was a rally of half a million people in Hyde Park, in support of the Tichborne claimant. This legal case had created such a distraction, and furor in the press, that the weeks before, and after Easter were not good for the theatres. The case was very convoluted, but boiled down to a battle over a large amount of money, between a rightful, but very stupid heir, and a greedy, wrongful, bureaucratic, and sanctimonious church body. The latter kept the money, and the former eventually perished in squalor.

At the Standard the season was a fortaste of things to come. It was dominated by women; plays about women, and strong actresses were to become a major feature of the operations at the Standard. The first was Sarah Thorne in the perennial *East Lynne*. This was followed by Marie Litton's Court Theatre Company, Rose Hersee in several weeks of heroine dominated operas, then Miss Furtado in a new sensation drama by the Douglasses. *Rank and Fame*, (fig.132) presented a novel technical innovation. A Revolving stage, which had been developed for panto transformations, was used to unfold various phases of the hero's dramatic escape from a German prison.

---

91.   The *Era*, (3 January 1875).

224

In May of 1875 Ada Cavendish (1847–1895) performed at the Standard in her recent vehicle called *The New Magdalen* (figs. 131 and 134). She played the heroine, a reformed fallen woman, Mercy Merrick. Albert recounted a story about his Shakespeare quoting, and punning Uncle Thomas and Miss Cavendish:

> Ada Cavendish, in making a hurried exit tore her dress on a door knob. She was very angry and complained that a small screw was the cause. Thomas admitted that there was a screw loose somewhere, adding that her dress was rather thin. 'Nonsense, ' she replied, 'the material is of excellent quality.' 'Yes,' came the answer like a flash, 'but you should see that the quality of Mercy is not strained.'[92]

The story of Mercy Merrick in Wilkie Collins's *New Magdalen* is a relatively simple-minded one, but it afforded a strong role for an actress. Ada Cavendish made this part her own, and performed it up and down the country for years. The theme was that a woman may stray from the path of

Fig. 132. *Rank and Fame* by Leonard Rae (John T. Douglass) and Frank Stainforth, 29 March 1875. *From the Illustrated Sporting and Dramatic News.*

92. Douglass, *Memories of Mummers*, p. 31.

virtue, lie, cheat, steal, but, if she repents, in the end she is sure to become saintly, and marry a clergyman. Collins is able to enlist the sympathy of the audience for the adventuress, rather than the poor victims of her frauds. Ada Cavendish is said to have found the role to her liking because the character is constantly under the influence of conflicting emotions.

Before the theatre was closed in July for renovation, the first time since it was built, Julia Matthews performed through June in *Girofle Girofla* by Lecocq. The changes in the building included a new proscenium, a domed ceiling, and embellishments on the boxes. A new act drop was painted by Richard Douglass with human figures added by his friend D. M. Friston. The press found the redecorated front foyer to be: ". . . in the shape of a grand hall with tesselated [square mosaic] pavements, and a magnificent stone staircase four yards wide. It was constructed on the model of the Grand Opera Paris."

Fig. 133. The front of the National Standard Theatre with Willing and Company gas-lit advertising signs for *Rank and Fame* by Leonard Rae (John T. Douglass) and Frank Stainforth, 29 March 1875. *From the Rose Lipman Library, Hackney.*

Fig. 134. Ada Cavendish (1847–1895). *From the Rose Lipman Library, Hackney.*

In 1865 roller skating had been invented by an American, Mr. Plimpton of New York. It had grown as a fad, and John Douglass capitalized on this by converting the hall above the lobby entrance from Shoreditch into a skating rink. A special asphalt-like floor was poured. It took longer to finish this than the rest of the remodeling, and the rink didn't open until 1 February 1876. *The Builder*, on January 1st, took notice of the interesting construction underway.

The National Standard Theatre in Shoreditch, although admitted to be the largest dramatic establishment in the metropolis. . . has hitherto had such an unpretending main frontage to High Street, opposite the Bishopsgate Railway Station, that a stranger would have some difficulty in finding its whereabouts. With the view of improving its external appearance, and at the same time giving increased facilities of approach to the auditorium of the theatre, the High-street elevation has just been entirely rebuilt, and the frontage to Bishopsgate [station] increased in length from 12 ft. to 54 ft., and now presents an architectural exterior. In addition to the rebuilding of the frontage, the lobby has also been reconstructed to a depth of 110 ft., extending to the audience part of the house. The new Shoreditch elevation is 60 ft. in height, and the style of the architecture adopted is Modern Italian. The ground-floor portion consists of pillars, from which spring three bold arches. [See figs. 119 and 133]. The upper portion is built immediately over the arcade, above which is a balcony with balustrade.

Fig. 135. *The Children in the Wood; or, Harlequin and the Wicked Uncle*, **with real deer, National Standard Theatre 1875.** *From the Rose Lipman Library, Hackney.*

From the balcony to the cornice the elevation is continued with piers, between which are three arched windows, and in the center the elevation is surmounted by a pediment. The elevation at the north angle is surmounted by a tower rising to a height of upwards of 80 ft., and at this portion of the frontage there is a separate entrance, with a stone staircase to an intended skating-rink in the upper portion of the building, altogether distinct from the theatre. In the center, under the arcade, there is an entrance and staircase, 12 ft. wide, leading to the dress circle, stalls and boxes. The walls of this entrance are divided handsomely by decorated panels, in which are placed mirrors 5 ft. in width and 12 ft. in height. The floor is laid with encaustic tiles. Immediately adjoining the central entrance is another of exactly the same dimensions, and similarly finished and decorated, leading to the pit-stalls and upper boxes. New entrances have also been made at the south side of the building, which now

228

face the new street from Oxford Street and Old Street to Shoreditch, at present in course of construction. . . . These entrances are four in number, one to the pit stalls, two to the pit, and one to the gallery. The newly erected building also contains a large additional saloon, 38 ft. by 24 ft. in height, in immediate connection with the several tiers of boxes. The skating rink in the upper floor of the newly erected portion of the building. . . is quite distinct from the theatre, is very spacious, having a floor covering an area of 4,000 superficial feet, and in connection with it are a number of retiring-rooms. No timber is used in the floors, which are constructed with Dennett's fire-proof arches, filled in and covered with asphalt.

The floor of the skating rink rests upon external and party walls of the building, from which spring concrete arches, the flooring being in asphalt.

The 27 December 1875 panto was *The Children in the Wood; or, Harlequin and the Wicked Uncle*. It held forth until March. One curious feature of it was that in the woods scene, real deer appeared (fig. 135).

Shoreditch had changed. The audiences educated by John Douglass, and Samuel Phelps, in their two theatres, could now take the new underground, or street trams, and go to the West End. Socially this was the thing to do. Shoreditch was now losing population to the middle-class suburbs to the north, and east. People who could afford to, moved from the declining area around Bishopsgate. Housing became run down, and crowded with the lower classes and recently arrived immigrants. Structures became factories and warehouses for the goods brought to the rail head. This further reduced the potential nearby audience. In this climate of decline, social unrest, and mundane daily existence, it is little wonder that "women in trouble" plays became popular, the way "soaps" have in the twentieth century. *East Lynne* is the archetypical play. It was based on a pulp novel by Mrs. Henry Wood, and first dramatized in 1866. It was a treatment of the sensational topics of divorce, infidelity, and the control of women by men. No *Doll's House*, the play demonstrates that a vile end awaits a woman who abandons her virtue and duty. Lady Isabel Carlyle runs off with a handsome sharper, leaving behind a

Fig. 136. Louise Moodie (1846-1934) as Lady Isabel in *East Lynne*. *From The Theatre*.

steady virtuous husband, and infant son. She is in turn abandoned when her money runs out. One can generate some understanding of the cad's action, because Isabel was a flighty and tempestuous woman no doubt hard to live with when the initial charm wore off. Some time later she is involved in a train accident, and a body is identified as being hers. Years pass, and a scarred Madame Vine applies for the governess position in her remarried husband's home. She becomes the nanny to her own son, little Willie. He, of course, falls ill (no doubt Carol Burnet's "Movie disease" caught from little Eva). In the third act the actress of the dual role of Isabel, and Madame Vine, is allowed to portray every emotion; and its concurrent suppression the death of Willie can generate. All the actresses of the period between 1870 and 1890 vied with one another in various versions of this story. None was better liked by the Standard's audience than that of Louise Moody (1846–1934) (fig. 136).

The Standard has been attended by large numbers nightly, and strong men and gentle women have alike been moved to tears by the touching sorrows of Lady Isabel Carlyle. This part, so well suited to test the capabilities of an actress, has been intrusted to Miss L. Moody, and could hardly have fallen into hands more able to do it full justice. In every scene in which she appeared she absorbed the attention of the auditors, and in the third act, where as madame Vine the unhappy wife tries in vain to suppress the emotions which fill her breast, clasps her child to her bosom, watches over its dying bed, and in its last moments reveals her identity, the house was hushed, tears filled many eyes, and cheers loud and long greeted the actress at the end, an irresistible call to the footlights rewarding her really artistic efforts.[93]

Between Avonia Jones's first presentation of the play at the Standard in 1866, and Louise Moodie's final performances for the Douglasses in December of 1885, *East Lynne* was acted one hundred and ninety nights at this theatre. Audiences had plenty of chances to see their favorite actresses in competition for the best adaptation, and interpretation of the dual role.[94]

The actresses who performed their various specialties in the spring and summer of 1876 were Louise Moodie, Mdlle. Beatrice (Marie Beatrice Binda (1839–1878), Ada Cavendish, Lydia Thompson (1836–1908) (of *British Blonds* fame), Emily Soldene (1840–1912), Kate Bateman (1843–1917), and Mrs. Rousby (1852–1879).

These ladies, for the most part, led provincial companies. The touring of London hits and stars had declined rapidly. The Douglasses found it increasingly difficult to find attractions

93. The *Era*, (18 March 1876).
94. Actresses performing *East Lynne* at the Standard were: Avonia Jones (1866), Ada Ward (1874 and 1875), Sarah Thorne (1875), Louise Moodie (1876, 1877, 1879 and, 1885), Mrs. Charles Viner (1877), Mrs. Rousby (1878), Dolores Drummond (1878), Bella Pateman (1879 and 1881), Mrs. Billington (1880), and Gertrude Norman (1883).

to fill their theatre. In July 1876 the Standard was closed two different weeks before Mrs. Rousby in Tom Taylor's (1870) *Twixt Axe and Crown* filled the theatre through August. William Creswick pleased his fans, for three weeks in September; but then business was slow until the Globe Theatre Company was persuaded to bring in Jennie Lee (1848–1930) in her career long role, Jo.

This clever little actress visited the old theatre many times always presenting the same drama, viz., *Poor Jo*, being a dramatized version of Dickens's *Bleak House*. Her performance of the outcast was memorable for its restraint and pathos, and to this fact can be traced its financial success—for many other dramatic versions of Dickens's novels produced about the same time were not exactly money spinners. Miss Lee's death scene never failed to create a deep impression on the audience. It was in this play that Dolores Drummond established her reputation as a great actress, giving a magnificent performance of Hortense. Miss Lee, who was the wife of J. P. Burnett, who played inspector Bucket in *Poor Jo*, was not quite content to 'wear the breeches' when playing her part only, but at times seemed inclined to assume them off the stage. One night when dying, she heard a little more noise than necessary behind the scenes, so

Fig. 137. *Open Sesame; or, Harlequin the Fourty Robbers of the Magic Cave,* **National Standard Theatre, 1876.** *From the Illustrated Sporting and Dramatic News.*

at the conclusion of the death scene rushed off the stage, and with a vehemence surprising in a corpse, seized the master carpenter by the arm and shouted: 'Understand, from tomorrow night, every stage hand must wear carpet slippers,' to which the carpenter replied: 'Well you damn well buy 'em.'A rude retort truly, but the offensive way in which the request was made partly justified it. Many in the profession today, are lacking in tact when addressing the staff, and the same remark applies to some producers when rehearsing the company, especially those early Victorian martinets, who deal with actors and actresses in the same manner that Simon Legree handled slaves, and egotistically imagine this method commands respect and cloaks incompetency.[95]

The pantomime of the 1876–1877 season was *Open Sesame; or, Harlequin the Forty Robbers of the Magic Cave*. The panto the year before had been declared beautiful, but it was not exciting and the box office had been poor. Douglass labored long, and hard to prepare *Open Sesame*. The money it could generate was needed to make up for the slow season before. E. L. Blanchard · (1820–1889), the great panto writer, has left his copy of the program with his hand written notes. He went around to the various theatres at Christmas time to see what the competition was up to. He was impressed with W. Corri's music, Cyrus Bell as Ali Baba, Rose Bell as the Captain of the Forty Robbers, Johnny Barnum (mentioned above as the cat), Miss A. Laurie, and Augusta Thompson.

They were all performers in the opening and transformation scenes. In the Harlequinade, he praised Mr. Vincent, and Ada Laurie, who were excellent dancers as Harlequin and Columbine. Richard Douglass's scenery was also commended especially that for the War Dance of the Vril Charmers, and the transformation of Ali Baba's Palace to the Golden Gardens of Enchantment. Most of all he liked scene eight, The Marketplace of Bagdad, next to which he wrote: "Never seen anything to surpass this" (fig. 137).

This is high praise indeed, and from the expert. The press found this scene just as effective, especially the use of ponies. Albert Douglass speaks of them and his boyhood friend:

I am writing of the celebrated author's son [T. W. Robertson Jr.], a clever young man, who came to the Standard as an apprentice to Richard Douglass, the scenic artist. Young Tommy and I became firm friends, and I have none but pleasant memories of our long friendship. Tommy could do anything required in the theatre except paint scenery. His great ambition was to become an actor. Poor Richard was distracted, for frequently when making an unexpected entry into the paint room he would hear young Tommy shouting Shakespeare, or perhaps holding an unfortunate fellow apprentice by the throat and

95.   Douglass, *Memories of Mummers*, p. 63.

Fig. 138. *Queen of an Hour*, **by John T. Douglass, and Frank Stainforth, 1 October 1877.** *From the Illustrated Sporting and Dramatic News.*

dancers to display their ribs. John T. Douglass was in despair, and hastily ordered forty embroidered cloths to conceal their 'good points.'

However, having several arches belonging to the North London Railway at our disposal, comfortable stables were prepared, and the ponies were so well fed, exercised and carefully groomed, that by the time the pantomime had finished the animals were in such splendid condition that they realized double the price originally paid for them.[96]

shouting 'Die! thou caitiff,' then stabbing him with a paint brush, dipped in vermilion to lend verisimilitude to the bloody deed.

Tommy, Clare Corri, and myself, were always together, and when any practical joke was played one could always rely on the culprit being one of the trio-christened by my dad, 'The Three Musketeers.'

Many clever business schemes were carried out by Tommy, one of which resulted in an unexpected profit. For our pantomime of The Forty Thieves, a similar number of ponies was required to carry the robbers. Tommy's offer to transact all the business in connection with the purchase of these animals was accepted, but his anxiety to obtain them in the cheapest market resulted in the greatest conglomeration of crocks ever seen. Some appeared to be suffering from house-maid's knee, whilst others were as eager as modern classical

This show proved a great success, and the enterprise was afloat again. Good productions were still hard to find. To fill in, Louise Moodie returned in *East Lynne*, followed by a touring comic opera company from the provinces. In May of 1877, a new production was finally staged when Hugh Marston's version of Jules Verne's novel *Michael Strogoff*, called *The Courier of the Czar*, opened on the 24th. This action melodrama got mixed reviews, but generated respectable business, and therefore was revived from time to time for several years. The next three months returned to the ladies, with a different *East Lynne*, starring Mrs. Charles Viner; Jenny Lee as Jo; Louise Moodie in *Lady Audley's Secret*; Isabel Pateman, with Johnston Forbes-Robertson, in *Lady Clancarty*; and other performers in the women's plays.

96. Douglass, *Memories of Mummers*, pp. 76–77.

Fig. 139. *Harlequin the Enchanted Prince: or, Beauty and the Bears*, **National Standard Theatre 1877**. From the *Illustrated Sporting and Dramatic News*.

John T. Douglass and Frank Stainforth climbed on the band wagon with their historical romance, *A Queen of an Hour*. The script was adapted from a French play about Edward VI, and Lady Jane Grey. The accuracy of the history depicted was very nearly a travesty, according to the press. Worse than that, Stainforth insisted on playing the role of Edward. He was called utterly incompetent. The play closed in a week, making it the worse failure at the Standard for over twenty five years (fig. 138). T. C. King in standard classics, and Buckstone, and the Haymarket Company were rushed in to fill the month and a half before the panto.

Harlequin the Enchanted Prince; or Beauty and the Bears, was a version of *Beauty and the Beast*. It was a considerable success, especially the ballet of the white bears, and the Python's Haunt (fig. 139).

About 150 members of the Corps de Ballet are called on to assume bearish character without bearish clumsiness. A number of the bears. . . take their stand upon an outspread base. . . and armed with clubs posture in fashion which presents the spectators a series of pictures effectively illustrative of 'chiefs in council,' 'peace or war,' 'trial by battle,'etc. Presently the bears have an alphabetical fit, and, armed with all the letters from A to Z by skillful combinations contrive to test the political feeling of the audience. . . . When the bears had put together the word Germany the spectators hissed; when Osman Pasha. . . they cheered most lustily;

234

and when the word Czar came to the front there went forth a howl of execration. The bears contrive to 'pile up the agony' in similar fashion by exhibiting flags of different countries. . . when they exhibit the standard of Old England [they] sing very heartily 'Rule Britannia'. . . .

The other scene to which we would like to call special attention, and which is calculated to create a sensation from a spectacular point of view, is called the charming of the serpent. It takes place in the Python's haunt, a marvelously clever bit of rock painting reflecting high credit on Mr. Richard Douglass, the artist, who also is responsible for the many other scenic beauties of the production. Some scores of serpent-charmers till the stage, their dark dresses being relieved in fashion, which is made more effective by a clever use of the lime-light. After sundry marchings and groupings, which prove very picturesque, the charmers introduce their serpents, which wriggle and writhe, and which presently shoot forth from their mouths volumes of flame. The dark rock work in the background is again and again illuminated in this way, and as often relapses into gloom, the result being a picture which is weird in the extreme, and which is calculated to make a deep impression upon the spectator (fig. 139).[97]

For the second year in a row the Christmas Pantomime was a big success. This again carried the theatre through the indifferent shows, and business of the spring and early summer. In August of 1878, Charles Wyndham was prevailed upon to bring his comic hit *Pink Dominos*. This play is rather like a modernization of the old *Cosi Fan Tutti* plot, disguised wives at a restaurant, husbands on the loose, etc. It was one of the most popular new plays of the quarter century.

After this sophisticated comedy Douglass reverted to an old hippodrama, and a shocking one at that. Liza Weber and Henry Vandenhoff and Astley's Theatre Company opened in *Mazeppa*. Albert Douglass tells of an incident connected with this production:

From the time Adah Isaacs Menken set the whole town agog by her daring performance of *Mazeppa*, at Astley's Theatre, many imitators sprang up to prove they were equally equipped by nature to enact the part; for Mazeppa is partially disrobed prior to being lashed to the Wild Horse of Tartary, so it was necessary to possess what might be termed a principal boy's figure. (Sometimes supplied by Raynes).

A big favourite. . . was Lisa Weber, who toured with this popular play of the period. Her 'wild horse' was really a beautiful white steed trained to perfection. When the hero was lashed to the horse's back it was thrilling to watch the noble creature dash up the mountain side. The scene where the exhausted animal eventually expired with Mazeppa still firmly bound to its back never failed to evoke great applause and volleys of cheers.

97.   The *Era*, (30 December 1878).

One Saturday night the management decided to play *Dick Turpin* as an afterpiece, with George Hamilton. . . in the title role. A brother manager kindly promised to lend a mare which had played Black Bess for many years, but unfortunately owing to a thick fog the train was delayed, and when the time arrived for the curtain to rise on Dick Turpin he was minus a mare.

After a lengthy selection by the orchestra, we prevailed on Miss Weber to allow her horse to undertake the part, she readily consenting, seeing it was the only way out of the difficulty. The stage manager stepped before the curtain to apologize, and in explaining the situation said, 'although two blacks did not make a white, with the kind indulgence of the audience, they would take the liberty of making one white do for a black.' Ironic cheers greeted his departure. The play proceeded rather smoothly-though every time Dick alluded to the pure white horse as 'my bonnie Black Bess,' the audience was convulsed with merriment. The horse probably dazed by the change of environment and its unaccustomed rider, seemed to stagger through the play in a bewildered manner, till the great Toll-gate scene, when Turpin shouted 'The Bow Street runners pursue us. . . The hounds of law are on our track. . . Come my bonnie Black Bess—take the gate, take the gate,' but by this time the horse had come to the conclusion that it was another performance of *Mazeppa*, so gracefully rolled over and died.[98]

The rest of the summer, and into the autumn was filled with these old plays. Meanwhile John T. Douglass, as Leonard Rae, had translated the Parisian version of *Uncle Tom's Cabin* that had been performed at the Gaite Theatre in 1853. This is ironic in that the Standard had probably the first dramatization of parts of the book in 1852. The French version was notorious for inaccuracies, escaping slaves barging down the Ohio River to Canada, and shooting Niagra Falls in the process, etc.

This version the Managers very truthfully say, although not pretending to faithfully follow the incidents of Mrs. Beecher Stowe's novel, has yet a continuity of action, and many original and genuine dramatic situations, which, with the rejection of superfluous characters, combine to render the piece in everyway attractive and interesting. The expressed desire of the Messrs. Douglass has been to obtain the very best drama on the subject. . . . Readers of the book will not, perhaps, be inclined to regard Simon Legree, and Cassy as 'superfluous characters,' but they have been rejected here. Those, too, who expect to shed tears. . . over the death of Little Eva will be disappointed. The French dramatist prepared a happier issue for the darling of the story, and in this version Eva's illness takes a turn for the better, and the physician is made to announce that the crisis has passed and that Eva will live. Of course this is somewhat a risky business. The English adapter was of the same opinion,

98.   Douglass, *Memories of Mummers*, pp. 57–58.

but, having made the experiment found it satisfactory, he has thought fit to let the matter stand as in the original. . . The drama has been placed on the stage with new scenery, appropriate costumes, and appointments, original effects, plantation dances, and choruses. . . the plantation festival in the third act being very merrily carried out by a crowd of darkies, headed by 'Beaumont's Black Blossoms,'—Messrs. M'Kee, Cotton, and Yankee Palmer— the doings of all exacting much attention and exciting much merriment. One of the most effective scenes of the play is laid on the deck of the 'Ohio' steamboat, on board of which we find St.Claire, Eva,Topsy, Uncle Tom, Julius Caesar (a fresh importation), Eliza and child, and Loker and Marks, slave hunters in pursuit. Eliza, when all other hope of escape is cut off, throwing her child into the stream and leaping after it herself. The whole action of the play is thoroughly unconventional, and those who visit the Standard may go with hope of seeing something new. . . .The important part of George Harris is intrusted to Mr. G. Hamilton, a valuable actor. . . . He played his part with his accustomed earnestness and vigour, and was deservedly applauded. Uncle Tom was personated by Mr. F. Young, who abjured all 'niggerism', and talked like a decently educated 'pale face.'. . . Mr. G. Byren, as the Captain of the 'Ohio,' plays with commendable spirit, and, of course, has the house with him when he shields Eliza from the brutality of the slave hunting Loker, well impersonated by Mr. Chamberlain; who, upon making his appearance before the curtain at the end of the act, found compliment in a storm of hisses. . . . Something like a genuine hit was made by Mr. F. Percival as Julius Caesar, the black boy who has 'notions' far above his station, and who considers that he owns his master rather than the master owns him. . . . The performance has concluded each evening with the farce entitled *A Chapter of Accidents.*[99]

Richard M. Douglass, the son of Thomas, who was head of staff and lighting engineer, was six years old when this production was mounted. He was small, and chosen to play the part of the infant Harry Harris.

When I was quite a little boy. . . I played Little Harry, the child of George and Eliza Harris. John's dramatization was so unlike Mrs. Beecher Stowe's novel she probably turned in her grave every time his version was performed. For instance, the last scene was a ravine with a cataract in the center spanned by a bridge (and it ought to be unnecessary to add; being John's production—it was a real waterfall). One side of this bridge represented slave soil, the other the Land of Freedom, a la the Mexico of the Movies today, and if any persecuted niggar born in slavery succeeded in negotiating that bridge he was a free man for evermore. The climax of the play was most sensational. George Harris, and his devoted wife after many hairbreadth adventures escaped across the bridge—[Loker] however held their child, seized an axe, hacked down the bridge which fell with a crash into the torrent

99.   The *Era*, (6 October 1878).

Fig. 140. *The Streets of New York*, by Dion Boucicault, Princess's Theatre, **1864.** *From the Illustrated London News.*

below, and triumphantly shouted, 'You may be on free soil, but your child is still in bondage.' At this moment Lawyer Marks appeared, shot [Loker] seized the child, and hurled him over the cataract to the out-stretched arms of his loving father; thus the curtain descended on the happy denoue-ment of mother, father, and son reunited, free from slavery, and villainy vanquished.

The effect of throwing me across the chasm was accomplished by an invisible wire from the flies attached to a belt beneath my tunic. All went well until Saturday, when my poor dad paid salaries in the forenoon—always a dangerous practice in those days. The performance that evening was memorable.

The actor portraying George Harris [G. Hamilton], on making his first entrance, delivered the whole soliloquy 'To be or not to be' from *Hamlet* before he realized the play was *Uncle Tom's Cabin*. How the actress playing Liza Harris [Miss Page] eluded her foes by crossing the ice with out dropping me, remains a mystery, and it is on record the stage manager warned her that unless she kept her mouth firmly closed the blood-hounds would find no difficulty in fol-lowing the scent.

. . . at length, the final scene was reached. George in a voice husky with emotion (and Johnny Walker) said 'Come, my darling wife, to freedom. Let me lead your faltering footsteps.' A case of the blind leading the blind—and they both staggered across the bridge. 'Ha! Ha! shouted [Loker], you are on free soil but your child is still in bondage,' and hissing these words he chopped at the bridge till it fell. Marks appeared—shot [Loker] and shouting 'Here is your child,' threw me over to my fond but foolish parents. Unfortunately, by this time, my stage father was in such a state of inebriation that he failed to catch me, consequently I went swinging back to the actor who sent me. His first intimation of my unexpected return was a kick on the ear. Turning quickly he made a grab—too late. I had gracefully floated back to my stage dad, but falling short, I swung back again and suspended over the yawning abyss, I defied the laws of gravity by revolving rapidly round like a joint on a roasting spit. The Curtain was rung down and the stage manager's language was really unfit for a child's ears. I never heard it equaled till I went on the music halls.[100]

The production managed to run for three weeks. One wonders, if they were really serious about these old style melodramas, or if the Douglass management was having a festival of nostalgia. The next production was Boucicault's *Streets of New York* (1852–1864) (fig. 140), Miss Heath in *Jane Shore* (1714), and in the final weeks of the season the return of Alice Marriott in *Jeanie Deans*. She had been touring this hit of 1862 on and off for sixteen years.

On 30 October 1878 Mr. Gough was allowed to use the Standard for his Blue Ribbon Temperance Army pledging. Six thousand people crowded into the house with fourteen hundred seated on the stage.

The year-end annual was advertised as John T. Douglass's fourteenth pantomime in a row at the Standard. *Harlequin Robin Hood; or,the Marrie Men of Sherwood Forest* began:

At the shop of Eustace de Smith, high Sheriff and butcher of Nottingham, we learn that Robin, the head man at the butcher's, has conceived an affection for his master's daughter. The master butcher has already promised her hand to. . . Guy of Gisbourne. . . The Sheriffs fete day arrives, with the procession for the shooting-match. . . Robin wins the match. The Sheriff refuses the prize to Robin, who thereupon seizes Marian and bears her off. . . The Sheriff, visiting the forest for a picnic with his friends, is robbed and maltreated; and a grand ballet of Merrie Men and Maid Marians takes place. King Richard now determines to proceed with the Crusades. A grand spectacular display follows, illustrating. . . a dioramic view of Famugusta bay from the heights overlooking the sea. The Crusaders, in gorgeous costumes and brilliant accoutrements. . . are seen descending the rocks by a rough circuitous passage. . . . Then follows a series of magnificent tableau, pending the arrival of the king, and the elaborate and costly pageant terminates with an entirely original and unparalleled combination of color and

---

100. Douglass, *Memories of Mummers*, pp. 110–112.

effect, representing the marriage of Richard I and Queen Berengaria, with attending festivities. . . in the Island of Cyprus. The whole of the magnificent scenery and the transformation scene, representing the Hanging Bowers of Fairyland are painted by Mr. Richard Douglass, assisted by John Neville.[101]

After the successful panto closed the husband and wife team of Robert Pateman (1841–1924), and Isabel Pateman (1844–1908) were engaged (figs. 151 and 163). Albert Douglass fondly remembered Robert and Bella in their version of *East Lynne*.

They were two of the most charming artists who ever appeared at the Standard, and were beloved by the whole company and staff. They were a devoted couple, and to be certain of no point being missed in the various parts they undertook they would watch each other's performance from the wings, and constantly rehearse scenes to gain every possible effect. They were exceedingly conscientious, and never rested content until every line and every situation was perfect.

When Robert Pateman created a new character it was positively thrilling to watch how thoroughly he got into the skin of the part as it were. I never remembered an actor working harder to obtain the success he never failed to achieve. Both were nearly always word perfect, though I recall on one occasion during the first production of Odette, whilst Mrs. Pateman was holding the audience

Fig. 141. *The Poor Engineer*, **National Standard Theatre, 1879.** *From A.S.J.*

spellbound, she suddenly paused. As I held the MS. in the prompt corner I gave her the word which saved the situation. At the end of the act she was so overjoyed at being prompted at the psychological moment that she gave me a hearty kiss and cordially thanked me. The next night I was presented with a very handsome scarf-pin with best wishes from Mr. and Mrs. R. Pateman.

I have never seen an actress who could equal Miss Pateman's performance of Lady Isabel in East Lynne; and for rugged power combined with dramatic intensity, Robert Pateman was unsurpassable, especially when portraying a character that had to depict terror. No playgoer who witnessed his Humpy Logan in *Master and Man*, can ever forget it.

101.   The *Illustrated London News*, (28 December 1878)

Fig. 142. *Flying Scud*, by Dion Boucicault, 1866. *From the Penny illustrated Paper.*

At the Standard he played the character of Mat Marsden in John Douglass's drama *No Man's Land*, which was toured for many years by John's daughter, Ida Millais. The part was undoubtedly what is now known in the profession as a 'Bob Pateman' part.

In one scene he was marooned on a desert island whilst a typhoon was raging. He blasphemed and prayed almost in the same breath-then tearing his shirt to tatters frantically waved it aloft in the vain hope of attracting the attention of a passing vessel. The effect was electrical.[102]

The spring and summer were filled with adaptations, most of which centered on women. *Une cause Célèbre*, and *Two Orphans*, both by A. D'Ennery and E. Cormon,

were closely followed by Tom Taylor's dramatization of Mrs. Braddon's novel *Henry Dunbar*. A short play by W.C. Chamberlain, from the Prince of Wales Theatre in Wolverhampton *Dora's Love; or, the Struggles of a Poor Engineer* filled the evening's bill with each of the other plays above (fig. 141). The Beatrice Comedy Company from the north then brought D'Ennery and Millian's *Women of the People*. A week of Adolphe Faucquez's adaptation of Bulwer's *Eugene Aram* was well attended.

In September, the D'Oyley Carte Opera Company came to the Standard for the first time. They brought all their original scenery and effects for eighteen nights of *H.M.S. Pinafore*.

The rest of the autumn season was very mixed: a revival of *The Ticket of Leave Man*, Sarah Thorn's Company in Boucicault's *Flying Scud* (figs. 142 and 143), and a number of weeks of opera in English. Of this last, the production of *Carmen* caused the most attention. The original *Carmen*, as an "opera Comique," had opened in Paris in 1875. By the time Emily Soldene brought this production to the Standard, the melodies, originally thought strange, had become so familiar that the reviewer believed they would be burlesqued in the Christmas pantos. Emily Soldene was considered one of the finest Carmens,

102. Douglass, *Memories of Mummers*, pp. 52–53. Robert Pateman must have played a character that was the equivalent of Benn Gunn because *No Man's Land* was an adaptation of Robert Lewis Stevenson's *Treasure Island*.

commended for her ability to act as well as sing.

The decade of the 1870s was one of hesitation in theatre aesthetics. No one playwright, type of production, or acting style dominated. The productions seen at the Standard were representative. Of the fifteen playsproducedintheLondontheatres in 1879, and considered important in the reviews, only two did not appear at the Standard by the end of 1880. The first of these was the touring Comedie Francaise's *L'Ami Fritz* (later an opera by Pietro Mascagni). It was described as an: "anti-Mal-

Fig. 143. *Flying Scud*, **by Dion Boucicault, 1866.** *From the Illustrated London Times.*

thusian drama so liberally supplied with real food, a real cherry tree, a pump with real water, and all the flesh-pots of theatrical Egypt."[103]

The second was Paul Meritt's *New Babylon*, described in the press as a mixture of *Tom and Jerry* and *Formosa*. The sensational scenic effects of this Duke's Theatre production included: a collision of ships on the Atlantic; the sale of real horses at Tattersal's; the Cremorne Garden's dancing platform, illuminated by a thousand lights; Goodwood on grand race day; the Thames Embankment; and the notorious Seven Dials by night. They were all described as "pictures of real life." This statement was the indicator of what popular taste was becoming.

The trend was toward naturalism; and it was first to be perfected in the settings, not the drama or the acting technique. With the benefit of hindsight, the elements had all been used in plays since the days of Charles Kean, and the antiquarian productions of Shakespeare in the 1850s. Three dimensional settings, real water effects, moving panoramas, revolving stages, scrim and gauze vision scenes, real props, furniture, three dimensional decor, rather than painted, and natural lighting effects. Now it was all coming together in a super scenic substantial way that was to eventually evolve, and transfer into the cinema.

The panto of 1879 somewhat obliquely continued the women in trouble theme, that had dominated the theatres since the early 1870s, with *Blue Beard Re-Wived*. The spectacle included a transformation scene to an underwater coral reef. Richard Douglass was commended for his use of color. In the opening scene, the main character retires to rest, and has fearful dreams being visited by various panto characters. In January of 1880, Francis G. Cheatham wrote a letter to the *Era* complaining that this incident, which was not in the original tale, had been stolen, as he had introduced himself in his panto at the Alexander Theatre Highbury in 1865. There he had treated it as a burlesque of the tent scene in *Richard III*. Cheatham said:

> The creations of a man's brains are as equally much his property as is his watch or purse, and appropriating one and 'annexing' the other appears to me to be nothing less than a distinction without a difference.
>
> If managers would content themselves to be only managers, and actors only actors, depend upon it there would be found plenty of authors to do the rest, and do it well, and I opine we should hear much less about the present 'moribund' state of the profession.

John Douglass's indignant reply to this "sour grapes" gives a picture of the nature of the composition of pantomimes, and his opinion of

---

103. Pascoe, *Dramatic Notes* (1879), p. 26. The reference is to T. T. Malthus, the English economist who proposed the theory that "Population increases faster than the food supply."

Cheatham's complaint:

Sir,—I am very much astonished, and I am sure many old Stage managers, authors, and pantomimists will be as well, to hear that Mr. Francis Geo. Cheatham, as lately as 1865, originated the business of the pantomime of *Blue Beard*, so far as the entrance of that potentate's headless wives into his bed-chamber whilst he sleeps.

Now, I never saw any Pantomime at High-bury Barn, either by Mr. Cheatham or anyone else. So much for the charge of plagiarizing that gentleman. But I know well I saw Mr. W. H. Payne twenty years ago do the same business in the bed room scene of *Blue Beard* and as the Wicked Uncle in *The Babes in the Wood*. (Payne always had a bed-room scene.) Many old pantomimists in comic scenes have used the same idea. Clown's wives, Policeman's wives, baker's headless wives. etc. To claim it as original business is ludicrous.

But I have a complaint to make. Some years ago I wrote a comic scene for the harlequinade of a pantomime. In addition to the introduction of the red hot poker, there was some very good acting business, steal-ing a bundle, also a very laughable incident of appropriating a lot of fish, joints, and loaves; these the Clown sat down to unequally divide with the pantaloon, when a policeman interfered, and removed them both. Would you credit it, Mr. Editor, all of these incidents have been since plagiarized by numerous pantomimists, without duly acknowledging the fact of my authorship. But I have bottled my indignation, and should not have written to you on the subject had not a brother author, by relating his own sad experience of 'the moribund state of the profession' probed the wound afresh. I as-sure you I have as much right to claim the originality of my comic scene as any author of a pantomime in 1865 has to the Bed-room ghost business of *Blue Beard*.

If Mr. Cheatham had paid his shilling for admission (we have no free list at the Standard), he would have known that. In the bed room scene of *Blue Beard Re-Wived* there are no headless wives, and only six pantomime hosts. The nineteen wives I have given the Bashaw, all retain their heads. This some authors find a difficulty in doing, when they ask where in the history of Blue Beard do I find nineteen wives. (By the way, in the blue chamber there are eighty wives.)

Your disappointed correspondent says Managers should be Managers only, not authors. But, surely where as much depends on stage management and practical knowledge as the production of a spec-tacular Pantomime, a Manager may be ex-cused if he objects to place the hands of an inexperienced author the power to peril the success of a Christmas season. (Of course, there are many authors of very great ex-perience in Pantomimes; these are always pretty well employed.)

Your correspondent's grievance seems to be that the Managers of the Standard Theatre object to Mr. Cheatham writing their Pantomimes. I cannot see how dramatic art suffers by this, or why legitimate authors should throw aside their pens in disgust. For many years the Standard Theatre has en-joyed a reputation for its pantomimes, and, during the last sixteen years, the same author has provided the entertainment. There being, I believe, only three writers in London, who can point to as many consec-utive years' pantomime authorship, viz., at

244

Drury Lane Theatre, Mr. E. L. Blanchard; at the Grecian, Mr. George Conquest; and at the National Standard Theatre. Yours etc. John T. Douglass.

P.S.—By kindly inserting the above in your next issue you will confer a favour on the author of *Blue Beard Re-Wived,* who has said his last word in a reply to a charge which old pantomime actors will think hardly needed refutation.[104]

Douglass knew he was killing flies with cannon since Cheatham had not published any of his works since 1870 and was a very minor author. He had worked at the Standard, writing the pantos of 1858, 1860, and 1862 under John Douglass Senior, only to be replaced by the manager's son the next year. It was a long time to hold a grudge.

Fig. 144. Charles Warner (1847–1909). *From Memories of Mummers.*

104. The *Era*, (11 January 1880).

12

SENSATION SCENES

By 1880 the public had many more methods and places of distraction than there had been in 1860. Parks and pleasure gardens, Music Halls, and Earls Court competed with the theatres. The area near the Standard continued to lose population, while those souls that remained were poorer. The Douglasses needed attractions that would draw people from afar.

After the panto of 1879–1880 closed, the Princess's Theatre Company with Charles Warner (1847–1909) (fig. 144), came with the terrifying play *Drink*. This was an adaptation of the 1879 Parisian hit, *L'Assommoir*, written by Bunach and Gatineau. Their play was, in turn, an adaptation of a novel by Zola. Charles Reade, a prolific novelist and playwright, provided the translation. Warner took the powerful role of Copeau, with Amy Roselle as the suffering wife Gervaise (figs. 145–150).

This production is considered to be the typical example of the naturalist school. Its settings were built with every attempt to look real rather than like stage sets. The conversation, for the time, seemed literal, not stagey, or dramatic. Warner's rendering of Copeau will always be remembered by those who were fortunate enough to witness it. His 'delirium tremens' scene, was undoubtedly one of the most masterly pieces of character acting, and every night after his realistic death scene he had to be carried to his dressing room to rest before removing his makeup.

Crowds always assembled outside the stage door to cheer Warner, although frequently failing to recognize the alert and debonair actor, and finding it difficult to associate him with the drunken sot they had just witnessed in the play. Warner was rather quick tempered but soon repented. One night when the property man, whose duty it was to dab the red paint on Copeau's hand as he thrust it through the garret window, was not at his post, so one of the great thrills was missing, for when Warner withdrew his hand it was not smeared with imitation blood. After the scene he was furious with the purveyor of human

Fig. 145. *Drink*, the construction scaffolding scene. *From A.S.J.*

gore, demanding his instant dismissal, but half-an-hour later Warner called the culprit into his dressing room and gave the astonished man a handsome tip.

I have often been asked how Warner, in the character of Coupeau, managed the fall from the topmost portion of the scaffolding to the stage, most people dismissing the idea of a dummy, truthfully asserting that they observed the artiste move and heard him moan after the accident. As a matter of fact it was a dummy placed on a plank on the roof out of sight, and as the actor trod on the board he shrieked, disappeared behind the chimney stack, and the dummy fell with a crash. The Act Drop descended quickly on this thrill, a few people rushed on for 'the picture,' the figure was removed instantaneously, and Warner sliding down a ladder hastily took its place, assuming the exact pose and position which naturally varied every night.

This dummy was indeed a splendid prop, made to Warner's exact measurements. The genial Willie Clarkson took a plaster cast of the actor's face, and a perfect mask, made up by Warner himself was the result, a duplicate wig, dress, and a pair of boots completing the illusion. So life-like was this

Fig. 146. *Drink*, the drinking scene. *From A.S.J.*

dummy that my little brother Dickey, would frequently prop it up on a chair in the wings, then hide in the O.P. corner to enjoy hearing people say 'good evening, Mr. Warner,' and impishly watch their indignation at getting no response. A curious accident occurred one night, when this dummy, falling only half-way down the scaffolding caught its legs in a piece of rope, turned a sumersault and concluded its entertainment by sitting on a plank, glaring at the audience. This acrobatic feat was received with roars of laughter, in which Charles Warner did not join [fig. 145].

Many ecclesiastics at this time were prone to preach from the pulpit on the moral influence of this realistic drama, strongly advising members of their congregation to witness it, as it was one of the great sermons on the evils of intemperance ever preached.

I am glad they did not quote the receipts of the Standard's bars in support of their statements, for during the run of Drink they broke all records.[105]

This play, and *Never Too Late to Mend*, filled the theatre to overflowing for the first time in several years for a

105. Douglass, *Memories of Mummers*, pp. 67–69.

Fig. 147. *Drink*, **the fight in the wash house.**
From A.S.J.

Mrs. Billington was Gretchen.

How curiously true to American life, and how curiously different from English manners, are the domestic scenes in *Rip Van Winkle*. Gretchen has the privileges of a feme sole, and owns house property in her own right. She beats her tipsy husband with a broomstick and turns him out of doors on a stormy night. In England things are managed in precisely a contrary manner: 'tis the drunken husband who beats his sober wife and turns her out of doors.[106]

In this happy environment Mrs. Billington created a perfect Xanthippe for poor Rip:

. . .in her original character of Gretchen Van Winkle, Rip's incomparably shrewish wife! I will trouble you for Mrs. Billington as Gretchen, if you please. I should like to place her on a pedestal and keep her in a glass case, and walk around her, and admire her, and analyze her—always keeping at a respectable distance; for Gretchen's arm is long, and her flexor and extensor muscles are wondrously tough and supple; and when she hits, she hits hard. And her tongue, I will not trouble you for her tongue, thank you. I hear it now, thrilling through the vasthouse in Bishopsgate; and it makes my ears tingle; and I tremble. Seriously, I look upon Mrs. Billington's Gretchen as one of the most original, the most powerful, and the most artistic dramatic conceptions the modern

production other than the panto. It set John T. Douglass to thinking about the nature of this success. And his own scripts began to take on the look of the naturalistic staging; this was obviously the audiences's desire.

While John Douglass thought about this and made his preparations, the summer and autumn season was filled with an interesting series of guest companies. After the perennial Moore and Burgess Minstrels, came the Hanlon Lees's *Voyage en Suisse*, a pantomimic magic show with wonderful sets, full of vampire traps, and other effects. Then came the American McKee Rankin Company. Their plays were *The Danites* by Joaquin Miller, and Boucicault's *Rip Van Winkle*. In the latter J. A. Arnold copied Joseph Jefferson's representation of Rip, and

106. *The Times*, (18 September 1880).

Fig 148. *Drink*, **the fight in the wash house.** *From A.S.J*

stage has seen. Were it not wicked to take liberties with Shakespeare, I should like to see a new version of Katherine and Petruchio, with Mrs. Billington as the heroine of a play, to be called The Shrew Whom Petruchio Could Never Have Tamed. [This actress is at the far left in fig.105].

The same West End critic, lured to Shoreditch for the first time, was surprised at how well and tastefully the Douglasses operated the Standard. He called it a vast, handsomely decorated house with wide stone staircases, spacious vestibules, mirrors and hangings.

The usherettes were: . . . neat-handed Phyllises in 'Pinafore dresses,' and 'Goody Twoshoes,' otherwise 'Kate Greenaway,' caps to conduct you to your seat, and with smiles as sweet as those of Fielding's Amelia . . .these dainty damsels handed you programmes with embossed edges redolent of Rimmel [Meadow flowers or Stephanie Bouquet].[107]

107. An unidentified newspaper clipping (18 September 1880).

Fig. 149. *Drink*, **the saloon.** *From A.S.J.*

Following this specimen of American characters, the first exciting Shakespearean production for some years arrived on the scene in late September of 1880.

George Rignold was undoubtedly one of the handsomest men in the profession. He was not exactly unaware of that fact, being the only actor I ever knew who demanded that the limelight from both perches should be focused on his face, whilst taking a call before the curtain. This necessitated two men to pull back the Act drop to allow the rays to reach his countenance. At the Standard he gave a very fine performance of Henry v, looking a perfect picture mounted on his white charger, and cheered by an enormous stage crowd. The scene depicting his entry into London, never failed to rouse the audience to great enthusiasm, so I was naturally surprised on the first night, at the conclusion of the play, to hear Rignold remark 'Well, Henry v is a damn failure at this theatre.' No one could understand the reason for such a false statement, but we learned later that he made the same remark at every theatre he visited, presumably to prove that such a reception was incomparable with his previous successes. . . . Rignold migrated to Australia, where he became an immense favourite.[108]

108. Douglass, *Memories of Mummers*, pp. 82–83.

The rest of the autumn was the normal comic operas, and a drama by the relatively new playwright Sidney Grundy. *Mammon* was his first significant success. It returned to the feminine centered themes. This also was the autumn that Edwin Booth toured London, opening at the Princess's Theatre on November 28th to mixed reviews. The panto of 1880 was *Harlequin and Wide-Awake Sleeping Beauty*. Aside from the title, the use of lighting effects was the chief achievement of this production.

Fig. 150. *Drink*, **the Boulevard Rochechouart.** *From A.S.J.*

When it is said that the coryphees become living candelebra no mere figure of speech is intended. The grouping here is extremely fine, and when, at a signal from the stage manager, there is what may be called a regular flare up, contrived by some mysterious means, the effect is positively dazzling. When the candelabra are done with, the ladies who have acted as the supports come trooping in with wands, which. . . are instantaneously crowned with blazing stars. We have seen gas employed here on more than one occasion in a novel way, but this scene, it must be said, is altogether unique, and is certain to exact the admiration of all who see it. The transformation is entitled the Harebell Groves of Wonderland. It is chaste in design and marvelous in execution, and, with the illuminating display just referred to, won for Mr. Richard Douglass, the scenic artist, the deserved compliment of a hearty call to the front.[109]

Except for the first appearance of William Creswick in four years, the spring of 1881 consisted of revivals of recently produced contemporary dramas. It also proved to be Creswick's final appearance at the Standard, Shakespeare being on the wain.

The summer of this year did offer a notable series of performances from the Saxe Meiningen Company at another London theatre. The press found their realistic, ensemble style and their settings excellent. But, it was remarked that Charles Kean had perfected this technique in the late 1850s, and Robertson, and the

109. The *Era*, (2 January 1881).

Fig. 151. Isabel Pateman (1844–1908) as Lady Isabel in *East Lynne*, 1878. *From The Theatre.*

Bancrofts had done the same thing in comedy. It is interesting to note that Saxe Meiningen had seen Kean's work at the Princess's Theatre. Douglass, in the meantime, with nothing exciting ready, took a page from his father's book and closed the theatre in July for a thorough overhaul, and redecoration.

Then, in September the one major artist of the 1860s, and 1870s, who had not materially figured in the seasons at the Standard, came with a full compliment of his plays.

Dion Boucicault was a remarkable man from every standpoint—brilliant as dramatist, producer, and actor. He played Con with us in his own play *The Shaughraun* [1874], supported by an excellent company including Shiel Barry, as Harvey Duff, a performance quite equal to his famous Gaspard in *Les Cloches de Corneville*, and Edward Sass as Robert Ffolliott, and Mrs.Bernard Beere as Claire Ffolliott. [He opened with] *The Colleen Bawn*, and on the first night I remember him sitting in the prompt corner whilst the opening scene was being set, grumbling and cursing all the time. 'By Heaven,' said he, 'we shall never be ready, my play will be ruined. What a theatre! What a staff!! Oh! why did I come?' As a matter of fact all the scenes were ready in ample time, and the scenery came as a revelation, for Richard had taken special pains, and the beautiful cave scene, was put on in a manner Boucicault admitted he had never seen equaled. At the termination of the play the head of every department was congratulated by the great man. Surely the true Irish temperament.

Speaking of the *Colleen Bawn*, I once saw the operatic version [*The Lilly of Killarney*] played in a theatre where the stock of scenery must have been limited, for a room in Hardress Cregan's Castle, was an old act drop representing King Humbert's Palace in Naples, and the cave consisted of a pantomime back-cloth of a fairy grotto, two wood wings and a water row not too firmly fixed, for when Danny Mann requested Eily O'-Connor to get out on to the rock, as the boat was leaking, her foot caught in the water which fell flat to the ground, revealing to the astonished audience that the rock was really a kitchen table.

Some years after Dion Boucicault's visit, John Douglass produced *Colleen Bawn*, with real water in the cave scene, though I recall long before that period a stirring melodrama at the Standard, in which a shipwreck was the great sensation. The huge vessel was built on rockers and at a given cue sank through the stage. The raging sea effect on this occasion, was secured by placing numerous small boys in various positions under a cloth which was painted to represent water, and by waving their arms and performing a series of miniature kangaroo hops they gave the most realistic imitation of a turbulent sea.

These youngsters, finding their duties rather strenuous, and very dusty, held a round table conference, at which it was decided to send their spokesman to interview the management and request that the salary of 6d. a night, which they were receiving should be increased to a shilling per night, an unjust demand that was promptly refused, being considered a cowardly blow at capitalism. On the following night just as the great shipwreck scene was about to commence, the impudent face of the delegate appeared from beneath the sheet, the boy shouting to the stage manager. 'Hi, Mister, what about it? Are you having six penny or

shilling waves tonight?' 'Six penny ones, you young scoundrel,' roared the stage manager. A muffled order was issued which penetrated to the bed of the ocean and sure enough the scene was completely spoilt, for the ship was wrecked in almost a dead calm.

Directly the act drop descended, the irate stage manager sought the ring-leader, and taking the law into his own hands administered a sound thrashing, which had the desired effect, for at every subsequent performance, we had a rough and very angry waves at sixpence per show.[110]

After Boucicault had finished his retrospective, another group of Americans arrived with a feminine centered play called *Baffled; or, Parma Violets*. Gertrude Irving was the star. The review stated that the play was written by one of the actors, Leon Sauveur. However, in October the *Era* received a letter of complaint from A. C. Gunter of New York who stated the script was a pirated version of his play *Two Nights in Rome*.

On the whole one might feel, with the benefit of hindsight, the author, whoever it was, should have forever remained anon. It is so very typical of the more turgid plays, with the feminine theme, that it is downright fun to recount its action.

Herbert Granville, a young artist, finding his proffered love rejected by Edith Beaufort, has in a fit of pique married

110. Douglass, *Memories of Mummers*, pp. 55–57. This effect was used in several productions including *Robinson Crusoe* in 1874. However the story sounds suspiciously like that in M. J. Moynet's *L'Envers Du Théâtre* (1873); as in fact do a lot of the effects the Douglasses produced; and they surely had a copy of the book. See *French Theatrical Production in the Nineteenth Century*, Chapters XVII and XVIII.

Antonia, who has gained, as he learned afterwards, the by-no-means complimentary appellation of the Calabrian tigress.

Their home is a palace in Rome; but, according to their own report, they are terribly poor. If not for the patronage of a certain Marquise de Villefrote, and the activity of a Yankee dealer in art (one Abija Lankton), they would run some risk of starvation. Herbert is confronted by his wife who demands money of him to supply her extravagant wants. He has it not to give. She insists that he sell his favorite picture; but this, he positively refuses to do. The picture is a portrait, that he has painted from memory, of his first love, Edith Beaufort.

Antonia has suspected this; when her suspicions are verified by her angry husband, she threatens to destroy his handiwork. This is prevented. But she has better revenge at hand. She takes from her writing desk a paper that she regards with fiendish gratification. It is the final reply of Edith Beaufort to his offer of his hand and heart; and it expresses her love for him and her resolve to share his fate whatever it may be. Antonia wrings Herbert Granville's heart by telling him that two years previously she had intercepted that letter in order to secure him for herself, for Herbert was the son of a Baronet, and was thought to have brilliant prospects. Presently, there comes upon the scene Captain Keer, a needy cousin of Herbert's. His interest is, by all means in his power, to prevent Herbert's succession, or that of any possible child of his, to the estates, since Captain Keer is the next in line. He also has discovered a dark secret of Antonia's past: that a certain Fernando Bassi has vowed to take her life. Bassi is none other than her first husband, whom she treated even more heartlessly than she now treats Herbert. She contrives to make her escape, and this brings us to the end of the first act.

In the second act, we have Edith and her friends visiting Herbert's studio— little thinking to whom it belongs. The Yankee dealer has cannily guessed that the most likely buyer of Edith's picture would be Edith. He guesses right, for she makes no argument when he sets the price at a thousand pounds.

There follows an interview between the old lovers, and the bewailing of the evil fortune that has separated them. Suddenly, out of the darkness comes the river police with the information that Antonia is drowned. Her clothes have been discovered on the roaring Tiber's banks. Shrewd people see through this ruse of Antonia, to avoid the vengeful pursuit of Fernando Bassi; but Herbert says, "It is fate, it is fate," hides his head between his hands upon the table, and brings the curtain down for the second time.

The third act introduces us to Lady Carrington's boudoir. And who is Lady Carrington, you may well ask? Well, Herbert Granville, the ex-seedy artist, has, through the accidental death of his father and elder brother, succeeded to the estates, and is now Sir Herbert Carrington; and has for his wife Edith

Beaufort, his first and only love. The old portrait hangs in a conspicuous place in the room. It actually gives rise to the first tiff between the young couple, who now boast a baby boy. Herbert has promised that his picture shall be lent to grace the *conversazione* to be given at the mansion of the Marquise. Edith is slightly jealous of this lady, who pays too much attention to Herbert. She determines that rather than let her portrait go to her! house for exhibition to her! friends, she will destroy it. This is a rash resolve, and it is soon repented.

But the picture is to be destroyed. There has been introduced to Edith a certain vocalist calling herself Viotti. Viotti, by chance, gets a look at the picture; learns to her astonishment who her patron is, and reflecting that she herself should hold the position Edith occupies, savagely rends the canvas.

Herr Karl, briefly introduced in the first act as an African explorer, having just returned, hears the noise from an adjoining room, sees Antonia—for Viotti is none other—and supposes she is Lady Carrington, whom he had never met. Antonia orders him into another room. Then Antonia hears to her dismay that Fernando Bassi is expected at nine o'clock, and she must make good her escape.

Her way, however, is blocked by the sudden return of Herbert. The Yankee dealer breaks the terrible news of the destruction of the dearly prized picture. Here follows the "effective scene." "Who has done this?" is the general cry. Herr Karl's face reveals he knows something. He is asked to speak; he hesitates, for he would not implicate his friend's wife. Smarting, however, under the harsh questioning by Herbert he blurts the words, "your wife." Herbert is distracted. He knows not what to believe. He remembers Edith's threats; but he cannot, will not think, her guilty. Edith steps forward to defend herself, and Karl is staggered by the discovery that Edith is Lady Carrington. Here is a greater dilemma than before. He knows he has seen Antonia, the others think her drowned. If he speaks now his friend's happiness will be destroyed, and his child branded with the stain of illegitimacy. To speak, however, he is compelled.

In the final act Antonia, having been discovered, is brought to face her accusers. She is defiant; boldly she proclaims that she is not the wife of Herbert. All she wants is to be permitted to leave the house before nine o'clock. The "cute" Yankee is again to the front. He has a letter showing there is some intimate relationship between Antonia and Fernando Bassi. "Now!" he says, as the clock points to nine, "Fernando Bassi is on the other side of that door, make a clean breast of it or I open it."

For only a moment Antonia is terrified, but the tiger in her returns; and she is once again defiant, now asserting she is the rightful Lady Carrington. Poor, tearful Edith speaks up, in behalf of her rival. She forbids the American to open the door, and utters words of kindness that go straight to Antonia's heart. What she would not yield to threats, she will yield to kindness, especially from such an unexpected quarter. She acknowledges

256

at once that Fernando Bassi was her husband; and that if he is living, her husband still, and that Edith is Herbert's lawful wife.

Here with her penitence, reparation, and forgiveness, was a good ending to the play. No such thing! The author, having awakened some sympathy on Antonia's behalf, suddenly destroys it by the rudest of rude shocks. The Yankee confess that Bassi is miles away, and that her confession has been extorted by a trick. The curtain falls upon the picture of Antonia, with all her old evil passions again aroused, expressing hatred for all about her.

The acting of the play was very uneven. Augustus Glover carried off the lion's share of the honours by his bluff, hearty, outspoken impersonation of the Yankee dealer, a gentleman who was prepared, if necessary, to furnish a portrait of General Grant by Mike Angelo, or one of Napoleon I by Phideas. . . . Walter Brooks made a fair Herbert, but has yet to learn how to express emotion. It should not be expressed through the shoulders too much. Leon Sauveur, who in certain quarters is credited with the authorship of the piece, was too deliberate in speech as. . . , Karl, but he gave due vigor to one part of his great scene at the end of the third act. . . . Fernando Bassi is a stupid part, and of it Mr. E. Shepherd could make nothing. . . . Miss Ella Strathmore made much of Edith Beaufort, and pleased us greatly by the grace and tenderness with which she invested the part. . . . Miss Gertrude Irving

as the wicked woman of the play, if she did not make the most of her opportunities and justify her appearance as a star, yet exhibited acting power which seemed to meet with a great deal of appreciation expressed at the hands of the audience. . . . Between the acts of *Baffled* the orchestra tortured the ears of those present with some most execrable 'music.'[111]

Following this folly was the Folly Theatre Company in Arthur Wing Pinero's *Imprudence*, the first of his plays at the Standard. The season of 1881 ended with the return of Emily Soldene in *Carmen*, then Haverley's Minstrels. The panto was *Harlequin Sinbad and the Sailor; or, the Genii of the Diamond Valley*. The scenic exertions of Richard and the gas engineering of Thomas Douglass were at the forefront of theatre technology. The ladies, spelling the names of various jewels with gas-lit letters, mentioned in a previous chapter, appeared in this production. But for novelty, the moving panorama and storm scene was the most remarkable.

Polly and Sinbad having plighted their troth to a sufficiently senti-mental tune, Mr. Augustus Glover as Captain Spanker, with tremendous gilt epaulettes and a telescope at least seven feet long, and accompanied by Bowsprit and Jibboom, after dancing a comic hornpipe, declares that as Polly's guardian he will never consent to her union with Sinbad. It happens that Spanker has an

---

111. The *Era*, (24 September 1881).

exceedingly ugly daughter, Matilda Jemima, whom he intends for that young gentleman; to avoid the proposed distasteful match Sinbad ships on board the 'lively polly,' bound for nowhere in par-ticular. . .

Whilst the 'Lively Polly' is supposed to be proceeding on her voyage Copperstick sings a couple of topical songs, much to the delight of the audience, who are evidently well posted in all the news of the day. Of course no one is surprised to find that Polly—still in pink and crimson, and with her beautiful blond hair hanging down her back—has shipped as a stowaway, or that Sinbad—in pale blue satin trousers and a white satin shirt—saved her from an intended rudeness on the part of Captain Spanker. By way of revenge the Captain proposes to sink the ship, and with it the bold but unruly young tar. Nature, however, saves him all the trouble in that direction, for while the prin-ciples, assisted by the Jack Tars, are en-gaged in dancing a hornpipe ballet and parading the ensigns of all nations. . . a storm creeps up the sky, darkness supervenes, and, with a tremendous roar, the 'Lively Polly' sinks beneath the waves. Whilst the people are struggling in the sea a huge paddle-wheel steamer appears and rescues a large proportion of the crew. This great sensation scene of the pantomime, following closely upon the spirit-stirring song of 'Rule Britannia,' and the waving countless flags and banners in the limelight, is received with rapturous applause. Sinbad, Captain Spanker, and Copperstick, after floating about on a raft, are landed on one of the Tum Tum Isles, where they become so hungry that the two younger ones agree to kill and eat the skipper. And that personage might have been sacrificed except for the timely arrival of Master Dicky, as Hanky Pankyebus, the old man of the sea. The Tum Tum Isles are ruled over by King Henpeck-erini, a musical monarch, whose tunefulness is answered for by Mr. Henry Nordblom. This potentate has a daughter, Princess Pretty Pans, more familiarly known as Miss Violet Hunt, and an unfriendly giant, Mr. Isaacson. Somehow the king is dethroned, and Cop-perstick reigns in his stead. The ex-king falls in love with Polly. Sinbad rescues her from his embraces, and Copperstick. Polly and Sinbad escape the island by way of a panorama to the [transformation scene in the] Valley of Jewels, where, amid gorgeous surroundings, the famous Roc appears. Next in order comes an Eastern slave market, where the captives taken on the Islandof Tum Tum are sold, and the numerous char-acters are turned to stone. The truly mag-nificent transformation scene. . . is followed by an amusing harlequinade, in which Little Ellis appears as Clown, Mr. Wallis as Pan-taloon, Mr. Westbourne as Harlequin, and Miss Carrie as Columbine.[112]

. . .a stupendous effect was obtained by the appearance of a very large, solidly built steamship that sailed onto the stage and having rescued one of the characters who was drifting in a small boat, proudly turned completely round in full view of the audience, and gallantly ploughed its choppy course back again through a most realistic 'vasty deep.' This magnificent scenic effect was

112. *The Daily Telegraph*, (27 December 1881).

achieved solely by a turntable, or revolving stage, fixed on a low platform (or flat rostrum) which ran smoothly on steel rails. As the huge craft, which was the full length and width of the stage, rotated to the amazement of the audience, the bow of the vessel came to within a few inches of the floats. This manoeuvre was only possible because the dimension of the scene-dock was even larger than the enormous stage.[113]

The period between 1878 and 1883, was one of turmoil for Britain. In South Africa there was the Zulu War, followed immediately by the Afghanistan War (the one where Dr. Watson was wounded); trouble with the Boers, in turn followed by the Mahdist uprising in the Soudan, and the death of 'Chinese Gordon' on 26 January 1885. One can understand the pageant of flags in the panto.

It had been a tumultuous one for the Douglasses as well. Amy Steinberg had been working in touring companies, but wanted to have a London base. The Standard was such a large theatre, and she wanted to perform in the more intimate drama of the new school. In December of 1878 the family became the owners of the Park Theatre in Camden Town. Here they opened with a small version of the Standard's panto

of 1876 *Ali Baba*. In 1879 various dramas and farces were performed by the young stock company, with Amy Steinberg and Stella Brereton as the stars. Amy, who was running the show, also imported provincial groups to fill the bill. A number of her husband's scripts were revived or previewed at the Park.

In July of 1880 his adaptation of Ouida's[114] novel *Held in Bondage* was produced with the title *Delilah; or, Married for Hate*. In August a new adaptation of Charlotte Bronte's masterpiece called *Jane Eyre; or Poor Relations* opened to mixed reviews. It ran until October, then went on tour to the provinces. Petite Stella Brereton played Jane, Amy Steinberg was the director, and she played Blanche Ingram, Rochester's previously intended. The Park was not a money maker, and the Douglasses tried to rent it to provincial actors, or even amateurs.

A panto was gotten up for the 1881 Christmas season, *Harlequin Little Red Riding Hood*. In March an amateur theatre group of the First Surrey Artillery presented *All That Glitters is Not Gold* by T. and J. Morton. A reviewer said, "they were well up in their parts."

---

113. Douglass, *Footlight Reflections, p. 103.*
114. Marie Louise de la Ramee (1839–1908), pseudonym Ouida from the way she pronounced Louise as a child, was a prolific author of children's stories, novels, and shorter works. A number were grist to playwrights, inspired incidents in plays, or led directly to stage adaptations. The best known of these are *Granville de Vigne; or, Held in Bondage* (1863), which became Douglass's *Delilah; or, Married for Hate* (1880); *Strathmore; or, Wrought by His Own Hand* (1865) which became C. H. Stephenson's *Wrath; or, A Message From the Dead* (1882); *Chandos* (1866); *Idalia* (1867); *Under Two Flags* (1867), which had four versions by 1883; *Tricotrin, the Story of a Waif and Stray* (1869), which became the American actress Estelle Clayton's favorite vehicle *Favette* (1883); and *Moths* (1880), which had six versions, and a burlesque by 1883. There are numerous others.

Fig. 152. Amateur actors in *Still Waters Run Deep*, December 1882. *From A.S.J.*

All was not well with the Park and the following letters appeared in the *Era*:

Sir—wishing to produce *Still Waters Run Deep*, at the Park Theatre, under our Management, we applied through our representative to Mr. Arnold Taylor for permission and terms (as directed to do by the Dramatic Author's Society tariff), stating it was for a week or fortnight's run, this being only a local theatre. We received the following reply from the party addressed, who succeeded to the property of a great name, apparently without inheriting the courtesy of the same; or, indeed the civility we should expect from a ploughman:—

My Dear Sir.—In the interest of my late brother's estate, I am, as trustee, very loath to see his best plays jobbed about by their haphazard representation in London for short periods. The playing of *Still Waters* at your Theatre for six nights appears to me to come within the above definition, and I am thereupon obliged to decline the proposal made to me in your letter of the 16th inst. Believe me faithfully yours Arnold Taylor.

Some weeks after the receipt of the above we found *Still Waters Run Deep* announced for representation by an amateur Club. [See fig. 152]. So that in the future we are to understand Mr. Arnold Taylor's phrase, as being played by a regular organized company under one of the oldest managements,

means jobbing a piece by hap-hazard representation; whilst the representation of the
same by amateurs is the perfection of
dramatic art, and consequently beneficial
to the interest of a late brother's estate.
Trusting you will kindly allow this statement
a place in your paper, that it may prevent
other managers who may wish to apply (as
directed in the Dramatic Authors' Society
tariff) from meeting with the unmerited
rebuff accorded to us. We are yours sincerely John Douglass- Richard Douglass.[115]

The Douglasses were looking to get
rid of the Park Theatre by the summer
of 1881. The building suddenly burned
to the ground on September 11th. The
press called it untended; but the
Douglasses stated there was a
housekeeper and five stage hands in
the building. When the fire started they
got a hose on it but it was too late. The
insurance covered the building, but not
the stock scenery, props or the
instruments of the band. A benefit was
held at the Standard December 19th to
help make up these losses. They were
probably well out of it. The Park was not
a good investment, perhaps a bit of
self-indulgence on Amy's part.

In the spring of 1882, the ideas
that John T. Douglass had been
formulating, based on the thirst
audiences had shown for naturalistic
sensation scenes, were realized in
*Humanity; or, a Passage in the Life
of Grace Darling* (fig.153). This play is
not remarkable for the majority of the
plot. Grace is the supposed daughter of
an old lighthouse keeper, who saved
her from a shipwreck as an infant. She
is, of course, an heiress; a locket she
has can prove it. She will, in the end,
succeed in recovering her identity
and heritage. The naturalistic
sensation scene was unlike any
staged anywhere before.

Grace is charged with stealing the locket
and chain from Mrs. Rowstock, but Barton
recognizes them as having belonged to
Grace, they having been stolen with the
papers. Jenny, a child, also tells how she
saw the Earl put the locket in the mantel, and
Grace is proved innocent. The Earl now goes
to Silvani's apartments at Hempstead to
demand the return of his money, and a
fearful struggle ensues. A chair is dashed
through a window; the furniture is smashed;
the fire-irons are thrown about; pistols and
decanters are used as weapons; and, to end
with, there are a struggle upon and the fall
of a staircase, the death of the combatants,
and the righting of Grace. This struggle alone
should make the fortune of the piece. It is an
attempt to realize the extraordinary affray
which took place some years ago between
solicitor Roberts and Major Murray in
Northumberland-street, and which will be
within the recollection of many of our
readers. It seems almost too real for the
stage, and we venture to say that nothing
more exciting has been witnessed behind the
footlights in the history of terrific stage
struggles. The spectators never take their
eyes off the combatants, but follow their

---

115. The *Era*, (26 March 1881).

Fig. 153. *Humanity; or, a Passage in the Life of Grace Darling*, by Leonard Rae (John T. Douglass) and Hugh Marston, 1882. *From A.S.J.*

deadly strife with the greatest eagerness, and when that staircase falls with a crash and leaves the villains struggling upon the floor, each seeking the life of the other, the effect is nothing short of thrilling. The actors who take part in this are Mr. Edward Sass and Mr. Arthur Dacre, who are to be warmly complimented upon the way in which they execute their arduous task. They do not spare themselves in the least, and by the time the catastrophe comes they must, we are sure, be thoroughly exhausted. Mr. Sass represents Langley and Mr. Dacre is Silvani, and throughout both play with that cool determination which is, as a rule, the most noticeable characteristic of stage villains.[116]

Humanity was one of the great successes, and ran for many weeks, chiefly owing to the scene depicting a thrilling rescue at sea of Grace Darling, and another in which occurred a terrific struggle for life in a handsomely furnished apartment. In this desperate encounter between two men, they used revolvers, fire-irons, champagne bottles, chairs-in fact anything available, the climax coming whilst the furious fight was raging on the top landing of a staircase which suddenly collapsed, thus killing both combatants. The original exponents of the two scoundrels who came to such an untimely end were Arthur Dacre and Edward Sass. The real reason for the sensational success can only be attributed to the terrific fight and wholesale destruction of crockery and furniture involved in the struggle, and for this John Douglass was solely responsible. True,

the great Northumberland Street tragedy furnished him with the idea, but he planned every move of the fracas, every detail being carefully rehearsed under his supervision.

He designed the scene, modeled the champagne bottles (manufactured of India-rubber in Paris), invented the collapsible staircase, which was made to appear as if it fell—but really was lowered from the prompt side by invisible wires, the landing being studded with sofa springs to break the fall. When the drama was first produced at the Standard a most unfortunate contretemps happened. Just before the struggle, Dacre in his incisive manner had to deliver the following lines 'You see I am calm, cool and collected. To prove how steady my hand is, I can snuff a candle, even at this distance.' He then proceeded to the back of the stage and fired at two lighted candles, one placed on the right table, the other on the left table, in each case extinguishing the flame.

This simple trick was accomplished by placing under each table a man who tugged a wire which pulled the candle down in its socket, thus extinguishing the light. The men who were effectually concealed by the table cloths reaching to the ground, only had the revolver reports to guide them, so it was arranged and rehearsed that Dacre should put out the left candle first, but alas! always a nervous 'first nighter,' he took deliberate aim and fired at the candle on the right table, and of course it was the flame of the candle on the left table that went out first; and when he fired point blank at the left candle (already out) the flame of the right candle was

116. The *Era*, (10 April 1882)

extinguished. Poor Dacre's next line was unfortunate. Turning to Sass, he said, 'You see what a wonderful shot I am.'[117]

The furniture smashing scene was later detached from the play and became a music hall sketch, toured by John Lawson. He changed the basis for the destruction to that of a "mental storm induced by a wife's unfaithfulness."

The play was quite a triumph yet, when it was not on the bill, the theatre was still not being scheduled to anything like capacity. Lillie Langtry came for a few rare morning performances in late April. The crowds and carriages in the street were "numberless," for everyone in the area wanted to see this friend of the Prince of Wales (fig. 154).

A weak spring season was followed by closing the theatre in July. *Humanity* was put on tour to raise some ready cash as the operation was in financial trouble.

Rose Hersee brought her opera repertoire for a week beginning 6 November 1882, but except for this the other productions were by small-time provincial companies.

John T. Douglass had been writing with might and main to get his next sensation drama ready. *The Ruling Passion* opened in mid-November. It was essentially a morality play with various characters representing vices, virtues, and the like. It was composed of seven moral "tableaux."

The great sensation scene of *The Ruling Passion*, was a balloon ascent from the Crystal Palace. A crowd of Easter Monday excursionists was discovered dancing, skipping and indulging in various kinds of horse-play, when suddenly, the guy lines being severed, the huge balloon, with its basket car containing an escaped lunatic and [clinging balloonist], was observed skimming through the clouds. On, on it drifted—another change, and the monster (for it was a real balloon with gas) was seen to be descending into the raging sea. As it gradually crumpled up, and the car was seen to be sinking owing to the inrush of water, a life boat manned by eight men came dashing through the surf, arriving just in time to save the occupants. This play afforded opportunity to Louise Moodie, and E. J. Odell. . . who, as Dr. Erasamus Dwining, gave a wonderful performance of a wily, oily proprietor of a private lunatic asylum.[118]

In the asylum scene, Amy Steinberg was found hanging by the wrists on a wall. A sailor in search of his sweetheart came into the cell only to discover it was not the right girl, but this gave her the chance to escape. She is next seen climbing into the balloon's car. After she cuts the tether, a balloonist tried to hang onto the basket to prevent it from flying away. Amy, the lunatic, chewed his fingers to make him let go—a novel reverse of cliff-hanging. Perhaps more

---

117. Douglass, *Memories of Mummers*, pp. 93–95.
118. Douglass, *Memories of Mummers*, pp. 88–89.

Fig. 154. Lilly Langtry (1853–1929). *From the Theatre.*

influential for future production techniques was the shower of real rain in an accurate set of Piccadilly. Real cabs and omnibuses came and went. In regard to this effect John Douglass said:

> In the notice on *The Ruling Passion* at this theatre your critic misquotes the lines both of Mr. Odell and Mr. Vincent. Also in speaking of the real rain shower he says—'If Mr. Willing imagines he has discovered a novel sensation in a real rain shower on the stage, we may remind him that the thing was done a year or two ago by the Salisbury Troubadours at the Alexandra Palace.' Will you allow us to remind your critic that we have never regarded the real rain shower in any of our advertisements. But still the origin of the effect belongs to the Standard Theatre, as a real rain shower was exhibited here in 1868, in a drama by Mr. Alfred Rayner, called *Danger*. The effect was repeated with improvements, in the year 1871, in the drama *Germans and French*. The latest development of the idea is to be seen nightly in The Ruling Passion, the situation at the end of the first act naturally suggesting such an effect. We are, Sir, Yours, J. and R. Douglass.[119]

Aside from many novel and innovative uses of lighting effects, the Douglasses believed they had invented the use of revolving stages (1875): moving panoramas (crudely done with flats in 1851, showing the principal shops in Shoreditch in *Harlequin Buttercups and Daisies*, and again in 1861 in the more conventional way); and the use of down stage rain troughs (1868). The method by which this last effect was accomplished was explained by Albert Douglass.

> In *The Ruling Passion* there was a downpour of real rain. This was accomplished by having two long zinc-lined boxes the whole length of the stage, with holes a la the kitchen colander, fixed up above in the flies. These troughs were supplied with water from three enormous vats filled each day by the aid of the fireman's hose. These vats were placed high up in the roof, thus ensuring a good and steady pressure as the water was liberated from each vat separately. By this ingenious arrangement, the whole scene, which represented Piccadilly Circus by night, was swamped, as the drenched pedestrians, carrying umbrellas and wearing macintoshes, stampeded for shelter; and a real bus, laden with rain-sodden passengers, proceeded on its storm-bound journey. The main difficulty was not so much in producing the real rain as finding an outlet for the water once it had descended. For this purpose the whole stage was covered with waterproof material, and the rake of the stage increased, to allow the water to pour down to the footlights. The space beneath them was cut away, and thus the water flowed into large tanks hidden beneath the stage.

> How the audience cheered this realistic scene! Yet, if emerging from the theatre after

119. The *Era*, (18 November 1882)

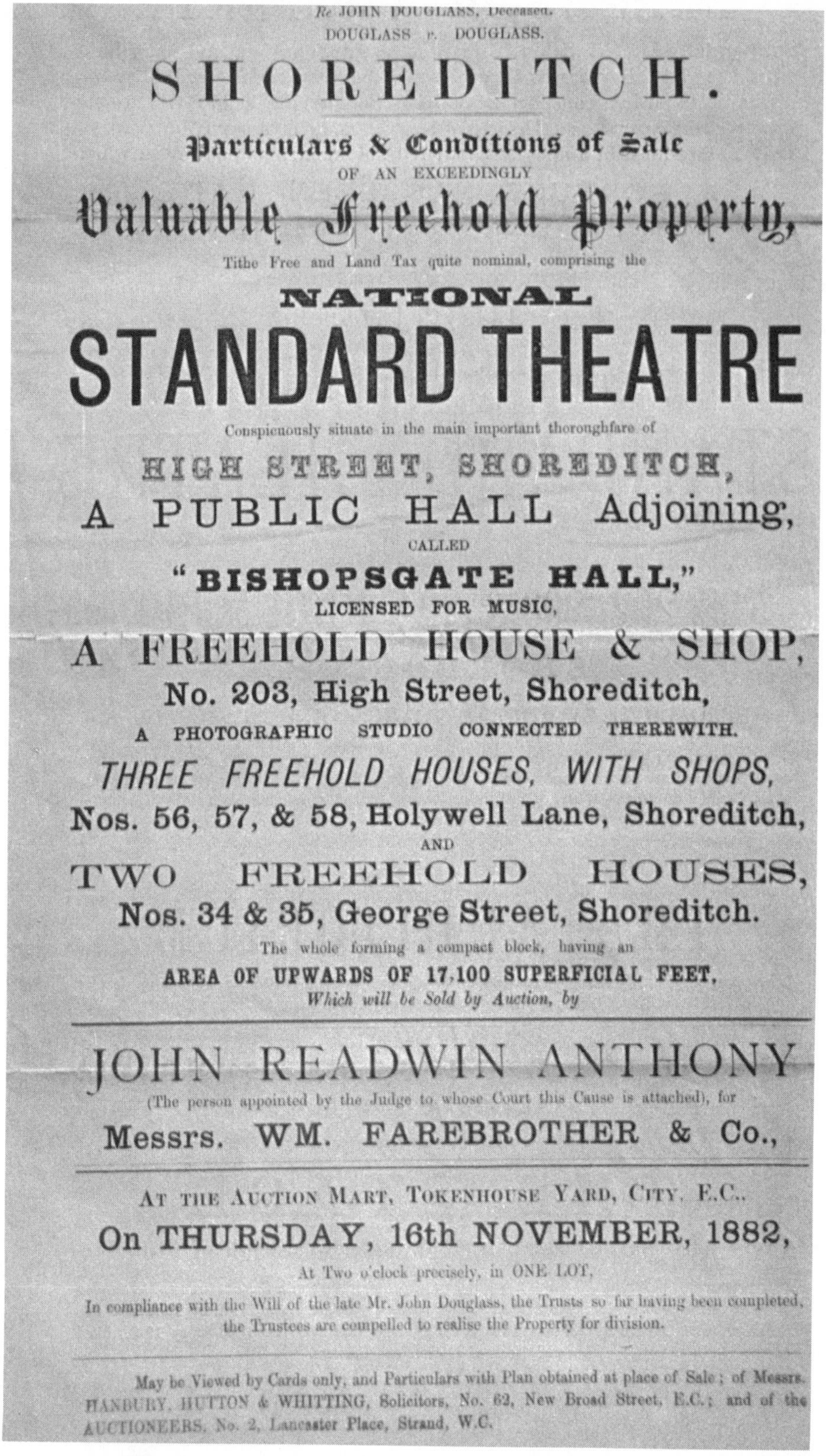

Re JOHN DOUGLASS, Deceased.
DOUGLASS *v.* DOUGLASS.

SHOREDITCH.

Particulars & Conditions of Sale
OF AN EXCEEDINGLY
Valuable Freehold Property,
Tithe Free and Land Tax quite nominal, comprising the
NATIONAL
STANDARD THEATRE
Conspicuously situate in the main important thoroughfare of
HIGH STREET, SHOREDITCH,
A PUBLIC HALL Adjoining,
CALLED
"BISHOPSGATE HALL,"
LICENSED FOR MUSIC,
A FREEHOLD HOUSE & SHOP,
No. 203, High Street, Shoreditch,
A PHOTOGRAPHIC STUDIO CONNECTED THEREWITH.
THREE FREEHOLD HOUSES, WITH SHOPS,
Nos. 56, 57, & 58, Holywell Lane, Shoreditch,
AND
TWO FREEHOLD HOUSES,
Nos. 34 & 35, George Street, Shoreditch.
The whole forming a compact block, having an
AREA OF UPWARDS OF 17,100 SUPERFICIAL FEET,
Which will be Sold by Auction, by

JOHN READWIN ANTHONY
(The person appointed by the Judge to whose Court this Cause is attached), for
Messrs. WM. FAREBROTHER & Co.,

AT THE AUCTION MART, TOKENHOUSE YARD, CITY, E.C.,
On THURSDAY, 16th NOVEMBER, 1882,
At Two o'clock precisely, in ONE LOT,
In compliance with the Will of the late Mr. John Douglass, the Trusts so far having been completed, the Trustees are compelled to realise the Property for division.

May be Viewed by Cards only, and Particulars with Plan obtained at place of Sale; of Messrs. HANBURY, HUTTON & WHITTING, Solicitors, No. 62, New Broad Street, E.C.; and of the AUCTIONEERS, No. 2, Lancaster Place, Strand, W.C.

Fig. 155. Sale Catalogue for the National Standard Theatre, 16 November 1882. *From the Rose Lipman Library, Hackney.*

In conjunction are

THREE FREEHOLD HOUSES,
Nos. 56, 57 and 58, Holywell Lane,

The upper parts being used as dressing rooms, the shops and basements of two let off, the other being used as the Stage Entrance to the Theatre. Also

TWO HOUSES,
Nos. 34 & 35, GEORGE ST., SHOREDITCH,

Containing Five Rooms, occupied by Housekeeper.

The whole forms a Compact Block of Freehold Property,

STANDING ON A SUPERFICIAL AREA OF UPWARDS OF

17,100 FEET.

ABOVE A PORTION OF WHICH IS BUILT THE

BISHOPSGATE HALL and Offices adjoining,

WHICH STAND ON

AN AREA OF UPWARDS OF 4,000 FEET.

The Property is situate in an important position of a main thoroughfare of London, near Six Railway Stations, facing Commercial Street, having entrances on three sides, and is unquestionably

AN INVESTMENT SELDOM TO BE MET WITH.

The Tenure of the whole is Freehold. Tithe Free, and subject to the small Land Tax of £3 per annum. The underlettings are:—

Saloons and Refreshment Counters of Theatre, producing per annum... ...	£520	0 0
No. 203, High Street, Shoreditch, and Photographic Studio	105	0 0
"BISHOPSGATE HALL," estimated to produce per annum...	300	0 0
No. 56, Holywell Lane, Shop and Basement only, let at 10s. 6d. per week, or per annum...	27	6 0
No. 58, Holywell Lane, Shop and Basement only, let at 10s. 6d. per week, or per annum...	27	6 0

No. 57, Holywell Lane, used for Theatre.

Nos. 34 and 35, George Street, occupied by Housekeeper.

Possession and use of the premises and of the fixtures, properties, wardrobe, and scenery will be retained by the Vendors until the 1st day of March next, and up to that date they shall be at liberty to carry on the business of the Theatre, and to receive the profits thereof (they paying all expenses) without interference by the purchaser, or any liability to him for any payment or otherwise for damage to or deterioration in the theatre, fixtures, properties, wardrobe, or scenery.

Fig. 156. Description of the National Standard Theatre. *From the Rose Lipman Library, Hackney.*

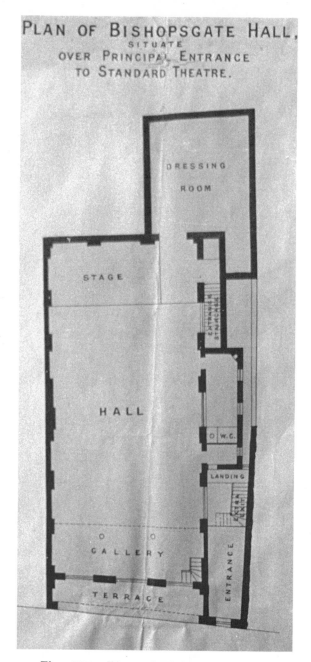

PLAN OF BISHOPSGATE HALL,
SITUATE
OVER PRINCIPAL ENTRANCE
TO STANDARD THEATRE.

Fig. 157. Plan of Bishopsgate Hall in the National Standard Theatre, 1882. *From the Rose Lipman Library, Hackney.*

the performance they found it was raining outside—how they cursed! Playgoers are a problem![120]

It was at this time the terms of John Douglass Senior's Will was exercised. The property was to be sold and the proceeds divided into appropriate shares. The sale was announced for 16 November 1882, and to show they were serious an extensive catalogue was printed (figs. 155-159). The auction took place but turned out to be a great disappointment. *The Builder* described the bidding commencing at £10,000 advancing only to £40,000. This did not meet the reserve price, the auctioneer stated that this was less than the value of the land alone withdrew the property. The family was forced to continue operations.

Albert Douglass said:

I can here make the first public announcement of the keen desire of Sir Augustus Harris to become the proprietor of the Standard Theatre. He offered £50,000—and later £55,000—for the property, both offers being refused, though en passant it may be stated the theatre was sold some years later at a very much lower figure to the father of the brothers Melville, the present popular proprietors of the Lyceum."[121]

Under the terms of the proposed sale the family would have retained the building until 1 March 1883. Therefore

120. Douglass, *Footlight Reflections*, p. 102.
121. Douglass, *Memories of Mummers*, p. 83.

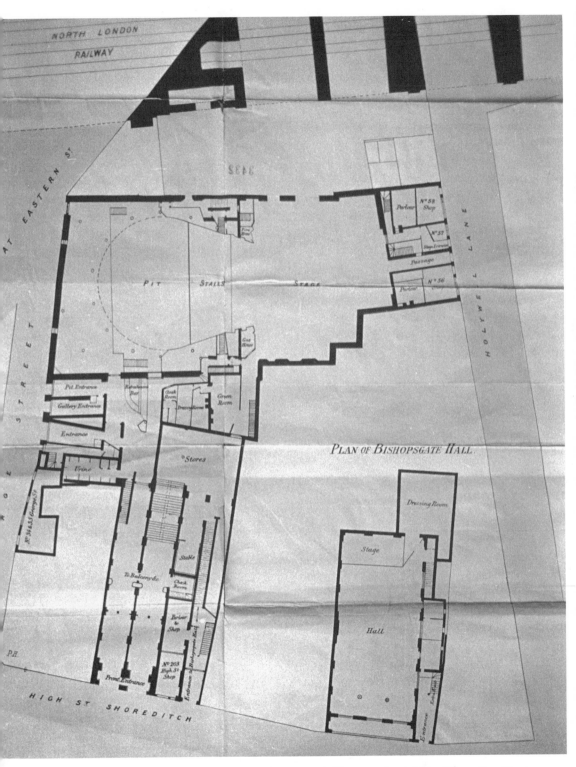

Fig. 158. Site plan of the National Standard Theatre in 1882. *From the Rose Lipman Library, Hackney.*

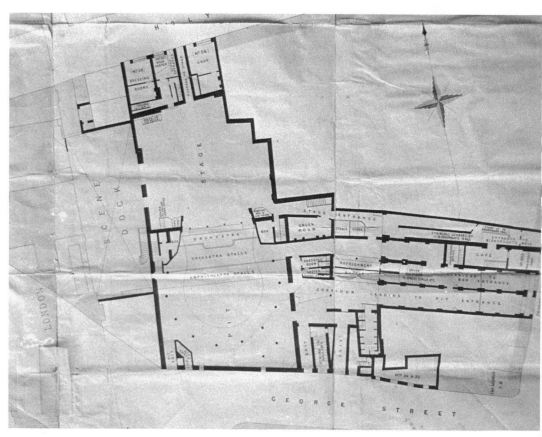

Fig. 159. Ground plan of the stage level, National Standard Theatre, 1882. *From the Rose Lipman Library, Hackney*.

they had resolved to produce the pantomime, even if they sold the theatre; it always made money. Since they had intended it to be their "swan song," they had pulled out all stops for *Little Red Riding Hood; or, Harlequin Boy Blue, Miss Muffet, the Wolf, and the Bears*. Richard Douglass produced some of his "happiest works of art." The gas lighting was spectacular for the corps de ballet, dressed as the Follies, bore wands,whichinaninstantbecame sun flowers in glowing flame, while similar adornments burst out from the tops of their glittering hats. Thomas Douglass, the inventor of the effects, in an interview with the press asserted that gas was not to be beaten by electricity as a means of stage effect.

13

FINAL BURST OF ENERGY 1883-1886

After the pantomime of 1882–1883 Amy Steinberg began to take over the leading roles in the plays *Humanity* and *The Ruling Passion*. Louise Moody and Bella Pateman had moved on to other engagements. John T. Douglass was again at work, and excitement began to build in regard to what it was to be:

A whisper had gone around to the effect that all sensations of the past were to be put in the shade; and that in the way of realism there was to be that which would eclipse all that had gone before. The performance was announced to commence at seven, but even at that early hour the house was fairly packed, the box office was besieged, and the cry was 'still they come.' Scores of faces familiar on first nights, at fashionable houses at the other end of town were to be noticed."[122]

The Referee reported among the first-nighters were A. W. Pinero, H. Pettitt, G. Conquest, Tinsley, Reece, Wilmot, Amy Roselle, and a host of other managers and theatre people. The play was *Glad Tidings*. The plot centered on a true disaster, the sinking of the pleasure craft "The Princess Alice," called in the play the "Glad Tidings."

The hero, one Arthur Pierce, discarded nephew of a baronet, has become the husband of Isabel Morton, a parson's daughter, and in doing so has greatly offended both Margaret Musgrave, who meant to marry him herself, and Godfrey Golder, his rival for the hand of Isabel. The disappointed ones are extremely unscrupulous, and coming by accident across the sister of Arthur's deceased wife, they put her forward as the real Mrs. Pierce, partly in order that they may prevent the reconciliation of Arthur and his uncle, and partly out of sheer malice, and desire to separate the happy couple. As

122. The *Era*, (29 August 1883).

274

a matter of fact, Arthur's wife, a mad half-cast whom he married in India, is dead long ago; but the conspiracy got up by his enemies and forwarded by his sister-in-law cannot for a time be defeated. Isabel is reluctantly convinced, and leaves her husband, after which her troubles culminate with her presence on board the ill-fated steamer, 'Glad Tidings,' when it is sunk in the Thames by a collision [fig.160]. After her rescue, she is agonized by the belief that her child has gone down, whilst her husband, on his part, believes that she as well as the little one has perished. All, of course, comes right in the end with the exposure of Margaret Musgrave's base plot, the death of her ally, and the confession of the sham Indian wife [fig. 162] . . . Miss Amy Steinberg, displays real pathos in the part of Isabel, the much-enduring heroine. . . It is not, however, by the labours of the company, any more than by the dramatic achievement of the authors, that Glad Tidings secures the triumph most likely to be talked about. This is won by two scenes, one illustrative of Rotton Row at the height of the season, and the other of the circumstances attendant upon the well-remembered 'Princess Alice' disaster. In praising the first of these there need be no arriere pensee. It is a marvelous piece of stage realism, singularly full in detail, and, as a whole, highly effective; indeed, it may be pronounced the best of the many good things of its kind accomplished by Mr. Richard Douglass. As to the other hit—for we suppose it must be credited as one—we can only say that opinions differ. To some these tragedies of real life evidently appear perfectly admissible incidents of an evening's entertainment. To others—and we confess we are of the number—it seems repulsive in the last degree to make capital out of the incidents of a calamity still fresh in the memory of many a widow and orphan. The better the 'Princess Alice' catastrophe and its consequences are rendered on the stage the greater it seems to us the reason

Fig. 160. *Glad Tidings*, **shortly before the collision, National Standard Theatre, 29 September 1883.** *From the Illustrated Dramatic and Sporting News.*

for regret that a morbid taste should be so successfully gratified.[123]

In...*Glad Tidings* the stage was converted into a realistic picture of Rotten Row in the season. Dozens of smart society folk mounted on restless steeds cantered up and down the row, which was covered with tan, whilst well-groomed men, and smartly gowned women lazily lounged on the park seats, or stood idly chatting, by the railings, which were real and firmly fixed in case the prancing horses should make them wobble and ruin the stability of the set. Only the huge dock on the O.P. side made this scene practicable. Another remarkable scene was the wreck of the Thames pleasure steamer. The deck was crowded with a merry crowd of excursionists singing and dancing, when the bows of a large vessel crashed into the side of the steamer, and the confusion, cries and subsequent sinking of the boat, were most realistic.[124]

The Referee commented that when the other managers—Pettitt, Wilmot, and Conquest—saw the production, they must have shed bitter tears on not having thought of the realistic Rotten

Fig. 161. *Glad Tidings*, **Rotten Row scene, National Standard Theatre, 29 September 1883.** *From the Illustrated Dramatic and Sporting News.*

123. The *Sporting and Dramatic News*, (8 September 1883).
124. Douglass, *Memories of Mummers*, pp. 89–90.

Row scene. It provided "East Enders, who never have been in Hyde Park during the season, when swells, and belles, and equine beauties abound," with such an accurate treat (fig. 161). The play was a smash hit, running, eighty three nights, to the last day of November. It was toured, and then revived, at the Standard in 1884.

Jenny Lee in *Jo the Outcast* then filled in until the panto. *Harlequin Puss in Boots* had new scenery, and new effects as always.

Certainly nothing could be better than the stage pictures [Richard Douglass] has presented to the Standard's audience; each cloth is worthy of a place in an art gallery, and a more brilliant, and, at the same time, a more chaste design for a transformation scene than that entitled Dream Land of the Star in the Realms of Blue Ether, it would be difficult to conceive. The Mill scene, the Mirror in the Woods, the City of Cats, and others, deserve much praise; but the inventive ability displayed in the scene of the Ogre's Castle merits a special comment. Here is a massively built-up scene, wherein a fight is being carried on by a number of auxiliaries, which glides away marvelously while the combatants are fiercely contending on every stage and battlement, and dis-

Fig. 162. *Glad Tidings*, **an exciting moment in Act II, National Standard Theatre, 29 September 1883.** *From the Illustrated Dramatic and Sporting News.*

covers, as if in a panorama, a lovely picture of sylvan scenery. Such an artistic and mechanical triumph is seldom attempted, and at no other house in London could it, in all probability, have been worked with so much success. When it is born in mind that the whole width of the stage is occupied with this scene, and that it is fully tenanted by super-numeraries while it is moved, the task may be imagined, and the success with which it is accomplished may be realized. The spectacular and choreographic effects in the Castle of Cats, where all the ballerines represent an army of cats of various kinds, and introduce the marvelous gas lighting effects, for which the Standard pantomimes are always famed, was a picture of magnificence not to be excelled upon any stage, and elicited much enthusiastic appreciation.[125]

The fire and safty regulations for public halls had begun to be strengthened because of a number of disasters in major cities of Europe, and America. Once the officials had examined the Royal Patent Theatres, it was only natural the huge Standard be scrutinized. The Metropolitan Board of Works listed twenty-one alterations they required for fire and safety reasons. A proscenium wall of brick, fourteen inches thick, with no more than three access doors in it, was required. The small doors could only be three by six feet, and hung with iron doors one-fourth of an inch thick. Also, the theatre had to be

separated by brick walls from all the other premises adjoining. New internal staircases to handle panic problems and new passages had to be constructed, and old ones closed. External entrance hallways, and carriage alleys had to be cleared of scenes, props, and materials stored there, aisles in the auditorium widened to a minimum of three feet six inches. Doors were to be properly hung to open out, and hinged in such a way as not to block any other passages. Hand rails were to be added in some places. Iron grills were to be placed under skylights, and all doors used by the public were to be a minimum of four feet six inches wide, hung in two-folds to open outward.[126]

The Douglasses complied with most of these, but disputed a few. In any case, the alterations took the spring and most of the summer to complete because the theatre stayed open.[127]

Bella Pateman was engaged for the revivals of *Ruling Passion* and *A Bitter Wrong* (fig. 163). These were followed by opera and minstrels, then the July closing for vacation that had become a regular practice. In the 1890s, at the time that the Melville family was running the Standard, further alterations were required for fire and safty reasons. The capacity of the theatre was therefore at its highest at the Christmas season of 1883–1884 perhaps as much as five thousand four hundred. After 1884 this figure gradually eroded to the forty nine

125. The *Era*, (29 December 1883).
126. *The Builder*, (29 March 1884).
127. *The Builder*, (12 April 1884).

hundred range. The drawings of the proposed 1890 renovations reveal the basic interior arrangement of the theatre as it stood between 1884 and the mid-twentieth century (figs. 164–170).

At the end of the summer, Schoolbred and Company of Tottenham Court Road finished the renovations. The redecoration included painting the theatre in crimson and gold, and removing the private boxes at the back of the grand circle.

During the construction period, two plays of interest were performed. The first, by George Lander and John Douglass, was *A Bitter Wrong; or, A Wife in England, No Wife in France*. This was a social-criticism play that revealed the inequities of French marriage laws. It was based on a true story, and the reviews compared it with the corrective dramas of Dumas, Charles Reade, and Wilkie Collins.

A French adventurer has temporarily fled to England. There he weds Mary, an Englishwoman. He loots the family funds and deserts wife and child; returns to Paris and there marries a rich widow. His destitute English wife follows him to France. In the confrontation he explains that by French law they are not married. She then turns to the French wife who becomes enraged, and takes vengeance on Armand, the cad, by throwing acid in his face, something like Holmes's *Adventure of the Illustrious Client* (1927). Mary, after much trouble, gets back to England only to be followed by the disfigured Armand who demands his rights as an English husband. Rejected he abducts his child, is tracked by the police, and in the end dies by his own hand after confessing to the murder of his French wife.

The second play gave Richard Douglass a chance to construct the mountain scenery of the California gold rush. Its title was *Karl; or, the Love that Wins* This play, compared to the plots of all the plays described above, is turgid; improbability collided with

Fig. 163. Isabel Pateman, and Arthur Williams in *An Interrupted Honeymoon*, Avenue Theatre, 1899. *From the Enthoven Collection*.

coincidence to such a degree that even the ardent devotees of the romantic drama turned away. It closed after two weeks.

In September, the press reported the Standard had been noticeably empty ever since the fire and safety reports had been published in March of 1884. The Douglass's advertising machine went to work, extolling the virtues, safety and comfort of the newly renovated building. John T. was also preparing to top his last sensation with his play *Daybreak*.

May, the daughter of a Vicar, has two suitors: Owen Landside, a young man with expectations, and Frank Fuller a rising barrister; Fuller seems the better match, but May, with suitable feminine perversity, prefers Landside. The Vicar, at the bedside of an old parishioner, is told the man paying court to May is a

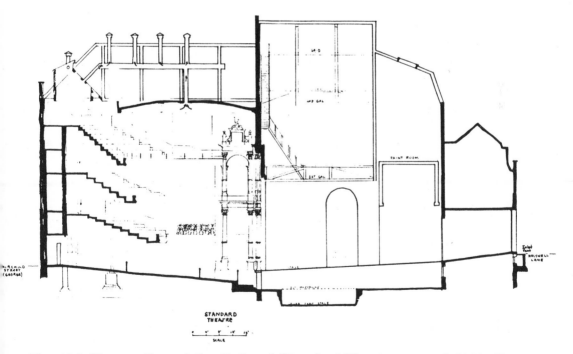

Fig. 164. The section of the National Standard Theatre around 1888. *From A.S.J.*

280

libertine who seduced the old man's daughter. Accused, Landside turns the tables by denouncing his rival, offers to meet the supposed victim, and denies any guilt.

In the meantime, he arranges to elope with May at daybreak; and she goes to bed. Five years have passed. May is discovered in shabby rooms in London, a deserted wife and mother. To add to her distress, Landside has repudiated the marriage, claiming it was a sham ceremony. He intends to

marry a rich heiress. An acquaintance of May's appears. She makes her living by bringing actions for breach of promise against all eligible men who fall into her clutches.

Landside's uncle dies leaving him a country estate, The Oaklands, some racehorses, and a mortgage for ten thousand pounds against Ivy Hall, the home of Sir Gregory Welbourne. Among the horses is the famous Fairy Queen, first favorite for the Derby. It was entered in Landside's name, there-

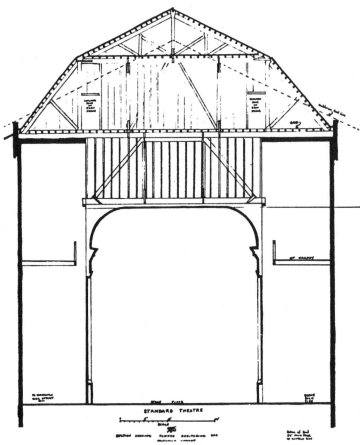

Fig. 165. The proscenium of the National Standard Theatre around 1888. *From A.S.J.*

fore, its running is not effected by the uncle's death. The dead uncle's wish had always been to join Ivy Hall with his own estates. To that end he threatened to foreclose if Clara, the niece of Sir Gregory, would not marry his nephew.

Mrs. Abigail introduces May and Clara to each other. May explains she is Landside's wife, but he says the marriage was illegal, for he had previously married May's eldest sister who is now dead, but was alive at the time of the supposed wedding.

Fuller, the barrister, stumbles over an old parchment at Ivy Hall that gives Sir Gregory the Right of Heriot, over the estate of Oaklands. This gives him the right to claim any three beasts from the estate. Fuller tells Landside he will claim Fairy Queen on behalf of Sir Gregory if Landside does not release the mortgage.

Landside laughs with scorn. But to revenge himself he steals May's child, and gives her to one Lysander Jones, who conceals the child at a mysterious old inn, "The Curfew," near Regent's Park. The scoundrel Jones is an inventor of infernal devices. He is also the genuine husband of Mrs. Abigail.

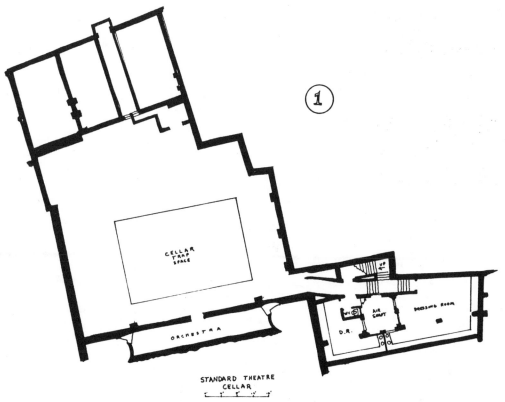

Fig. 166. The cellar and trap room level of the National Standard Theatre around 1888. *From A.S.J.*

She has overheard the plot, and tells May where the child is. Jones is quite ready to take money from both sides, and sells the information to Fuller who is thus able to follow May to "The Curfew." At the Inn, May hears strange cries, and finds a maniac, who she recognizes as her supposed dead sister. In a rare lucid moment, the sister tells May that she married someone else; and May's marriage is perfectly legal. Landside plans to capture Fuller at the inn in order to prevent him from seizing the mare at the Epsom races. Fuller escapes, and forces Landside to release the mortgage just before the race is run.

Jones, the double dealer, drugged the horse, and she comes in last. Landside is ruined. When he goes home, the police are waiting, and arrest him for forgery. He believes May has set them on his track, pulls a revolver, and shoots her.

The scene suddenly changes to the bedroom of the first act. May is in bed;

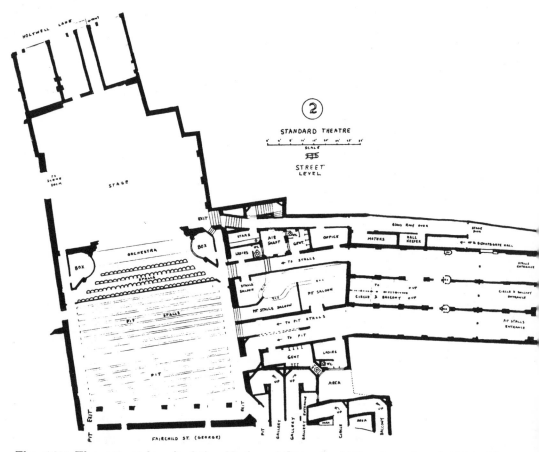

Fig. 167. The street level of the National Standard Theatre about 1888. *From A.S.J.*

she wakes up and realizes the whole story of five years has been a bad dream of a single night, hence the title *Daybreak*.[128]

Pre-expressionistic scenes of mesmerism, visions, and dreams had been common in the 1850s and 1860s, in plays such as *The Corsican Brothers*, *The Bells*, *Free Labour*, and *The Wandering Jew* where the audience saw a graphically staged scene, as the character saw it in his mind. But *Daybreak* was a bold step because two whole acts were the dream; and the audience was not in on the device until it was over, much like the use of this technique in *The Cabinet of Dr. Caligari*.

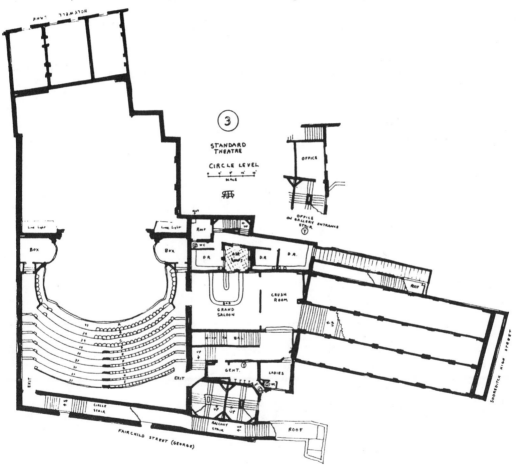

Fig. 168. The circle level of the National Standard Theatre around 1888. *From A.S.J.*

128. *Under the Clock*, (3 September 1884).

Some of the scenes and tricks of the evil Cerfew inn were of interest including "the chamber of death," on the second floor, that contained a bed, that at the touch of a button lowered the occupant into the lunatic cell, where murderers come in to polish him off.

Epsom Derby was relentlessly reprod-uced; and the newspaper described the "road home from the Derby" scene as a "triumph," with a real four-in-hand driving past the Cock Pub at Sutton,"An ever greater triumph of picturesque realism."[129]

John produced a complete representation of The Derby, in which real racehorses were utilized for the first time. [Ponies were used in *Tom and Jerry* in 1823]. Only the almost isolated position of the theatre made this scene possible. On the P. side was a large open space known as Bessell's yard, leading to Holywell Lane. On the O.P. was a long dock and a raking piece [ramp] also leading out to the same thoroughfare. The scene and vast crowed can be imagined. The horses at

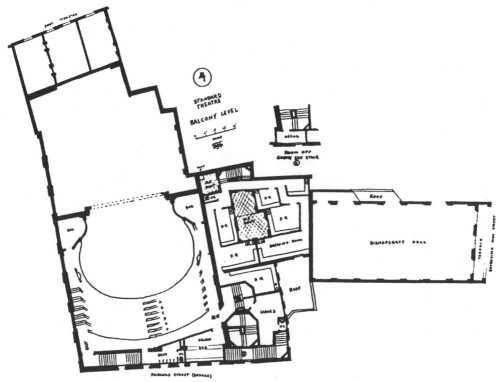

Fig. 169. The balcony level of the National Standard Theatre around 1888. *From A.S.J.*

129. *The Referee*, (3 September 1884).

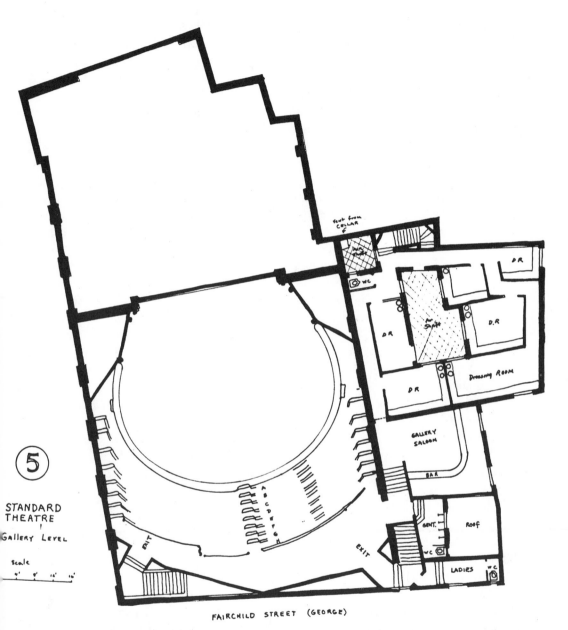

Labels within the figure:

Vent from Cellar

WC

DR

DR

For Stage

DR

D R

DR

Dressing Room

GALLERY SALOON

BAR

GENT.

Roof

W C

LADIES

W C

EXIT

EXIT

A B C D E F G H

⑤

STANDARD THEATRE

Gallery Level

Scale

FAIRCHILD STREET (GEORGE)

Fig. 170. The gallery level of the National Standard Theatre around 1888. *From A.S.J.*

the cry of 'They're off,' started from the O.P. side, cantered down the dock, dashed into the street, down Holywell Lane, through Bessell's yard, and by the time they came into full view of the audience they were going hell for leather; indeed the jockeys found it difficult to pull up until they had almost completed the course a second time. This will explain what puzzled so many, who naturally imagined that horses going at such a pace must inevitably crash into the wall before being pulled up. It was a real race every night, both John and Thomas offering cash prizes to the winner, and as great a rivalry existed between jockeys, each one strived his utmost to be first past the post. Betting was always brisk, the keenest punter being the constable who held up the traffic in Holywell Lane whilst the mimic race was in progress.

Another triumph of stagecraft was the Road Home From the Derby. This scene represented The Cock, at Sutton, and was a beautifully executed piece of scenic art. Here passed in full view of the audience real hansom cabs, . . . Donkey barrows, wagonettes, coal carts, and a couple of four-in-hands, all crowded with noisy revelers and pleasure seekers cheered by a swaying and excited multitude. Holywell Lane was again in demand for this scene, and the street was nightly thronged with spectators eager to obtain view of the procession in the street before it entered the theatre.[130]

Shakespeare had declined in importance throughout the British theatre. At the Standard, where there was virtually an Elizabethan play festival each season in the fifties and sixties, now there was almost none. By autumn of 1884, the only actor presenting any of professional quality was W. H. Pennington. The press called him "elocutionary" and "capable."

> In this somewhat pedantic age, it is refreshing to hear Shakespeare's magnificent English, so naturally and unaffectedly given. In his general rendering Mr. Pennington emphasized the reflective and melancholy side of Hamlet's character, rather than the impulsive and fiery.[131]

Amy Steinberg played Pauline in *The Lady of Lyons* for Pennington's benefit night. This was to be the last season of Shakespearean plays at the Standard. There was a short run by a provincial company; and six more nights of Pennington in 1888, but that was it. Oddly, the minstrel show disappeared from the bill at this same time.

The National Standard Pantomime for 1884–1885 was *Cinderella; or, the Fairy of the Little Glass Slipper*. The cart ponies used in *Daybreak* were worked into the production in the arrival at the Fancy Dress Ball scene. The palace gardens were created, and the ponies dressed in brilliant liveries pulled up to the entrance with the carriages of the arriving guests. The most notorious guest to arrive was

---

130. Douglass, *Memories of Mummers*, pp. 90–91.
131. The *Era*, (14 December 1884).

General "Chinese" Gordon, who, in reality at the moment, was desperately defending Khartoum. The press said he was a "most welcome visitor." Although the truth was not known until months later, he was killed at the end of January 1885 while this show was still running.

The first transformation scene was the Kingdom of Flame, which was speedily changed under the influence of the water genii to the Realms of Perpetual Winter. The second transformation was the traditional un-folding type. There were eleven distinct "unfoldings" of the beauties of the Floral Kingdom beneath the glitter of the ever-changing color of the gas lights.

The old Harlequinade, once the heart and soul of the panto, was a dying institution. It became difficult to find good performers for the traditional roles. Music hall and burlesque comedians began to take their place. It was like replacing Harlequin and Columbine with Abbot and Costello.

In this case, Arthur Roberts of the Gaiety Theatre's Burlesque Company made fun of all the popular plays of the previous season. He played Ophelia, Pauline (a character in a drama titled *Called Back*), Wilson Barrett in *Claudian*, minstrel shows, and the like in the character of Cinderella's ugly sister, Clorinde.

By this time Richard Douglass had become one of the major providers of scenery for the British theatre. The Standard's dock was fully supplied, and although he had to design and supervise the sensation drama and panto each year, the Standard had few other requirements. Therefore he kept his staff busy making scenery for other theatres. An article on this described the number of miles of canvas, and the tons of drops. For example, he supervised painting of several hundred tons of scenery for fifteen operas for the new Comedy Theatre in Manchester.[132]

In March of 1885 the aforementioned play *Called Back* was transferred to the Standard from the Princess's Theatre. The problems of the smog irritated throats of the East-Enders, plus the quiet "domestic" style of the actors points to the changes in drama and acting style that were beginning to take hold.

We were struck, on our visit, with the difference in the general effect of a play which results from its transfer to a larger house, where the bulk of the audience is seated at a great distance from the performers on the stage. The space through which the sounds of their voices have to travel is an important factor in the sum of general satisfaction, and we would suggest that, especially as regards the earlier part of the piece, those engaged might with advantage make some acoustic experiments with a view to deciding whether the pitch of their voices should not be raised in order to carry their utterances to the farthest

132. *The Referee*, (4 January 1885).

recesses of the pit and gallery. *Called Back* is a play which demands for its thorough comprehension a dutiful attention to every line of its explanatory dialogue; and we are inclined to think that many of these must have been lost amid that chorus of coughs which, at this period of the year, is certain to arise from time to time in a large East End theatre. We recognize the value of quiet acting in domestic and social scenes; but think that, in this case, realistic softness of tone should yield to the practical requirements of a large house and a deep stage.[133]

The reviewer went on to say, the actor playing the blind protagonist needed to study real blind people to capture their mannerisms. He goes on to report the realistic death scene of the villain, ". . . the way in which after being shot, he turns round, and round in agony, and finally falls, his limbs stiffening in the death pang, is capital."

This problem of the size of the Standard, not being suitable to the coming dramatic styles was insoluble. This was one reason the Douglasses continued to try to "top" their last sensation scenes, rather than moving toward the rising naturalism in drama. In the mid-1880s the size of the Standard proved to be a handicap to the maintaining of the theatre's reputation as a microcosm of the theatrical picture of its time.

Problems relating to copyrights continued to plague the dramatic profession. This was an age of constant adaptation of short stories and novels to the stage. In April of 1885, Amy Steinberg was praised for her role in a new play called *Two Women*. Edward Rose, the author, had originally intended to call his adaptation of *Marie Tudor*, the little-remembered work of Victor Hugo, *Too Late*.

When this was advertised W. H. Patterson, and Charles Quayle were put forward as authors of two plays of this same title, each of which had been performed in the provinces. After the complaint was registered, Rose reported that his research showed that John Douglass Senior led the field in the use of this title for a play called *Too Late: the Anchor's Weighed*. It had been performed in 1849 at the Standard. The 1849 playbill does not use the phrase "Too Late." There may have been some confusion on the part of John T. about his father's script, or perhaps the hand-written manuscript. of this old T. P. Taylor-John Douglass play had such a title attached.

Another controversy surrounded the production of a play based on Florence Warden's *House on the Marsh*.[134] This provincial play opened at the Standard 1 June 1885 with Florence Warden herself in the lead (fig. 171). The review stated she had adapted the story for the stage following the lead of Wilkie

---

133. The *Era*, (14 March 1885).
134. Florence Warden was the pen name of Florence Alice Price (afterwards James), (1857–1929). She wrote a hundred or more novels and short stories. Her novel *The House on the Marsh* was first published in 1877.

Collins and Charles Read, who adapted their own works.

The story is an old-fashioned thriller. A band of burglars is headed by a seemingly respectable business man. Violet, the heroine, stumbles over the gang. After much movement through trap doors, and the like, the villain, Rayner, is shot by Sarah Gooch, a woman he had used as a "cat's paw." The detectives, and Violet's affianced arrive in the nick, and all ends well. The play had a modest success, but the story of its dramatization is of more interest. After it opened, a writer named Augustus M. Moore complained that most of the drama was his work, and he was not being given credit. He wrote to the papers:

> In a paragraph on the subject of my action to prevent Miss Florence Warden playing my version of *The House on the Marsh*, you say Miss Warden 'offers Mr. Moore £10 as remuneration for his trouble over the original version.' This is scarcely correct. In one of her letters to me Miss Warden says, 'You had better keep this letter.' She will be pleased to hear I have done so. In her first letter to me on the subject she offered me £10 down, and £100 if the piece was produced in the provinces, and £200 if produced in London, or any fairer terms I could propose so long as those terms admitted the withdrawal of my name as part author. These terms I, of course, refused. Miss Warden then agreed to burn the play since we could not come to terms, and to give me an agreement, the draft of which is in her own handwriting, to have no hand, act, or part in, or derive any benefit from any version of the book, I giving her a like agreement on my side. To this I willingly consented, and considered the matter settled. I heard no more from Miss Warden till, in reply to a letter of mine desiring to know if she still intended to fulfill her word of honour, she wrote me, through her solicitor, that she did not; but that she had rewritten the drama, omitting all my suggestions, and would shortly produce it, leaving me to take any course I liked, or did not like. If Miss Warden's idea of re-writing a play, omitting all my suggestions, is copying it out and making such important changes as altering a child's name from Mona to Haydee, she certainly has kept her promise. Since I have seen a short-hand writer's copy of the piece I am more inclined than ever to think she has stuck more to my work than her promise. Miss Warden is not good at admitting, but I happen to have two letters of hers in which she admits that the situation at the end of the first act, of which there is no kind of hint in the book, is mine, and that the substitution of the violin-scene to conceal an abduction instead of a robbery is also mine. These she has reproduced in the drama.

> In my play I invented a rescue at the end of act three. I have the original MS. of this act, so can prove it. A Nottingham paper censured Miss Warden for not having a dramatic rescue at the end of act three, and for introducing some light comedy scenes, on the first representation. Miss Warden has since taken the hint, and inserted my rescue. This and the introduction of an old bore, who lightens the play by stopping the action to talk about 'pickles' in every scene in which he is on, are the only original innovations in which Miss Warden, as far as I can remember, has introduced since the first

Fig. 171. Florence Warden (Florence Alice Price, James) (1857–1929), writer, and sometime actress. *From the Theatre.*

presentation. I have a letter of Miss Warden's in which she proposes that Rayner should commit suicide off the stage. I find in her 're-written' play she adopts my idea of his being shot on the stage by Sarah Gooch. This is, with the exception of some abuse which I will not trouble you with, the summary of Miss Warden's letters to me.

As Miss Warden has published her pleas of defense in the Scotsman, perhaps it may interest your readers to read my grounds for praying for an injunction.

One word more and I have done. Miss Warden, as reported in the *Scotsman*, accuses me of having represented myself as being responsible for *Claudian* and *Called Back*. My experiences teach me that two men, or a woman and a man, as a natural consequence, becoming deadly enemies as soon as they have collaborated in a successful play which has brought them fame and all the good things of this world, quite forgetting that their strength lay in their union, and that alone they would have earned none of these good things. My old friends Mr. Wills and Mr. Herman still shake me by the hand when we meet. Mr. Comyns Carr has not publicly or privately horse-whipped me (as Miss Warden would like to do). Mr. Hugh Conway and myself are collaborating on a new and original drama which, for the sake of our friendship, I hope may turn out a failure. Under these circumstances, Queen Mab must have been with Miss Warden. If I told her so, as indeed I did not, she is far too credulous for this wicked world. All I know of dramatic construction and dramatic writing I

learned from my best and oldest friend Henry Herman. I really ask everyone to believe me when I tell them I am not half generous enough for the post of public 'property ghost,' and I have never been able to persuade managers that I had any cerebral eggs worthy of their learning to suck. The day may come. Faithfully yours, Augustus M. Moore.[135]

Some sort of agreement was eventually made that permitted the production to proceed; but not before another writer, Charles Percy Emery, had inserted his oar, insisting he had written a play in 1873 from which Miss Warden had stolen her whole plot for the book.[136]

In this spring of contention, the Standard survived with a diet of beautiful Alice Atherton in *Babes* from Toole's Theatre, Charles Warner in *Drink*, and Wilson Barrett in the big "crime" drama *The Silver King*.

In August the Standard's box office got a telephone (number 1229) to permit the audience to call for reservations for the coming exciting attraction: Lillie Langtry in Sardou's *Peril*. As in the case of her previous appearance, a morning performance was arranged for Saturday, September 5th. She perhaps had too much to do of-an-evening for more conventional appearances.

Lillie Langtry, and the Christmas pantomimes were the only theatrical

---

135. The *Era*, (2 May 1885).
136. The *Era*, (9 May 1885).

attractions that were so sensational (or notorious) that such a thing would have profitable. The critic of *The Referee* was suitably impressed with her interpretation, despite the fact that he believed her version of the play was the worst of the five translations that had been seen in London.[137] Her cut of the box office for these performances was double that which most stars received, and it was even more in the provincial theatres.

Waiting in the wings was a new but traditional action melodrama. *The Broad Arrow* by Gerald Holcroft was a throw back, almost a parody, of the Boucicault style of play. The critic for The Referee had great fun describing the production.

Old Mr.Medwin has two sons, Saul and Oswald, who in no way resemble each other, or their parents, or anything else in this world or the next, except people nailed-up in plays. Saul, the elder, is the heaviest and most atrocious villain in a frock coat ever seen upon any stage. Oswald is by turns a diamond digger, a convict and a fugitive, but is virtuous all the time. Oswald, having been sent to seek his fortune, returns with a bag full of diamonds, but pretends he has come back destitute, and his father reviles him. Therefore, Oswald calls at his brother's office and asks him to buy the diamonds. Saul is evidently a connoisseur as well as a capitalist, for, after three seconds' inspection of the stones, he agrees to give £20,000 for them. Also, having the exact sum—twenty

notes of £1,000 each—lying on his desk, quite handy and promiscuous like, Saul pays for the gems there and then, and Oswald goes on his way rejoicing. But only for about three minutes. Within that time Saul has told his father that Oswald has stolen £20,000 of his, and Oswald, turning up with cheerful innocence to claim his lady-love, Beatrice, and explain that he is not quite so hard up as he pretends to be, is promptly arrested by perhaps the smallest policeman on record, and is (as it seems) marched off to penal servitude there and then. Saul meanwhile sent the diamonds off to Amsterdam by a 'Husker' who happened to be busking in the street outside. These are some of the doings of Act I.

In Act II Oswald is doing time in Dartmoor, which ought to be called Dark Moor because of the fearful fog which arises there when Oswald knocks down an objectionable warder, who is presently and more permanently knocked on the head by Ikey Shaw, another convict. Oswald having escaped, is supposed to have committed the murder. Meanwhile Old Medwin, Beatrice, Saul, and Saul's young woman seem to be living together at a place called Birdhurst. Old Medwin thinks he is going to die, and in order to save legacy duty executes a deed of gift of his whole fortune to Saul, who presently, because Beatrice refuses his proposals, turns both her and his father out of doors— to starve! At this juncture Oswald turns up, and, introducing himself as Beatrice's long lost brother, proposes to watch over and work for her and Old Medwin. It seems Oswald escaped from Dartmoor by train, and

---

137. *The Referee*, (6 September 1885).

in the railway accident, which naturally ensued, he changed cloths with a dead passenger who luckily turned out to be Beatrice's brother. Of course no one has any suspicion that Oswald is aught else than he now pretends to be.

There are three more acts in which many curious things happen. . . It is enough to say that Beatrice, becoming very hard up, goes down to the Thames Embankment to drown herself. She jumps in at the O.P. side of Cleopatra's Needle, . . . and Oswald, who happens to be passing that way, jumps in and pulls her out. (And thus the whirligig of time brings in his revenges—but no matter.) Meanwhile Saul has been playing hide-and-seek around the Needle, and when Oswald and Beatrice come out of the water the eyes of Saul are opened and he denounces Oswald as an escaped convict, but at this moment up comes the busker (now a Lion Comique) who took the diamonds to Amsterdam—or rather didn't take them. He hasn't got them now anyhow, but he helps to expose Saul and to get Oswald away from the little policeman who is again on hand. And by-and-by Oswald conceals himself in a Punch and Judy show, and Ikey Shaw (now a shoeblack) shoots Saul dead, and, being also about to die himself, explains that he not Oswald, murdered the warder; and then Old Medwin finds that Saul has (by mistake) burnt the deed of gift, and all the survivors have nothing else to do but live happy ever after.

All this hotch-potch is illustrated by the singularly beautiful scenery which is the specialty of the Standard Theatre. The rep-resentation of Higate Woods in the first act is charming. The fog scene in Act II is the best managed thing of the kind that I can remember. The Thames Embankment scenes—by night and by day respectively—will bear favorable comparison with their prototype. . . Miss Amy Steinberg plays Beatrice, but the part is unworthy of her.[138]

The work necessary to mount these plays was considerable, Holcroft wrote to the *Era* and stated his play was typical in that it was accepted in April (the first no doubt), and the sets were painted throughout June in order to be ready for a September 7th opening. The Pantomimes took even more time.

The next Douglass special was now ready, and the hokum of the Holcroft play was replaced with *A Day Of Judgment* in which the entire process of the courts was brought on the stage in a most realistic manner. The title was simplified to *Judgment* on the suggestion of *The Referee* (fig. 172).

The dramas of Mr. James Willing [J.T.D.], whilst containing plenty of healthy sympathetic interest, invariably present some striking picture of contemporary life, such as can be accurately realized on few stages so vast and convenient as that of the Standard. It seems but a few years ago that all London was startled by the appearance on stage of a real Hansom Cab, built by a well known maker, attached to a serviceable horse, and driven by a licensed cabman. Down to that time the stage cab had only been a creditable

138. *The Referee*, (13 September 1885).

makeshift. A pasteboard vehicle and a profile quadruped. . . On the boards of the East-end theatres there had been attempts at striking realism long before West-end managers condescended, or rather yielded, to an imperative cry . At the old Victoria, in the New Cut an advancing steam-engine was used to illustrate a terrific accident, prior to the time when the dramatists of the Princess's, Adelphi, or Drury Lane competed in the great race for sensation. When Mr. Andrew Halliday wrote A Great City [1867] and produced his play on the boards of the 'National Theatre' the sacred dignity of the drama was said to be threatened by the appearance of a real Hansom Cab. But what would the playgoers of those days have said could they have seen the pictures presented at the Standard Theatre in 1885 to illustrate the sensation act of Mr. Willing's drama of *Judgment*? The heroine of the play is unjustly accused of murder, and she has to stand trial at the Central Criminal Court. So Mr. John Douglass, and his clever brother Richard go boldly to the fountain head, and take their sketches from actual life in the immediate neighborhood of Newgate and the Old Bailey. First we see the yard at Newgate on the morning of a celebrated trial. Barristers in their robes, witnesses with their summons to attend, erratic jurymen, and official policemen prepare the scene for its subsequent excitement. First one Hansom cab drives up, and then another, depositing in the courtyard lawyers or officials of various degree. Judges and aldermen arrive in their broughams, and the whole stage is filled with vehicles of varied shape and size; but the excitement is not complete until the arrival of the prison van, a veritable 'Black Maria,' such as may be seen any day in Bow-street, which is driven bodily upon the stage, and then, at the entrance of the court, deposits the weeping prisoner. This is no stage property cleverly made to imitate a prison van, but the actual thing, built by the government contractor and furnished with the latest improvements. The scene changes to the interior of the Central Criminal Court, with its sword of Justice, the judge in full robes, and the attendant aldermen who happen to be on the commission. Often before there have been trials upon the stage, but few have been realized with greater accuracy. Once more a change and we arrive at the room where the jury empanelled to try a murder case decide upon their verdict. At this point the dramatists have availed themselves of a license that is scarcely justifiable. There may have been instances where juries have 'tossed up' sooner than remain to convince an obstinate colleague; it is not beyond the bounds of probability that twelve honest men and true have, when shut up to consult, indulged in indecent levity, swallowed surreptitious stimulants, and even played 'nap' to while away the tedium of waiting; but surely not on the occasion of a serious trial for murder. . . Juries make mistakes, and grievous ones, but it is surely a grave instance of dramatic license when such sarcasms are leveled at an ancient English right and privilege. In a civil case and for the assessment of damages it is conceivable that an English jury of tradesmen could toss up; but not to decide a matter of life and death.

. . . apart, however, from these blemishes, the new drama is admirably direct, well constructed, and interesting. When convicts escape from Portland and assume the habit of respectable citizens they have murdered the position gets exciting, and the career of

Fig. 172. *Judgement*, National Standard Theatre, 26 September 1885. *From the Penny Illustrated Paper.*

Richard Gurnon, who in his new existence, has to act as father to a naturally willful child, is watched with extreme interest. In fact, the audience breathless with attention when this accomplished and ingenious scoundrel finds his would-be daughter walking in her sleep, and uses the sonnambulist as a cover to one of the murders he has committed in cold blood. Amina has hitherto been accused of no graver crime than stealing the family teaspoons; but a sonnambulistic Amina, who is dabbled over with a victim's gore, and charged with murder through the accident of sleep-walking, is decidedly a new feature in modern drama. Down to this time Mr. James Willing can lay claim to the prize for a new dramatic motive. . . a sonnambulistic murderess never yet occurred to the combined or separate brains of a Jones, a Herman, or even a Wilson Barrett.

The weight of the play falls on Miss Amy Steinberg, who plays the heroine with great intelligence and effect, and some remarkable acting is shown by Mr. Austin Melford, a young actor of considerable promise and individuality, as the convict villain. Mr. Melford is full of resource and invention, and acts as so few young actors do—with his head. . . . The new drama is beautifully mounted by Mr. Richard Douglass, who can paint a cloth of sunny landscape as well as he can model the dock and Judge's canopied seat at the old Bailey.[139]

Other critics also saw the travesty enacted in the jury room as offensive to the British sense of justice and fair play. *The Referee* said, "This we consider a blot upon the play."

However, in regard to the sweeping scenes of city life, the Douglasses were anticipating the techniques of David Belasco, and the cinema, more than inventing long-term useful techniques for the live theatre. Despite the sharp criticism, *Judgment* was able to engender acceptable houses for twenty-five days. Then *Ruling Passion* was substituted for four weeks. Several small-time companies, including a terrible American group with something called *Capers*, closed out the autumn. The Douglasses had planned for *Judgment* to run to the panto then pick up again in the spring. But when attendance fell off, it was too expensive to operate with its huge cast, and the outside cabmen and carriage drivers.

The pantomime for 1885–1886 was *Harlequin Whittington and His Cat* again. A comparison between the books of words for this show, and the one for 1873, reveals they are similar, with some revisions. This is the first time in twenty-one years a panto was repeated. The previous production may have been remembered by John T. Douglass as his favorite, or perhaps the most popular with the public.

The new elements included "The largest real Bells ever used in a theatre," put in a belfry near the roof, to ring the Bow Bells tune; and a pageant representing the city companies in

139. *The Daily Telegraph*, (23 September 1885).

liveryin the Lord Mayor's procession. The transformation scene was "From Winter's Frost unto Ethereal Spring," a harmonic triad in grey, mauve, and gold.

In the early spring a sensation scene drama with a twist moved in to the Standard. *The Foreman of the Works* was an early example of "labor verses management" theme plays.

Mr. George Manville Fenn, the well known novelist, who is never at a loss for scenes which are at once stirring and picturesque, has handled an awkward subject with considerable judgment and tact. Years ago when Boucicault wrote *The Long Strike* [1866] there was not much risk in describing on the stage angry discussions between masters and men, threats and recriminations, or in arguing the cause of the workman as against the capitalist. But today it is a different matter. With the unemployed crowding the streets and conversation turning upon 'social-democracy,' it requires a very skillful pilot to steer a working man's play through the shoals and quicksands of danger, particularly when the author elects to give us boldly the meeting of a secret society in full conclave, the room hung round with revolutionary texts, and the president of the locked-out men leaning on a barrel of blasting powder. A sample of a 'ruined home' underlies the passion and excitement of Mr. Fenn's new play. . . produced last night. It will not surprise anyone to learn that the foreman of a bell foundry down in Yorkshire has a pretty daughter, who has fallen into the toils of the oppressive and aggressive master, or that the interest of the play depends upon the war of the working men

democrats against the sensual capitalist, who is about as bad and tyrannical a young man as has ever been presented on the stage (fig. 173).

Because of the usual wrong committed against the foreman's daughter by the slavering capitalist, the angry father reluctantly joins the secret society. They plot to destroy the factory; and the foreman himself, to prove he is worthy of the society's trust, must place the blasting powder. Knowing the Douglasses' reputation for naturalistic spectacles the audience, at this point in the play, must have laced up their shoes, collected their bonnets and handbags in preparation for a mad dash to the new convenient emergency exits. The reviewer continued:

The gunpowder is smuggled into the factory, the train is laid, the slow-match is lighted, everyone expects a stack of chimneys to come toppling down, the ladies in the audience prepare for the excitement with a little twitter of fear, when Joe Banks, the foreman, discovers that his child is in the deserted factory, and is within an inch of destruction. So he stamps upon the slow match, puts it out, and saves the child, without any sensation or destruction of property. The drama is certainly constructed on a new principle, and that is, to lead the audience gradually to expect something that never comes. Apart, however, from the scenes in which the workmen air their grievances when on strike and harangue violently, there are several well-drawn characters, one of the best of them being a 'muscular Christian,' the young liberal parson, who talks excellent sense and has a love scene into the bargain. A clergyman making love on the stage is a new feature in dramatic history.[140]

As if to atone for the trick played on the audience, the next two productions, designed in the true spirit of Douglass scenic naturalism, reached new heights of their technique. On 22 March 1886, *Our Silver Wedding* presented breathless audiences with a children's Sunday School excursion in a leafy glade of Epping Forest. There were over two hundred and fifty children engaged as extras. A dozen wagons and green grocer's vans, with flags flying and real horses, were employed from the Whitechapel area. The children sang choruses of popular songs, entered races, played games, and had contests (fig. 174). In the midst

Fig. 173. The characters in *The Foreman of the Works*, National Standard Theatre, 20 March 1886. *From the Illustrated Sporting and Dramatic News.*

140. *The Daily Telegraph*, (9 March 1886).

of the happy throng was a downcast clergyman who had just been handed a note, from a wife he adored, saying she had left him forever.

. . . the reading of this epistle by the broken-hearted man, whilst the children were dancing around him, was an intensely human situation that gripped by sheer contrast, and when the children had departed, the vision of that lonely and sorely stricken vicar remained in the memory long after the real horses were forgotten.[141]

Two other bucolic scenes followed. The first was a badminton game on a green lawn, and the second was a real fox hunt (fig. 174).

All at once Master Reynard breaks covert, and sneaks across the stage, dodging through the hedge and making for the open; the hounds follow in full cry. . . Then quickly come horsemen and horsewomen pell-mell, shouting at the top of their voices; some take the leap in fine style, clearing the hedge and water at a bound, others refuse; willing horses are encouraged, stubborn ones are whipped and spurred, and the interest of the play being luckily over before the hunting tableau is presented the audience is so overjoyed at the novelty of the scene that it actually insists on the curtain being raised and encores the whole chase from start to finish—fox, hounds, huntsmen, and all.[142]

---

141. Douglass, *Memories of Mummers*, p. 89.
142. *The Daily Telegraph*, (9 March 1886).

Fig. 174. *Our Silver Wedding* National Standard Theatre, April 1886. *From the Illustrated Sporting and Dramatic News.*

14

A DARK SECRET 1886-1889

The autumn of the Douglasses' next- to-last season at the Standard began with a play based on a novel by Whyte Melville called *Uncle John*. In it the wife of a country vicar had been married, when young, to a scoundrel. He supposedly was dead—fat chance! He returns, and tries to force his wife to lead a double life to help further his wicked schemes. She runs off, but the rascally husband pursues her, and makes her life miserable. It sounds like this is the wife of *Our Silver Wedding*. Eventually, after many affecting scenes, the villain turns out to have been a bigamist; and everything is worked out. Vicars's wives always seem to have such hard lives in these plays. Amy Steinberg plays the helpful friend of the long suffering wife. The review said she was a merry and lovable woman, whose bright face and manner brought her high honors from the audience.

However, it was the second play in October that reached the ultimate—the apex—of the Douglass effect. This is the play that was forever after associated with the National Standard Theatre, and John Thomas Douglass; the play that gave him his nickname.

The indefatigable John's most wonderful and daring achievement was in his drama entitled *A Dark Secret*. The river front of lovely Henley was shown on a July day, just before the race for the Diamond Sculls. The stage was a broad belt of real water, real flowers, real rushes, real boats, and real swans. House boats, steam-launches, gigs, wherries, outriggers, the tub of the minstrels were all there in a scene brimming over with animation and spirit. When the great race was over, the sky became overcast, and down came a torrent of real rain. Later the river was shown at night with the house-boats illuminated with lanterns, and just one boat, the crew of which sweetly sang a barcarole as they drifted by in the soft moon-light.

The scene earned for John (whose initials were J.T.), the sobriquet of John Tank Douglass. Of course he keenly relished the jest—was there ever a Douglass that did not enjoy a joke?—but the term 'tank' is somewhat misleading, for it gives one the impression that simply a huge tank was placed on the stage. It requires little imagination to conceive that such a device would be useless. How could boats pass, steam launches go off, turn round and return, or outriggers go out of sight, if only the stage were covered with a sheet of water? It was necessary to have far more water off the stage than on, a fact frequently forgotten.

Perhaps no stranger sight in London could have been witnessed than when my brother Dickey and I, alone in the vast theatre on Sunday, would unfasten a boat from its moorings and go for a row on the improvised river, followed by a couple of inquisitive swans.[143]

A Dark Secret: A Tale of the Thames Valley was based on parts of Sheridan Le Fanu's novel *Uncle Silas*. It was a grim story full to the brim with horrors that compared with those in *Sweeny Todd*, *Jonathan Wild*, *The Romany Rye*, and *The Hidden Hand*.

Papa James and Uncle Jonas are brothers. James is good, and rich, and has a dear little lady-like daughter, Nelly. Jonas is wicked and poor, and has a raffish son, Stephen. James has also a step daughter, May, but they do not speak as they pass by. Everybody but James knows Jonas to be a villain. Therefore James, in order to show his confidence, makes his brother his executor and sole guardian of Nelly, the money to come to Jonas after Nelly's death. All this being thus, James dies off—from slow poison implied, but not expressed. It may be, however, that his habit of sleeping on a

bench without being properly covered up hastened his end. The rest of the play—Henley Regatta excepted—consists of Jonas and Stephen's efforts to get Nelly's money, and the terrible trials that poor little girl successfully goes through before all is over prove conclusively that she has a stronger constitution than her poor father. Jonas is steeped in assorted crime. When May's sweetheart, young Mr. Raynes, came round to inquire about some forged acceptances, Jonas puts him to bed in 'The Tower Chamber,' and the next morning poor

Fig. 175. John Thomas Douglass, James Willing Junior (Arthur Douglass), and Richard Douglass (rear), 1886. *From the Entr'Acte.*

143. Douglass, *Memories of Mummers*, pp. 91–92

Raynes was found with his head cut off. The coroner's jury brought it in suicide; but May has no confidence in coroner's juries, and has sworn to devote her life to the unraveling of this 'dark secret'—so there you get your title, don't you know.

Jonas is a regular old viper, and sticks at nothing to gain his ends. Stephen is nearly as bad, and is a howling cad into the bargain. Stephen's notion is to marry Nelly and, as he would say, 'put the double on the old 'un.' Jonas is not averse to matrimony, but prefers murder. This precious pair are aided and abetted by Madame La Fontaine, a wicked Frenchwoman, whose front name is Emile, probably because of her masculine characteristics. . . . Emile pinches Nelly, shakes her, and finally flogs her with a riding-whip. Whereupon May, disguised as a housekeeper, rushes in, routs the foreigner with great slaughter, and thrashes her with the same whip, to the intense delight of the audience. But Nemesis is at hand, in scene fifteen, Clavering Tower. Here in an upper chamber, are shown Jonas, Stephen, and Emile, standing over poor little Nelly, who has swooned. They might very easily kill her now, but they prefer to do things elaborately, and besides they have got a big effect ready for the last scene. Meanwhile poor May has been stowed below in a vault, which is supposed to be an old tank, though why does not appear. 'Emile,' says Stephen suddenly to the wicked foreigner, 'What would you do if I were to promise to make you and honest woman?' 'I would go and turn on ze watarie in ze tank,' replies Emile, with much promptitude. No sooner said than done.

Emile turns on tap, water—from Henley probably—rushes into the vault, and May is about to be drowned, when the leading juvenile and May's new sweetheart rush in, knock holes in the wall, and drag her out. Picture.

The end approaches. Scene sixteen is the Tower Chamber, where Raynes cut his own head off, according to the coroner's jury. Here Nelly is brought to be drugged first, and murdered afterwards. She looks out of the window, and sees two men digging her grave. Horror! Enter Emile, with coffee-pot and cups to do the drugging. Emile pours out the coffee, and to inspire confidence drinks. Nelly (who was not born yesterday) says, 'No thank you.' Emile sits on the table, becomes conversational, drinks out of the wrong cup, and speedily becomes drowsy. She throws herself on the bed, and is at once fast asleep. Mysterious taps are now heard, and a creepy sensation comes over the house. Nelly, horribly frightened, hides behind nothing in particular. The shuttered window revolves on its own axis. Enter Stephen on one side, and an accomplice with a big lantern on the other. Enter also (by the door) Old Jonas. 'Be quick about it,' says Jonas, handing Stephen a sort of small pick-axe. Stephen poises this murderous weapon for an instant, and brings it crashing down into what is supposed to be the skull of the female figure on the bed, but which is really a block of wood—for even the Standard's realism must draw the line somewhere, and they couldn't afford to kill an actress every evening for the sake of vraisemblance. Nelly shrieks! They all rush on her—when suddenly enter leading juvenile, sweetheart, May, and police—and 'The Dark Secret' is a secret no longer.[144]

The Henley regatta scene was introduced to give cad Stephen a chance to further reveal his rascality, when he tries to bribe the other crew in the diamond sculls to "even up the odds."

> . . . when the hero, amidst all this excitement, wins the race from the villain there is such a shout of applause and congratulation as is seldom heard within the walls of a theatre. . . .It will be a strange thing if all London does not go to the Standard to see the Henley Regatta scene.[145]

The portable tank that Douglass had constructed, in order to take the play on tour, was probably smaller than the one at the Standard, because few stages were as big as it was. Even so the tank was twenty-three feet from foot lights to the up stage side, and seventy feet from wing to wing. It was three to eight feet deep, and held five thousand cubic feet of water.[146]

Of the actors, the ladies of the company took the honors. Dolores Drummond, playing the French adventuress, was described as playing feminine cruelty with such ferocity that it equaled that of the notorious Mother Brownrigge. Amy Steinberg, who was now taking roles in which she represented sturdy middle-aged women, played May.

A dea ex machina has been found in the sister of the persecuted heroine, a noble-minded woman who elicits cheers that nearly lift the roof off the theatre when, her kinswoman having been unmercifully thrashed, she tucks up her sleeves and gives the French woman a castigation that sends her writhing to the floor. If women fight duels in sensation pictures in the Salon it is no doubt considered in accordance with the spirit of the age that they should thresh one another on the stage. The excitement was here raised to fever pitch, a previous bout between bullies and boxers at Henley sank into insignificance, and shouts of 'Give it her well!' resounded through the house.

The weight of the acting fell on Miss Stella Brereton [Richard's petite wife], the persecuted heroine [Nelly], and on Miss Amy Steinberg [John T.'s wife], her protectress. Miss Brereton, hitherto recognized only as a pathetic ingenue, here displays remarkable vigour and unquestionable power. Her frame is slim, but her nervous strength is sharp and intense. With a voice clear as a bell, and all her energy braced for action [she had appeared in the Prologue as a child of fourteen], gave to the passionate pleading of the girl, the fierce despair of a woman. Miss Amy Steinberg. . . played the good sister, May Joyce, remarkably well. Artistic throughout and defiant in her devilishness was Dolores Drummond, the celebrated Hortense in *Bleak House* [Jo]. Her Scorn was terrible; her disgust at all sentiment, withering in its shamelessness. She never faltered in what

144. *The Referee*, (31 October 1886)
145. *The Daily Telegraph*, (30 October 1886)
146. Information courtesy of E. S. Stewart of Boston, whose father was involved in the technical side of the American tour, and who kept a diary describing some of the aspects of the tank.

she had to do, and never flinched under the reproaches of her audience.

The old villain of the play, Jonas Norton, was personated by Mr. Julian Cross with great intelligence and occasional flashes of power; and one of the most originally drawn characters in the play, Stephen, a slangy, unscrupulous, shifty blackguard, showed that Mr. Henry Bedford is an actor of considerable observation, and no little skill in the delineation of modern vice.[147]

The success of *A Dark Secret* inspired even quiet and droll Richard Douglass to take pen in hand. He composed the following piece that gives the best picture of back stage life at the Standard seen through the eyes of the theatre's black cat.

Am I the only cat here? Oh! no. There's Smellers, Carrots, Tom (the property-room cat), and myself. We lost a dear friend some time ago—Tib—nice cat, but so inquisitive (a 'she' of course). It is believed the *Dark Secret* was the cause of her death. She suddenly disappeared one night, and the four of us searched for her from the flies to the cellar, but in vain. The manager had previously produced a magnificent aquatic drama, and for one scene—'The upper Thames by Night'—the whole stage was covered with a huge tank of real water. Alas! when that scene arrived, and the large platform which covered the tank was lifted, the corpse of poor Tib was seen calmly floating on the top, bathed in a halo of white lime-light. Several hands were stretched forth to bring it ashore, but the manager excitedly exclaimed 'No! no!—let it alone. The upper Thames will look more realistic than ever tonight.'

Have I always succeeded with the actresses paying us visits? Oh no! One lady, whose name I must not reveal, but will call her Miss Gasper [perhaps Gurtrude Norman in the 1883 *East Lynne*], took a rooted dislike to me from the first. I heard her say 'she detested black cats,' and sure as I tried to coax her, my efforts were only rewarded with a kick. If I approached her at all during rehearsals, she used to exclaim, 'That horrid black cat again—that means failure—I know he'll ruin my drama!'—an exclamation to which the comedian replied sotto voce, 'It would be a case of one cat upsetting another.' I stood her insults patiently till the final rehearsal, when, not satisfied with unladylike epithets, Miss Gasper threw the manuscript at me. This so exasperated me I hid behind a wing and swore to be revenged. For hours I schemed and pondered. At last a bright idea struck me. She was starring for a fortnight, and the play was *East Lynne*. Of course she had her own version. What emotional actress hasn't? It was the first night. All went as the proverbial marriage bell till the scene where Lady Isabel, on a snow-white bed, dies. The audience were deeply affected, and when white handkerchiefs glittered and tears flowed freely there was my cue. I calmly walked on, sat in the center of the stage, and quietly washed my face. At first the audience tittered, then they laughed, and amidst the cries of 'Sh! Cat! Sh! Sh!! Rats! Meat! Meat!' I gracefully retired, being

---

147. *The Daily Telegraph*, (30 October 1886).

convinced there was an end to all sympathy with the dying woman, who was muttering fearful things about me under her breath, in diction totally unfit for one thinking of departing this life.

I had to pay dearly for this; for, fearing the consequences of my escapade, I rushed through the scene-dock, dodged a well-aimed blow with a broom, and sought refuge in a large red bucket labelled 'Fire.' Unhappy plunge! It was full of water. Half drowned, I hastily scrambled out, and beat an ignominious retreat, taking shelter in the carpenter's shop. But as I dried myself on some new shavings I pondered deeply, how that pail came to be full of water was beyond my feline comprehension. For months it had been as empty as a dude's head, and dry as a carman when he brings you a Christmas hamper. Why! Sally had actually given birth to a family of six in that very pail, only two weeks previously, and now it was full to the brim with water—clean water, too. I thought at first some scene-shifter had suspected my humble abode, and this was his revenge; but in the morning it was all explained. The manager had received an official intimation that some members of the London County Council were coming to examine the fire appliances.

Eh? Will I have a drink? Why, certainly. What's yours? Rum and milk. Oh! no rum for me. Too early. I'll have a saucer of milk, please, neat.[148]

A Dark Secret was performed for forty-five nights until 18 December 1886, when they had to mount the pantomime. *Aladdin* was a rewrite of the 1871 production. It was successful the normal length of time through mid-February, but, it was clear the Douglasses were concentrating their creative energy on the sensation dramas.

After the panto, *A Dark Secret* was able to fill the house for another two months. Then, after a provincial troop or two, the Gaiety Theatre's popular hit *Dorothy* came for two weeks in June.

The attendance at the Standard, and the other theatres as well, plunged. There was a new distraction in town, and a very great one indeed! Buffalo Bill and his Wild West Company performed all summer in the large triangle of land between the underground railway junctions in South Kensington, called Earl's Court. This was on the opposite side of the City from the Standard. There had been bad press as well. A reporter came to the Standard one night; and the next day reported in his column on the safety of London Theatres, that he found the Standard rather dangerous, an extra gallery fire exit barred and padlocked, one of the pit entrance doors half bolted up, as well as some other exit doors in the same condition.[149]

The Douglasses didn't need this kind of publicity when houses were almost empty anyway and they closed up for the rest of July and part of August of

148. Richard Douglass, "Interview with a Theatrical Cat," *The Era Almanac*, London, 1893, p. 89.
149. "The State of the London Theatres," *The Saturday Review*, (23 July 1887).

1887. *A Dark Secret* reached the high-water mark of the tank dramas. The family haunted the bookstalls looking for another story John T. could adapt to fit the expensive tank. One was settled upon and went into rehearsal while the theatre was closed. *The Royal Mail* and the two other tank plays that followed it in the next ten months represented a rapid decline. They were written to fit the scenery rather than the other way around.

[In The Royal Mail:]. . . the period of the prologue is somewhat vaguely described as 'The Burmese War,'[1886]. Operations commence in the interior of a Houghla fort, upper Burma. Here Colonel Wade, his sister Catherine, a White-chapel idolmaker, and Legorra, or Begorra the Burmese maiden, and a few redcoats are beleaguered by rebels who spare neither age, nor sex, nor pains. Shots are freely exchanged, and the excitement is intense. [Echoes of Buffalo Bill's Wild West ?] Nobody knows but the next moment may be his or her last, and were it not that every two minutes hostilities are suspended to allow Colonel Wade, Catherine, and the White-chapel boy to give off explanatory dialogue, the tension would be too great to be borne. Enter Bosquet a Burmese spy. If Colonel Paton doesn't come to the rescue, all is lost. Wherefore Wade sends off Bosquet with dispatches to Paton, and immediately after is informed by Begorra that Bosquet is a traitor. 'Aha! say you so? I will go myself.'. . . Scene changes to a Ravine. Enter Bosquet on a dark bay horse with carmine mane and tail—which is probably Burmese Local Colour. The steed would come into the orchestra if he could,

but Bosquet prevents him. Exit Bosquet right, after sticking half way for a brief space at the wing. Colonel Wade is on his track. Scene changes to a Burmese hut, apparently belonging to Bosquet, who explains that his real name is Lawes, that he is of Irish birth, and that he has vowed vengeance on the Saxon oppressor. [Charles Parnell, the Phoenix Park murders, and the Irish question was much in the news in this spring.] Lawes has a comic Irish confederate—Curly—who is the divorced husband of Wade's sister Catherine, and who is generally drunk. Enter Paton. Laws and Curly hide in opposite corners. Enter Wade. The two Colonels collogue, and exchange confidences. Each having a presentment that his end is near, each makes the other his executor, and they exchange papers. Enter softly a Burmese mob. Enough having now been said to let the audience know what is going on, Lawes, Curly, and the mob rush upon the two Colonels. Wade is shot dead in his tracks. Paton is taken out to be shot. Lawes searches Wade's body and finds papers. 'Aha! What is this? A letter—commending my dear wife to the care of my dearest friend—no name mentioned—and signed Paton! By Jove; how lucky! I will personate him and marry his widow, and say that Wade and Paton Quarreled, and that Paton having shot his friend, was shot down by our soldiers while trying to escape. . . .' The scene suddenly changes to the Cataract on the Irrawaddy—which is voted so splendid a stage picture that Richard Douglass has to come on and bow his thanks before anything more is done. The bank nearest the orchestra is fortified, and held by British troops. The opposite bank seems to be held by rebels. Independent file firing. Suddenly a raft comes floating down the river with the rescued garrison on board. Some of the occupants fall into the Irrawaddy, and swim therein, in order to prove that the river is real water, and just as something or other, which is not obvious, is about to be done, the British Troops rush in and rescue everybody. End of prologue.[150]

In this scene the waters that cascaded over the rocks and down into the river fell from high-set pieces that stretched into the flies, being conveyed thence by a patent steam driven centrifugal pump.

When the drama proper commences Lawes is living in furnished apartments near Neath, southern Wales. Passing himself off as Mr. Conway, the dearest friend of Colonel Paton, he has married that unfortunate officer's chuckle-headed widow, and, having wasted her substance, now treats her with malignant cruelty, and proposes to allow her a pound a week out of her own money, while he marries somebody else. Catherine, now a robust invalid, is obliged to have a doctor for her sweetheart. Presently, on the Swansea road, Conway runs against the Whitechapel idol-maker and Begorra of Burma. They are running a waxwork show, but times is werry hard, and Begorra has developed a wonderful talent of making waxen faces. Let me think! says Conway. Yes—she shall make me a waxen mask, the counterpart of the face of this portrait. Photograph handed over, bargain struck, and exit Begorra dissembling.

Catherine, having discovered much, now meets Begorra, got up to resemble the Wild Huntress of the Mississippi. 'Aha!' says Catherine, 'We will change cloths—and I will take the waxen mask back myself.' Scene changes. Conway and Curly having heard somehow that a consignment of rubies from Burma is coming per mail tonight for Mrs. Paton, resolve to rob the mail. Meanwhile there is other fish to fry. One of these is Mrs. Paton, who implores Conway not to desert her. 'Fool! you are no wife of mine!' says he. 'Your husband was living when I married you!' 'Then he is alive!' 'No; he died last night!' 'Where—O, where?' 'Here!' says the miscreant, pulling open the curtain of an alcove and disclosing the semblance of a corpse laid out upon a bed. Mrs. Paton gives a wild shriek, and falls senseless. 'Now, if that don't driv'er her mad, I'm a bad judge,' sneers Conway, as he turns on his heel. Catherine disguised as Begorra, has heard all, and now enters. Conway offers her a glass of sherry. 'Do you object to smoking?' 'No.'—'Thanks.' Catherine joins Conway in a cigarette—and then shows him that she knows all! He secretly puts poison in her sherry, and Curly advances from behind a screen with a rope to strangle her. Catherine produces a revolver, and makes the game— even all. 'Fool! You are a dead woman! that sherry was poisoned, and, being this being thus, I will tell you that I did murder your brother, and that Paton is alive and innocent' etc. 'Aha!' says Catherine, 'At last you are in my power!' 'Fool! Where is your witness?' 'Here!' shrieks Mrs. Paton, who has revived during these proceedings. Discomfiture of

150. *The Referee*, (21 August 1887).

Conway and change of scene. N.B.— The poison was only aniseed (fraudulently supplied by the artful doctor), and the corpse was only Curly, disguised in Bigorra's wax mask.

It is now time to rob the mail, and Conway and Curly wait for the cart upon a lonely road. A shot is heard 'off,' and presently Conway and Curly rush on dragging the mailcart man, whom they bash till he falls senseless. Mailcart (and horse) walk to the center of stage, and Curly holds horse's head. Conway freezes to mail-bags, and goes over them secundum artem. 'Aha! here is the packet!' Enter Catherine, the Doctor, and several policemen. They fall upon Conway, and convey him to prison. Catherine, in order to show her agility, jumps up on the mailcart and drives it off.[151]

This gave Amy Steinberg as Catherine a chance to get in one of the humorous tag lines John would write for her. As she is in the process of starting up the mailcart, a chance question stops her: "What will they say? A female driving the mail!" Her answer is obvious: "Don't they always do it?"; and admidst shouts of laughter the curtain falls on the middle act.

Presently there is a terrible storm off Swansea, and the tank is again exposed to view. It now represents some of the Bristol Channel. Mumbles Head is thereabouts, but where is not quite clear, for it is a wild night.

A Royal Mail Steamer is in trouble somewhere, and it is known that Paton redivivus is on board. Rockets are fired. Agony is piled up. Suddenly a lifeboat (built expressly by builders to the National Lifeboat Institution) appears on the tank. Though the Bristol Channel is here comparatively calm, probably owing to Mumbles Head breaking the force of the ocean surges, the lifeboat—full of passengers—rolls and pitches terribly. I fancy they threw overboard one of the passengers to lighten the boat, for presently a man was seen swimming ashore with a neat overhand stroke. Heroic conduct of three women, who haul him ashore. Perhaps he was Paton. Let us hope so! The curtain fell to thunders of applause, which were renewed when a few seconds after it rose to another tableau representing the morning after the wreck.[152]

The final scene, representing the ocean off Swansea, eclipses all the others. The mail steamer has drifted on shore in a storm And while the lifeboat is putting off to it, waifs from the wreck, among them being Colonel Paton (who was not executed after all by the rebels), float towards the shore and are rescued by his wife and Wade's sister, who stand waist deep in the turbid water, among the rocky boulders.[153]

The seaweed used to give authenticity to this scene was especially imported to London each day.

---

151. *The Referee*, (21 August 1887).
152. *The Referee*, (21 August 1887).
153. *The People*, (21 August 1887).

Assuming that it is necessary to put the Irrawaddy and the Bristol Channel on the stage, it is difficult to see how it could be done better. The acting is about up to average Standard form. Miss Amy Steinberg as the all-conquering Catherine played brightly and humorously, and her views on matrimony pleased the audience hugely.[154]

It is a given, in theatrical things, that after an aesthetic style, technique, or form has been popular for a decade or so, it runs out of dynamic force; the consequence of this is that it gradually becomes a caricature of itself. You wonder if the Douglasses really were serious or whether they were beginning to laugh at it themselves.

When the Americans heard about it, somewhat after the fact, John Douglass saw a chance to make some money from a whole new, as yet unexposed, multitude. While *The Royal Mail* continued at the Standard John T. Douglass had readied its replacement, and had gone to America to rehearse *A Dark Secret* for its Philadelphia opening.

John Cobbe informs us that he has secured the American rights to *The Royal Mail* for the Anglo-American Attraction Agency, of which he is the English manager. Cobbe's American colleague produced *A Dark Secret*—tank and all—at the Walnut Street Theatre, Philadelphia, on September 5, 1887. John Douglass is to go out and put the

finishing touches at rehearsal. They have engaged Teemer and Hosmer, the well known oarsmen, to appear on the tank in the Henley Regatta scene.[155]

Back at the Standard *Tongue of Slander* was opened, 17 October 1887. Written by T. G. Warren and "improved" by John T. Douglass. This relatively old-fashioned heroine imperiled melodrama utilized the tank only in the last scene.

Picture, then, the inner harbour of a seaport town, the lighthouse in the distance, the wharves, the drawbridges, and the vessels at their moorings—a kind of idealized Ramsgate. Thither the heroine is lured, and, having secured the secret of the villain she is pounced upon by a couple of desperate men. They overpower her and drag her screaming along the tottering bridges of the quay, and then there she is thrust backwards into the water. There is no doubt about it; in she goes. The splash is a real splash. Battling and struggling, she swims to the slippery side of the quay, when, in an exhausted state, she is thrust again into the dark water. Whereupon the villain is shot, and the hero appears to rescue his beloved. He takes a splendid header, and, admidst the frantic cheers of the audience, he goes under; he swims to the drowning woman, clutches at her, a boat puts off, and the pair are rescued. . . . *The Tongue of Slander* is not so bad as such plays go. It wants concentration and unity of purpose. It is interesting by fits, and

154. *The Referee*, (21 August 1887).
155. *The Referee*, (21 August 1887).

Fig. 176. A North London Railway 2-4-2T "Scotchman" locomotive built in 1864–1865. This train is on the Liverpool Street Line that passed the west side of the Standard Theatre. *From A.S.J.*

starts, and is not wholly satisfactory as regards construction and sustained interest. We get a little bit of *Old Robin Gray*, a scrap of *Othello*, a scene from *Peril*, and a recollection of *Editha's Burglar*; but the acting is good. . .[156]

Amy Steinberg was not in this production, having probably gone to America with John. The play only managed a two-week run. Richard Douglass, left in charge, rushed the stock tank company of actors into a revival of *Colleen Bawn* with the tank

and the scenery for *The Royal Mail* used for the Lake of Killarney scene. This sustained the operation to the panto.

Fe Fi Fo Fum; or, Harlequin Jack the Giant Killer was the Douglasses' last pantomime. The scenes were supposed to be a child's dream on Christmas Eve: a snow scene by moonlight, Hemstead Heath with a crowd of Donkeys, holiday makers, and two trained elephants, Jack and Jenny. But, the main attraction was still the transformation

156. *The Daily Telegraph*, (22 October 1887).

scene.

Elsewhere the transformation scene may have lost much of its special glory; at the Standard it still holds its own as the great spectacular attraction of the evening's scenes.[157]

The spring of 1888 was the end for the Douglass dynasty at the Standard. After the pantomime closed, Sims Reeves gave several of his farewell performances to the old house in February. Then a new sensation drama was introduced. In *The Lucky Shilling*, a villain gives a poor girl a counterfeit shilling. For passing it she gets a year's imprisonment. She suffers many trials ending with her being shut up in a lunatic asylum. Her problems become solved through the agency of the villain's wife who has vowed vengeance on him for obvious reasons. She becomes an amateur detective and discovers and thwarts all his plots.

It is not the piece itself so much as the scenery that is looked to here, and thus St. Martin's Le-Grand with real mail carts—a railroad goods station with capabilities for shunting [freight cars] drawn by a real locomotive, and the capture and death of Fleming on the goods train—and a scene in which four rooms are shown at once; of the

Fig. 177. A Great Eastern Railway 0-6-0 switch engine. This is the type of locomotive and freight cars that Richard Douglass would have built for *The Lucky Shilling*, February of 1888. *From A.S.J.*

157. *The Illustrated Sporting and Dramatic News*, (1 January 1887).

Fig. 178. The characters in *The Lucky Shilling***, 3 March 1888.** *From the Illustrated Sporting and Dramatic News.*

two upper, one is occupied by a gang of coiners, and the other with an attempt to murder the sailor, the lower ones representing the cells of an asylum, with raving lunatic and revolt against the madhouse keeper—these formed the attraction, and that it would be an impossibility for such various characters to be all under one roof did not appear to strike the audience as incongruous. Miss Amy Steinberg filled her role of female detective in which she assumes various disguises, to perfection. Miss Stella Brereton as Hester. . . [was] deserving of praise.[158]

The various reviews of this play chafe and strain against the scenic realism. This sort of criticism had begun the year before, and it became clear that the critics had had enough even if the

158. *Dramatic Notes*, (25 February 1888).

314

audiences had not. The next step in naturalistic production technique was becoming obvious. The characters and the dialogue needed to be believable; plots needed to be like real life instead of cartoons of the most sensational crimes of the time. Yet, even with the new requirements becoming clear, the critics in the same breath could still commend the railway engine and switching of the freight cars in the rail yard for their accuracy (figs. 176-178).

One critic did sum up the problem of the sensation effects:

> It takes an inordinately long time between acts to get the stage ready for them, and when they come the sole reward for one's waiting is a subdued picture in the theatre of what one can see a good deal better outside . . . it is not worth either the trouble or the money in comparison with the opportunities for genuine emotion which the competent playwright ought to find in humanity itself.[159]

Despite this criticism (and also harsh words about the characters and plot development of the script), the critics found the acting enjoyable.

> I do not think I ever met a murderer whom I regarded with less abhorrence than I did Mr. W. H. Day, the triply-dyed villain here. Having killed the uncle of Hester Wyatt and claimed his name and money, he sends the young lady to jail; proposes to marry her, although he has a wife already; hunts her down as she seeks a livelihood; confines her

and her long lost father in a lunatic asylum; shoots her protectress, a female detective— and yet I was quite sorry when, after a scramble over a goods train, he was ultimately shot himself. The heroine, very fitly played by Miss Stella Brereton, ought to have won my sympathy. She suffered all that I have related, and was very graceful and nice about her suffering. But I fear I did not feel for them as I ought to have, because she endured a great deal more than any sensible girl should have endured from villains whose iniquity was so perfectly obvious. The assistant scoundrel, Erasmus Percival Flight in the playbill, will be understood from his name. He is a very traditional sort of rascal—does all the dirty work, but does it jocularly. Mr. Pardon plays the part

Fig. 179. John Thomas Douglass in the tank, with Richard Douglass in the background. *From Entr'Acte.*

159. *The Illustrated Sporting and Dramatic News*, (3 March 1888).

with too much self-consciousness for my liking. Flight is a sinner of even a worse type than his colleague Fleming. He has been imprisoned everywhere for everything, except for being too funny by half, which is his fault at the Standard. Among his many crimes is that of bigamy. It is this offense which makes an enemy for him and his colleague, of his second wife, who to their ultimate confusion becomes a detective. Miss Amy Steinberg takes the part. She assumes a number of female characters with considerable success—an old French beggar is especially good. But, like other stage detectives, she puts off everything until the last moment. . . The scene in which the madhouse is shown in section is perhaps the nearest approach to sensation that the piece

Fig. 180. John Thomas Douglass. *From the Entr'Acte Annual.*

affords. In the fourth [room]—the deserted wife of Fleming—tries to reach the trembling Hester by straining and biting at her rattling and yielding chain.[160]

Another reviewer found this scene too much to handle. After mentioning the railway yard, and switching trains, and the mail delivery dock scene, with the men in their scarlet coats driving the night mails, he said:

> However to make up for the quiet display of incidents of modern life we have a terrific scene of outrage as displayed in the four compartments of the London Lunatic asylum. Here, we may presume, realism ends and imagination begins; for we see at one glance two çoiners at work, an innocent sailor being drugged by a comic scoundrel, a sister of charity thrashing a hospital nurse, and a chained lunatic endeavouring to tear an innocent girl limb from limb, as both writhe and struggle on the straw [fig. 178]. Most uncomplimentary remarks from the Standard gallery are hurled at the head of the woman with the whip, who might contribute an extra chapter to Mr. Camden Hotten's celebrated work on 'Flagellation' as practiced in ancient and modern times.[161]

The play seems a parody of Boucicault with echoes of *Jonathan Bradford* (1833)(the four rooms). Despite the serious attention to realistic displays of contemporary places, all concerned were probably saturated with the form.

John T. Douglass was distracted by the tour of *A Dark Secret* with its tank. In fact, it was making a deal of money while the Standard was not. He allowed the affairs there to slide; and Richard became the sole licensee, probably for purposes of the sale of the building, on 28 September 1888. *The Lucky Shilling* ran just five weeks, to be followed by visiting companies and a few nights of the stock company in Shakespeare with Amy Steinberg for leading roles. The Douglasses closed forever their operations at the old National Standard Theatre 16 June 1888, just a few months short of forty years of family ownership. They had even out-lasted the Conquest family of the Grecian Theatre fame.

160. *The Illustrated Sporting and Dramatic News*, (3 March 1888).
161. Unidentified clipping, (25 February 1888).

15

EPILOGUE, ADVENTURES WITH A TANK

In October of 1888, the Standard Theatre was again offered for auction. The catalogue gives particulars about the alterations made between 1867 and 1888. The dimensions of interest are: proscenium, 34 feet each way, capacity 4200, average box-office take £200 per night; the stage was sixty feet on a side, fitted with first and second fly galleries, grave traps, vampire traps, and five sink traps.

The bidding only reached £31,000, and the property was again withdrawn as it had been in 1882 (the reserve was said to be £60,000). It was finally re-auctioned on December 17th, and the high bid of Andrew Melville was reluctantly accepted. It may have been about the same as the high bid of October. This money was then divided among the living relatives of John Douglass Senior, his sisters, brothers, Thomas and George, his sons, Fred, Henry, John Thomas, (Samuel) Richard, Arthur, and their sister Isabella.

Once the Standard Theatre was out of their hands, Richard Douglass moved his scenery painting company to the Grand Theatre in Islington, where he remained until after 1909. John T. Douglass possessed the tank, which was made of copper, and was portable in sections. He and Amy took it and several of their tank dramas on extensive tours. *A Dark Secret* was the principal production. It opened in Philadelphia at the Walnut Street Theatre in September of 1887, then toured the United States; back in England at the Surrey, Easter time of 1888, and in 1890; also the Marylebone, the Pavilion, and Sydney Australia in 1890; the Britannia in London, Vienna, Berlin, and in Hamburg in 1891; Milan, Antwerp, and in Amsterdam in 1892; back in London at the Britannia, then the Elephant and Castle in 1894; the Princess's in 1895; Stratford, Antwerp, Ghent, Brussels,

318

Fig. 181. John Thomas Douglass, (1842-1917). *From the Rose Lipman Library, Hackney.*

and Amsterdam in 1896; and finally in Antwerp in 1898.

In America, Jefferson and Taylor, two impresarios, bought the rights to the play and had a second tank built to John Douglass's specifications. The original tank was not used in America. As stated above, John and Amy came to the

United States to supervise the staging for the Philadelphia opening. After that engagement, the play went to Cincinnati, Ohio, Portland, Oregon, New York City, and Boston, all during 1889. In the American version, various "improvement sensations" were added to the Henley scene. As the institution of Henley, it didn't mean much to the American audiences. A steam launch called "The Dark Secret," was built at the cost of $1,000 by a Boston firm. The popular champion oarsmen Teemer and George H. Hosmer were hired to have an actual race in the play. Local champion life-guards leaped in and out of the tank, saving people, dogs, and children. Captain William A. Andreus, and his little twelve-foot sailing dory, also called "Dark Secret," attempted a solo west-to-east Atlantic crossing. They were picked up after a month because of straying off course, and storm damage. Then he and his boat were added to the Henley scene.[162] The villains still tried to drown May Joyce in the tower's tank, and bash the heroine in the bed. All of this mightily pleased the American press.[163]

Life on the road is no bed of roses, as any theatre person knows. Travelling around with a huge copper tank in pieces and directing local actors in different languages made for many adventures. John T. Douglass told of some, perhaps the most extreme, but

162. *The Daily Telegraph*, (22 October 1887).
163. Mr. E. S. Stewart of the old Boston firm, Charles H. Stewart & Co. Theatrical Scenery, sent me advertising posters of the Boston production. He also gave me information from his father's diary about the installation of the tank.

none the less typical.

They manage these things better abroad,' is a sentence frequently in the mouth of the average Englishman, but I question if the remark applies to 'things theatrical.' In some countries, as far as my experience goes, the bogus manager is as much in evidence on the Continent as in England or America. During my foreign tour with the tank drama, *A Dark Secret,* I was unfortunate enough to meet with at least two specimens of 'the thorough-going, down-on-his-luck-bit, but wouldn't pay-if-he-could' style of manager christened by our Yankee cousins as 'Mr.Bogus.'

One was a veritable diplomat—suave, winning, obliging (no hard words could make him lose his temper, always on his dignity when asked for money; always virtuously in haste (verbally) to discharge his legitimate indebtedness, and equally ready to excuse or explain his reasons for not letting his actions justify his words. In fact, no man ever possessed a more marvellous way of evading his responsibilities without in any way actually repudiating them. He was tall, handsome, so gentlemanly in his bearing, so liberal to his friends, so generous to his employees, that, although he was deliberately getting deeper and deeper into our debt, yet neither my partner nor myself dared to upbraid him for broken promises, or undue extravagance with moneys that should have been ours. So absolutely were we fascinated by this German Jeremy Diddler that, on leaving him (he came to the railway station to see us off, and never mentioned his debt), we cordially grasped the hand he extended to each of us in turn, and thanked him for his hearty good wishes for our safe journey. Yes, grasped the hand in friendship that had already picked our pockets of more than a hundred pounds. In his way he was a genius.

The second specimen was 'made in Holland.' A real Dutch actor-manager, a native of Amsterdam, whose acquaintance I made at a cafe in Antwerp in the spring of 1892, under the following circumstances: *A Dark Secret* was being played at the Flemish Theatre in Antwerp to immense business, and the manager (a charming gentleman) asked us to prolong the arrangement to the end of the season (another month), and then take the same cast to Amsterdam for our season there. We should have unhesitatingly accepted such a capital proposition at once, but we were due in Amsterdam in three weeks' time; it was therefore necessary to write to Mr. Bogus (whom I will designate Van Tromp) and ask him if he would oblige us by postponing our opening night for one week; to add weight to our appeal we hinted at being able to arrange to bring over the whole of the company then playing the piece in Antwerp. Two days after (preceded by a telegram) the manager arrived, attended by his friend and adviser, Mr. Bloc, who had acted as our agent and drawn up the business contracts between us.

From the first I instinctively had a strange dislike for Von Tromp. He was a tall man of very dark complexion and about fifty years of age, with long hair, a bald patch on the top of his head, and an unshaven face. He wore a soft felt hat and a very short kind of pilot coat. His suit of faded brown, carelessly folded neckcloth, ungloved hands, and elephantine boots did not inspire one with those feelings of respectful awe which ought to surround the ordinary individual on finding himself, for the first time, in the presence of the 'Henry Irving' of Holland, for such he was introduced to us by Bloc, his friend and our agent.

The great man declined to alter his date. I can see him now as he stood by the cafe window (as if posing for an instantaneous photograph) and delivered himself thus: 'My own theatre' (mark the possessive) 'not being large enough for your water scenes, I have specially taken the Parc Schouwburg. I have engaged a powerful orchestra, and gone to considerable expense to mount and produce *A Dark Secret* in a manner worthy the importance of the work'—I bowed, as he continued—'and of the traditions of the world-famed Van Tromp family, to which I have the Honour to belong, I cannot allow a moment's delay. As to your preposterous notion,' he added, 'of bringing over the Flemish company, native Dutch artistes,' he continued with withering sarcasm, 'would scorn to be compared with such actors as those of the Flemish school. No, gentlemen, no,' he observed in quieter terms, 'I keep everything in my own hands.' (I found the truth of that later on.) 'My system,' he urged, 'is personal. We Dutch have a proverb, The master's eye makes the horse grow fat. I never leave the stage whilst I am able to occupy it myself.' Then the great man paused, his eye with fine frenzy rolling, and, altering his pose with dramatic elegance, he continued: 'I play the lead and heroes generally. My wife plays the juveniles; she has done so for thirty years past. Her mother is our heavy lady. My sister trains the chorus and combines the grisettes; whilst my two sons divide the heavies and low comedy, thus forming the nucleus of a powerful company. As to the minor parts,' he observed thoughtfully, 'you will find them filled by specially selected artistes; artistes,' he repeated raising his voice, 'Dutch artistes, let me remind you.' (Dutch natives occurred to me.) And folding his arms theatrically, the roused tragedian desired the agent to draw Mynheer Dooglis's attention to the penalty clause of the agreement, whereby either party breaking the contract was to forfeit to the other party the sum of three thousand guilders (about £250 sterling); certainly more than from appearances anyone would have cared to credit Mr. Van Tromp with the possession of.

However he continued to talk loudly of the splendid production he contemplated, of his great reputation, and laid particular stress upon his command of a large and influential following. 'I am so well known,' he said; 'My name on the bill alone is sufficient guarantee.' We found, to out cost, his name was well known!!! and he certainly did command a large and influential following—of creditors.

It is necessary here to state in brief the terms of the contract we had entered into, that the reader may fully understand the trap into which we, as aliens, had fallen. We agreed to provide a translation in the Dutch language of the English drama *A Dark Secret*; to provide the boating costumes; to fix the tank, and in fact, to supply the scenery, boats, steam-launch, and everything belonging to or required for the two great water spectacles, Henley Regatta and the Upper Thames—with picture posters. Of course, our principal expense would be incurred before the curtain rose on the first performance—viz., for the construction of the tank, the lead lining, waterways, erection of the boilers to heat the water, and fixing the scenery. As we were to receive 50 per cent of the receipts nightly, it follows we had naturally based our calculations of possible profit on the minimum number of performances that would pay our outlay, reckoning the nightly receipts at one-half the holding capacity of the house. Consequently Mr. Van Tromp was bound to run the piece at least twenty nights.

A week before the opening night in Amsterdam I arrived in that city with my staff of workmen from London to commence fitting up the tank and scenery sent on from Antwerp. Arrived at the theatre (Parc Schouwburg), I looked about in vain for any traces of those vast preparations the great man had boasted of. Then I questioned the stage carpenter (a man of Falstaffian proportions who spoke a little French and less English) as to where Mynheer Van Tromp's 'a'elier' was. 'Never knew he had one,' answered the man.' 'But' I returned, 'he told me that all the staff of this theatre were engaged three weeks ago on the scenery and appointments for *Een Dunkle Geheim*. . . .' 'Why, you are green, governor,' said Falstaff, with a merry twinkle in his eye. 'We'd be very sorry if we had to look to him for our screws. Why, lor sir!' he continued almost bursting with laughter, 'he don't mean to spend a shilling on the show, if he had one, which I'm a bit doubtful of.' I own I was fairly staggered at the revelation, but I determined to know the worst at once. So I had recourse to that never-failing English method of starting an acquaintanceship—I suggested a drink. Falstaff accepted with alacrity; and in the cafe opposite I learned enough in ten minutes about the antecedents and theatrical history of Mr. Van Tromp to fully comprehend his anxiety that my attention should be drawn to the foregoing clause of the contract. Little

by little the truth dawned upon me that he counted on our being so thoroughly disgusted with his mode of doing business that we should decline to open on the specified date; then he was prepared to immediately appeal to the law to make us pay the penalty under our agreement. I was told he had boasted of how he would do the Britisher. Anyhow, it really seemed, from the sequel, as if he cared nothing for the success or failure of the piece, so long as he secured hard cash from us for breach of contract. Sadly I turned from the opera house and took a tram-car to 'The Dam,' determined to see one of the rehearsals which our agent assured us were progressing satisfactorily at Mr. Van Tromp's own theatre.

On making enquires for this temple of Thespis, I was directed to a narrow, dirty street called 'The Nes' (visitors to Amsterdam will recognize the locality). Almost every house in the street is a free-and-easy, sing-song, or low music hall—no charge made for admission, but you have to pay for drinks! Nearly at the other end of this disreputable street was the Tancredi (after the disclosures made by Falstaff, it was only what I expected to find the Irving of Holland's own theatre— no better than an English penny gaff). Although not astonished, I must confess my heart sank within me as I entered the dirty, grimy portals of the building, and the thought uppermost in my mind was: 'The man has already broken his contract; but what possible chance have we of getting even 250 pence out of Mr. Bogus? It wants thinking of. What ought to do?' I passed unnoticed into the back of the pit, from whence I could watch the rehearsal going on on the stage and yet be unseen myself by any of the actors! Truly, no English author and entrepreneur was ever in such a humiliating fix. Ye gods! The company—the family nucleus was there in all its hideous deformity. I could not believe I was living at the end of the nineteenth century! No, it must be Richardson's Show redivivus, without the talent that much-abused institution developed in its time. In half an hour I was out having a brandy at my hotel, and consulting with my partner as to whether we had not better sacrifice the forfeit-money and get out of the country rather than be mixed up in such an exhibition. The result of our interview was, my partner saw his consul (the Hungarian). I saw the British, a thoroughly genial, business-like, typical Englishman, who gave me some excellent advice, and recommended me a lawyer, who told me: 'Do not let the breach of contract come from your side. Endure any snubs, put up with any inconvenience—but carry out your arrangement, and insist under any circumstances on twenty shows.'

'But,' I urged, 'We are prepared to pay the penalty and have done with the matter.' 'But will you have done with the matter then?' he asked. 'I imagine so, ' I replied. 'Then undeceive yourself,' he answered. 'If an alien breaks a contract made with a native Dutchman he can be sent to prison for six weeks, and no appeal.'

'What?' I exclaimed, 'Rob us of our money and lock us up as well? What humbug!' 'Very likely; but still a fact. 'Then,' said my companion, 'Van Tromp has broken the contract now; let us see how he will enjoy six weeks in jail.' 'You are not a Dutchman, I presume?' asked the lawyer, addressing my partner. 'No, an Austrian subject,' said I. 'Mr. Richard Pitrot, the mimic, ' I added, introducing my partner. 'Exactly,' said the limb of the law. 'In that case you can do nothing against Mr. Van Tromp; neither can Mr. Douglass.' 'Why?' we exclaimed in astonishment. 'Why!' echoed the lawyer. 'Because only a native can punish a native. Your contract should have been drawn up as between one Dutchman and another. As it is,' he added significantly, 'do not let the breach come from your side. Pocket your pride, gentlemen, good morning.'

I pass over the effect of this advice, but we took it. . . . The dress rehearsal came. No furniture. The eminent tragedian remarked, in reply to my remonstrance, 'They will come to see me—not the furniture.' The extensive scenery he had prepared we were not permitted to behold 'at rehearsal,' he explained, but I heard Falstaff, inform 'The Eminent One' that the nearest thing he could let him have for 'The Restaurant at Henley' was the Banqueting Scene from Le Prophete.

The first night came. The location was excellent, and the house very full. The money taken was over 1300 guilders (about, roughly, £100). In fear and trembling I saw the curtain rise. The first scene was enough. The great actor-manager appeared as Jonas Norton, wearing the self same seedy brown suit and felt hat in which I had first met him at Antwerp. He had evidently walked over from his own theatre and onto the stage of the other house without changing his clothes or troubling to make-up. Then came the antique heroine, and then—I could stand no more. I rushed hastily out into the front lobby, where evidently something was wrong. My partner Pitrot (in the elongated box called in Continental theatres 'The Control') was surrounded by a mob of nearly sixty people, all clamouring and gesticulating vociferously for money (as well as I could make out). 'What is this?' I asked. 'Oh, Mr. Douglass,' returned Pitrot, 'see here. All these people want their share of the receipts.' 'But who are they?' I inquired. 'Van Tromp's creditors from the Tancredi,' said Pitrot, 'and he has sent word around to the cashier to pay them, but I've taken our half first, and they say I've no business to, and I must give it up.' At this moment Van Tromp himself appeared, and called us all the dreadful names he could think of. As he spoke in Dutch, which neither my partner nor myself understood, it didn't much matter, and of course we felt very hurt when it was translated to us later in the evening. How dared we to take his money!! WE ought to have waited until he was prepared to pay at the end of the week. Then he appealed to me in French: 'Was it just to rob his creditors of what he had promised them for weeks, viz., the entire receipts of the first night of *A Dark Secret*? Come, Herr Dooglis, tell Mr. Pitrot to return it, and I pay you next Friday.' Pitrot, however, on hearing the suggestion, cleverly came to the rescue. 'Herr Van Tromp,' he put in (speaking to the tragedian in German), 'here is our contract. It expressly says, 'our share to be taken nightly, and we must not break our contract on any account. You know how particular you were. We feel for the disappointment of your creditors, but if we yielded now, as our inclinations prompt us (Pitrot was visibly affected here), you would be justified in claiming from us the penalty under our agreement.' That settled it then; but the creditors turned up again a few nights after.

Needless to recapitulate the blunders of that opening night. Sufficient to record that the two water scenes were received with frantic enthusiasm, but with everything else the audience were disgusted. The press praised the water scenes, and abused the piece. 'Poor author!' Strange to say, the business continued excellent during the first week; it dropped a bit the second week, and then Van Tromp developed his scheme to make us break our agreement. The second Sunday he kept the drop down one hour between the acts, because he was playing in a new piece at the Tancredi. Then he cut the extras (those occupying the boats in the regatta scene) down to one-fourth. Then he said the gas was too expensive to allow the boiler of the steam launch to be heated by gas, so he cut off the steam. Then the water rate was too heavy to allow so much water for the rain shower, so the rain was cut off. Another night two characters were cut out. Then the band was an exorbitant item for him to find; he could not afford an orchestra, he said, so the music was cut off. We protested; but still we wouldn't break the contract. Then the scenemen struck for wages. The piece had to be played in two scenes, besides the two water scenes which Pitrot and I set ourselves—but we still fulfilled our engagement. In fact we told the agent if there was nothing on the stage and not a soul in the auditorium we should still carry out our contract. Then the actor-manager played his last card.

The valve of the boiler was broken (I have every reason to believe wilfully broken), and it became impossible to get it repaired by the following day, or in time to heat the water for the night. The lady playing May Joyce (prompted by the manager, no doubt) gave me notice at five O'clock that she would not go into the water the next evening unless it was the same temperature as usual. She would play the part, but she would not be thrown into the water. It was clear that, if we could not heat the water in the tank, that made us break our contract, as we had agreed to provide and maintain everything belonging to or required for the two water scenes. The Eminent one had us on toast, and he knew it. We couldn't very well leave the country with all our paraphernalia in the theatre, and I could get no double in Amsterdam to do the water scene. The only likely one I spoke to told me frankly she dared not, as she would have been boycotted all round after. There was one chance, and one chance only: could I get someone from England who had played the part? Pitrot suggested Miss Millais [J. T. Douglass's daughter]. I wired my wife 'Send Ida Millais in time to play water scene, *Dark Secret*, Amsterdam, tomorrow night.' That wire reached Surbiton 9:30 on the Wednesday evening. Miss Millais started from Holborn Viaduct Station 8:30 on Thursday morning; wired me from Flushing, 'Arrived at six O'clock,' so as to let me know she was on the road. I met her at Central Station, Amsterdam, at 9:50, and at 10:10 she was on the stage at the Parc Schouwburg, playing the part like a living marionette (i.e. the Dutch lady speaking the lines for her from the side). Her water performance was tremendously applauded, and she continued playing the part until the end of the run. It was a notable feat, besides which it saved us breaking our contract, and enabled us to checkmate the last attempt made to impose upon us by the impecunious manager.[164]

As one can see the Douglass family remained very active in theatrical circles. Richard painted scenery for theatres all over the United Kingdom, in his workshop next to the Grand Theatre. In addition, he created massive panoramas in the displays at the Earl's Court Exhibition grounds (figs.189–195).

Stella Brereton and Amy Steinberg occasionally took character roles in their "special lines" until about 1910. Amy also began to publish dramatic scripts in her own name. She copyrighted several including *Our Climate* (1888), *My Uncle* (1889), and *My Mother* (1890). She lived on in relative obscurity until 1920.

John Thomas Douglass, after finishing with the tours of *A Dark Secret* in 1898, helped to stage pageants in South America, Vienna, and at the Earl's Court. There his *Fighting the Flames*, about firemen, was considered thrilling. He also served as the stage manager of the Princess's Theatre in 1895–1896. He was asked to stage his own scripts at various provincial theatres during this same period. When the London Coliseum opened in 1906, he was stage manager for a while. In the period between 1896 and 1910 he was rather like a modern stage director.

John and Amy had several children. Byron Douglass—the character actor, and Ida Millais had toured for many years, the latter

---

164. John T. Douglass "The Impecunious Manager," *Era Almanac* (London, 1894), pp. 63–66.

Fig. 182. John Thomas and Richard Douglass. *From the Entr'Acte.*

Fig. 183. Amy Steinberg (Alice Rachel Koning), (1850-1920). *From The Theatre.*

accompanying Bransby Williams on his first visit to Canada.[165] The other son, Gordon, forsook the theatrical profession to become a consulting engineer. They were seldom brought to the theatre during the Standard years; this is why they are not mentioned before.

Poor John's end was indeed tragic. He lived in Hammersmith, and seldom visited the neighborhood which held such happy associations for him, but his elderly sister, Mrs. Roach, being an invalid, and needing a bath chair, John suggested an old firm he knew in Curtain Road, and promised to purchase it for her. For this purpose, with cheque in his pocket, and in excellent spirits he started forth on what proved to be his last journey, for it chanced to be the day [13 June 1917] selected by the Germans to attempt their first daylight air-raid over London. About twenty aeroplanes whizzed through the air. John was about to enter the shop—a bomb dropped—and all that remained of the brilliant dramatist, wonderful producer, devoted husband, and loyal friend was an almost unrecognizable mass.

Alas! Poor John. Was it fate that lured him east only to find death awaiting him within sight of his beloved theatre? Perhaps if that theatre had been situated in the charmed circle of the West, his genius might have been more fully appreciated, but, unfortunately, most of his best work was accomplished in the East End, therefore seldom treated seriously by contemporary

Fig. 184. Albert Douglass (1882–1940), call boy at seven, prompter at seventeen, assistant stage manager at twenty, stage manager at twenty-three. *From Memories of Mummers.*

critics, who preferred to reserve their praise until his original ideas were rehashed and served up the other side of Temple Bar—[166]

In her book on the Conquest family, Frances Fleetwood describes her three best friends Ida Millais (ca.1872–1952), Laura Conquest, and Cissy Farrall. They were all appearing in John's *A Dark Secret*.

Ida, then about eighteen, played the persecuted Nelly; Cissy was a gipsy girl, and Laura a vagrant. The three, who were all

---

165. Bransby Williams (1870–1961) was a mimic, actor and impersonator of Charles Dickens. He first appeared as a music hall entertainer in Shoreditch in 1896. About 1923 he went on tour to Canada.
166. Douglass, *Memories of Mummers*, pp. 22–23. This raid by the Moth bombers was probably aimed at the rail yard, but it was ineffectual, and the death of John T. Douglass, and a very few other poor souls was about its only result. Their obituaries were suppressed to confuse the German Intelligence Office as to the extent of the damage.

Fig. 185. The gallery door of the National Standard Theatre in Fairchild Street (now George Street), around 1915. *From the Rose Lipman Library, Hackney.*

taking singing lessons from the same master at the Guildhall School of Music, were great friends. Charming young girls, each in her different way: Ida with her innocent, open face and light-brown hair (it is white now, but still thick and curly—and sixty years have not faded the forget-me-not blue of her eyes); Cissy, pale and quiet, with dark curls tied back by a ribbon, usually sitting in a corner, her head bent over a book or script; and Laura filling the dressing-room with laughter, chatter and snatches of song. She was slightly older than the others, and she had a pull over them, for she had just become engaged. And she was pretty, in an obvious style that eclipsed her cousin's more subtle good looks: a figure like Clara Dillon's— plump and dainty at the same time; bright gold curls, and a complexion like the pink roses that she loved to wear.

Last left of the 'Three Little Maids from School,' Ida used to smile reminiscently as she recalled Laura's radiant vitality and happiness in those days. Their friendship

Fig. 186. The Standard Theatre as the Olympic Picturedrome, July 1939. *From the Rose Lipman Library, Hackney.*

continued to the end of their lives. Laura died in Brighton in 1950 at the age of eighty and Ida quite suddenly, of a heart attack, in May 1952.[167]

Ida toured for a time in her father's adaptation of *Treasure Island* called *No Man's Land* (Leicester, 1890; Grand, Islington, 1893). It also used the tank.[168]

Albert Douglass describes himself:

To be perfectly candid my youthful career could hardly be called a success. I am credibly informed that I was a 'bonnie baby,' but as Glaxo was not in existence at the time, I am unable to produce a photo in support of this statement. The first time I appeared was in a conventional melodrama. The heroine, in a blinding snowstorm that relentlessly

Fig. 187. The proscenium of the Standard Theatre. *From the Rose Lipman Library, Hackney.*

167. Frances Fleetwood *Conquest*, p. 209.
168. Douglass, *Memories of Mummers*, pp. 31–34. On page 7 of this book, Albert explained his own collection of memorabilia was destroyed before 1924, but on page 18 he said that Ida Millais had her father, J. T. Douglass's, scrapbooks. They may exist somewhere, if they were not destroyed in the Blitz.

pursued her all over the stage, many large flakes sticking firmly in her hair, entered carrying a bundle—(I was the guilty bundle)—and when the great dramatic scene commenced I yelled lustily all through the situation. For ruining this scene I received my notice.

Fred Payne attempted to teach me dancing, but realizing it was a hopeless case gave up in despair. Paul Valentine then took me in hand, followed by George Burt, both of whom agreed with Fred Payne's verdict. Such unanimity is rare. In spite of this trio of 'gloomy deans,' I received a gold medal for dancing (a most undeserved honour) from Brittain Wright when playing in pantomime with that celebrated Adelphi comedian.

Later I became call-boy—'the world's worst' was the opinion of H. J. Turner the prompter. (Poor man how glad he was to get away and open the Gaiety Theatre, Hastings, for Mr. Gaze). At rehearsal, when nearing the entrance of an actor, turner would whisper the name to me, and off I sped to The Unicorn opposite, being quite expert in running my quarry to earth in his favourite bar (saloon on Monday—four-ale department on Friday). Of course the whole tone of the profession has now changed for the better.

I frequently played boy's parts, such as Willie Carlyle, and it seemed strange that no matter who played Archibald the moment he entered I was conscious of a peculiar aroma reminiscent of The Unicorn. Dramatic critics were loud in their praises of these *East*

Fig. 188. The demolition of the Standard Theatre in 1939, looking at the proscenium from the south. *From the Rose Lipman Library, Hackney.*

Lynne productions, waxing enthusiastic over the atmosphere created, but I only remember that when these Archibalds bent over the cot in which I patiently lay awaiting the call to heaven, the atmosphere was calculated to despatch me to my destination without further delay. On pointing out this coincidence to my dad, and enquiring why all my stage fathers sought inspiration in alcohol, he sadly shook his head and said: 'My boy your performance drives them to it.'

My optimistic parents also decided that I should learn the violin, and two famous London musical directors became my tutors: the first Michael Connolly, and then Barry Isaacson struggled with me, and at the end of each term they were in such a nerve-racked condition that it is surprising that both were not certified insane. How well I recall that little front room over the pit entrance in George Street where I had to practice the violin for two hours every day. I never discovered why dad insisted on this, for he always lived on friendly terms with his neighbors. When the Great Mackney was the rage of London, I became the Inimitable Infant Mackney, vide programmes, small bills, and large frames of highly-coloured photographs. For this turn I was taught singing by a young lady who emigrated before any other charge could be brought against her. A small fortune was spent on costumes, songs, music, and other accessories. Result 'a trial turn' and as my turn was indeed a trial—a date book packed from cover to cover with vacant weeks.

At seventeen I became the prompter at the Standard, at twenty assistant stage manager, and at twenty three, stage manager, remaining at one place of amusement for nearly thirty years. I have now been at New Brighton twenty one years—making over fifty years in the theatrical profession—and daily I realize what a lot I have to learn (fig. 184).

One of the younger and perhaps best known members of the family is R. H. (familiarly called Dickey) the comedian and producer. Born in the Standard Theatre he too made his debut as a baby, playing the stolen child in the first act of *The Bohemian Girl*, before he was two years old, the Devilshoof being Richard Temple (afterwards the famous Savoyard), and later this part was played by Aynsley Cook. Dickey's first appearance was more successful than mine—because he was asleep. My dad often related how Lady Bancroft, when playing at the Standard, admired Dickey and graciously insisted on nursing him. I could not help recalling this incident a few months ago when my brother appeared in *Cast* at the Manchester Repertory Theatre. . . and ruminating on the whirligig of time, I found myself thinking how strange the great actress should nurse a future Eccles.

Dickey played every conceivable child's part for years, and when old enough took his share in managing the stage, filling every position to enable him to obtain a sound knowledge of the business. Having written several monologues, notably *A Pantomime in Ten Minutes*, and *A Comic Opera Rehearsal,* his services were much in demand for concerts, and his originality becoming a much discussed topic, Meyer Lutz, well known musical director of the Gaiety Theatre, who was taking a farewell benefit, asked Dickey to appear. Naturally there was a grand array of talent, including nearly all the London stars, but Dickey's success was electrical.

An exceptionally favourable criticism appeared in *The Referee*, and those connected with that popular publication followed it up by offering him the part of Tom Dutton in *The Trumpet Call,* a drama by George R. Sims and Robert Buchanan, about to be produced at the Adelphi. He appeared in this play for over a year—and never looked back—for at the termination of this engagement Arthur Blackmore (of Blackmore's Agency) lured him on to the music halls, a step considered very infra dig in those days.[169]

The old Standard Theatre just about out lasted all the family. Andrew Melville, a theatre proprietor from Birmingham, became the new owner in 1888. He produced melodramas, and pantomimes much in the Douglass tradition, until his death in 1896. His wife and sons continued to operate there until 1907, when they went to the Lyceum. After that the Standard became the Shoreditch Empire, a music hall, until 1926, when it was converted to the Olympic Picturedrome, a cinema (figs.185–186).

In 1939 the Film Syndicate decided the building, now seventy-two years old was too difficult to operate, or modernize, and began to tear it down (figs.187–188). It was to be replaced with a modest-size neighborhood cinema. The architect's colored drawing for this proposed yellow and glass brick building exists in the District Surveyor's Office. The site was beginning to be prepared in 1939 as the war began. The construction stopped. Some of the collected building materials were used to build a bomb-shelter next to the North London Railway Viaduct over Great Eastern Street.

On 19 July 1941 during a massive air raid, that heavily damaged the Bishopsgate railway goods depot across the street, a bomb fell on the site destroying the shelter although no one was inside at the time. After the war, this part of East London no longer had sufficient population to support a cinema as planned. The site was eventually sold.

In the 1970s a petrol station occupied the corner of the land, and other parts became businesses. The railway viaduct is now all that remains of the structures that were used by the theatre. In 1943 Gerald Morice toured many sites of older London entertainment establishments. He said that at the Standard's site:

> . . . all that is left are massive wooden beams (part of the flies machinery), which span what was the stage. The plan of the Standard can be made out. It was an L-shaped building one arm comprising the entrance hall and crush rooms, behind at right angles was the auditorium and stage. It would appear that the scene dock, next to

169. Douglass, *Memories of Mummers*, pp. 34–35.

and in the railway arches is still there. The big opening off the stage into this outbuilding is discernible, though bricked up.[170]

Thus ends the saga of the Standard Theatre and the Douglass family. The Douglasses had controlled the operation of the Standard Theatre just short of forty years. They had produced 10,663 nights of entertainment for the theatre-going public. By 1854, John Douglass Senior had risen, from a humble and little educated actor of nautical roles at outlying theatres to the position of the owner, and manager of, perhaps, the largest theatre in Europe.

After the summer of the Great Exposition of 1851 in the Crystal Palace, Douglass had established an operational pattern that made the bill of fare at the Standard the epitome of the Victorian theatre. This pattern was continued by the Douglass family until about 1874. Then the decline of the neighborhood, and the changes in theatrical aesthetics forced changes in the production techniques.

In a final burst of energy, John Thomas Douglass developed a decade of super scenic, naturalistally staged, sensation melodramas. Real railway locomotives, horses and cabs, fox hunts and pageants, rain showers revolving stages, waterfalls, rivers of real water, and three dimensional settings became central, even if the plots,

dialogue and acting styles remained rooted in older styles.

All through the era of the Douglass management of this huge theatre in an unfashionable suburb, the highest reputation was maintained. The Christmas pantomime, year after year, was described as: "if not the best, surely one of the two or three to see in the whole London area." If one wanted to see opera and other popular musical forms, with the greatest stars, and usually in English, you went to the Standard. The great Christy Minstrels treated the Standard as a summer home.

A comparison of the plays produced at the Standard for a forty-year period reveals the dramas, that were the heart beat of the time, were seen at the Standard. This is true of the performers as well, at least until 1878. If you had not appeared at the Standard, you were not yet an important artist.

The salaries paid at the Standard were high for everyone, even the minor performers. Costumes were of the best quality many being imported from Paris. Yet, because of the huge numbers of loyal audience, the Douglasses were consistently successful at the box office.

Eventually the changes in theatre caught up with the size of the building rendering it out of fashion. Even then, for a good show, the "take" continued to average £200 a night, which in 1888, when the theatre was sold, would have

---

170. *Notes and Queries*, (9 October 1943), p. 224.

added up to about £50,000 a year if the theatre was consistently in use.

The Douglasses themselves were humorous friendly people with high ethics and tact. They represented the best side of Victorian society. This was at a time when many around them bespoke one set of values, while following the opposite in their private lives. It must be true then—the National Standard Theatre was "the standard" for the mid-Victorian theatrical arts.

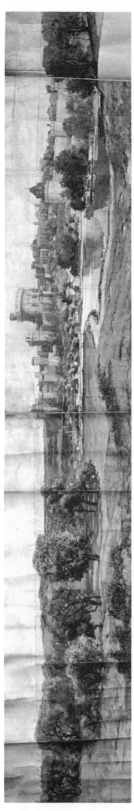

Fig. 189. Panorama of Windsor Castle by Richard Douglass, around 1900. *From A.S.J.*

Fig. 190. Panorama of Warwick Castle from the Avon by Richard Douglass, 1902. *From A.S.J.*

Fig. 191. Panorama of the exit of the rivers in Cornwall by Richard Douglass around 1900. *From A.S.J.*

Fig. 192. Panorama of the rocks at Injce by Richard Douglass, Earl's Court, 1908. *From A.S.J.*

Fig. 193. Panorama of Bothwell Castle from the Clyde, by Richard Douglass, 1903. *From A.S.J.*

Fig. 194. Panorama of the north end of the western section, "Hungarian,"by Richard Douglass Earl' s Court, 1908. *From A.S.J.*

Fig. 195. Panorama "Hungarian 1908," by Richard Douglass. *From A.S.J.*

Fig. 196. Design for a Mediterranean act drop by Richard Douglass. *From A.S.J.*

Fig. 197. Design for an oriental act drop by Richard Douglass. *From A.S.J.*

Fig. 198. Shanklin, the Chine, June 1870, by Richard Douglass, painted while on his honeymoon. *From A.S.J.*

Fig. 199. Shanklin, the Chine, June 1870, by Richard Douglass, painted while on his honeymoon. *From A.S.J.*

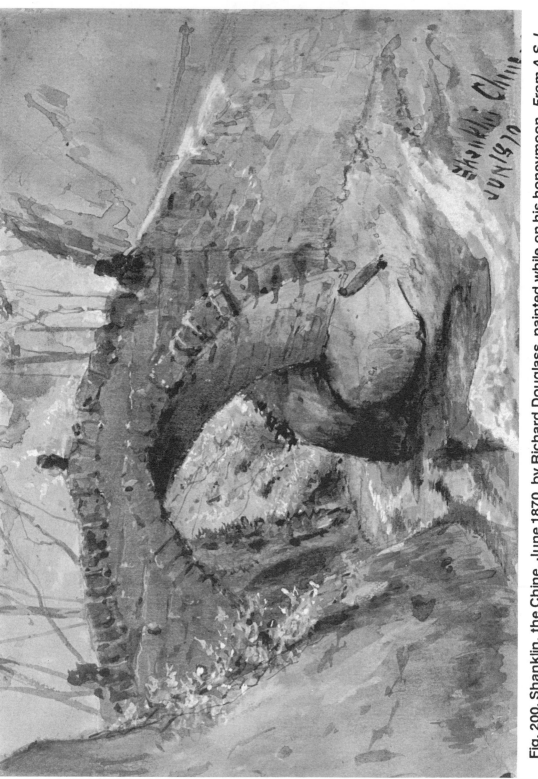

Fig. 200. Shanklin, the Chine, June 1870, by Richard Douglass, painted while on his honeymoon. *From A.S.J.*

APPENDIX 1:

THE DOUGLASS FAMILY

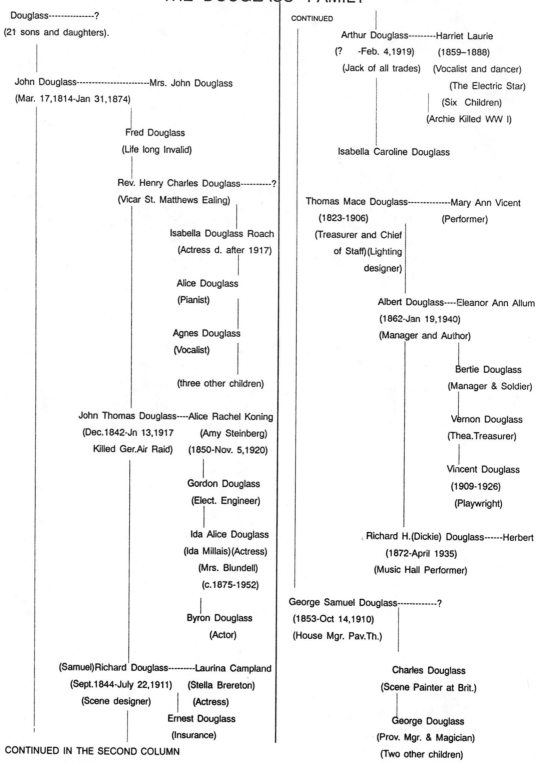

Douglass--------------?

(21 sons and daughters).

John Douglass-----------------------Mrs. John Douglass

(Mar. 17,1814-Jan 31,1874)

Fred Douglass

(Life long Invalid)

Rev. Henry Charles Douglass----------?

(Vicar St. Matthews Ealing)

Isabella Douglass Roach

(Actress d. after 1917)

Alice Douglass

(Pianist)

Agnes Douglass

(Vocalist)

(three other children)

John Thomas Douglass----Alice Rachel Koning

(Dec.1842-Jn 13,1917   (Amy Steinberg)

Killed Ger.Air Raid)   (1850-Nov. 5,1920)

Gordon Douglass

(Elect. Engineer)

Ida Alice Douglass

(Ida Millais)(Actress)

(Mrs. Blundell)

(c.1875-1952)

Byron Douglass

(Actor)

(Samuel)Richard Douglass---------Laurina Campland

(Sept.1844-July 22,1911)   (Stella Brereton)

(Scene designer)   (Actress)

Ernest Douglass

(Insurance)

CONTINUED IN THE SECOND COLUMN

CONTINUED

Arthur Douglass---------Harriet Laurie

(?   -Feb. 4,1919)   (1859–1888)

(Jack of all trades)   (Vocalist and dancer)

(The Electric Star)

(Six Children)

(Archie Killed WW I)

Isabella Caroline Douglass

Thomas Mace Douglass-------------Mary Ann Vicent

(1823-1906)   (Performer)

(Treasurer and Chief

of Staff)(Lighting

designer)

Albert Douglass----Eleanor Ann Allum

(1862-Jan 19,1940)

(Manager and Author)

Bertie Douglass

(Manager & Soldier)

Vernon Douglass

(Thea.Treasurer)

Vincent Douglass

(1909-1926)

(Playwright)

Richard H.(Dickie) Douglass------Herbert

(1872-April 1935)

(Music Hall Performer)

George Samuel Douglass------------?

(1853-Oct 14,1910)

(House Mgr. Pav.Th.)

Charles Douglass

(Scene Painter at Brit.)

George Douglass

(Prov. Mgr. & Magician)

(Two other children)

APPENDIX 2:
PLAYS BY DOUGLASS

JOHN DOUGLASS (1814–1874)

1848 *The Model Pantomime of 1848; or, Harlequin King Coppernose!, and the Fairy of the Golden Temple.*

1849 *Harlequin and the Magic Teapot; or, Chi-Ki Ski Hi, King of the Golden Pagodas.*

1949 *[Too Late?] The Anchor's Weigh'd.* (With Tom Taylor).

1850 *Jolly Jack, or, the Roscius of the Fleet.*

1850 *Harlequin Buttercups and Daisies; or, Great A, Little A, and Bouncing B, the Cat's in the Cupboard and She Can't See.*

1851 *Hoddy Toddy All Head and No Body; or, Harlequin and the Fairy of the Magic Pippin.*

1852 *The Triumph of the Standard; or, Ben and Bob the British Bulldogs.*

1852 *Uncle Tom's Cabin.* (By J. B. Johnstone and or others ?, from H. B. Stowe).

1852 *Harlequin and the Enchanted Milkmaid; or, the Fairy Queen of the Golden Alphabet.* (Also titled) *Harlequin and the Golden Alphabet; or, the Fairy Queen, One Eye'd King and the Enchanted Milkmaid.*

1853 *Plum Pudding and Roast Beef; or, Harlequin Nine Pins, and the Card King of the Island of Games.*

1854 *Fire Burn Stick; or, Harlequin Old Dame Crump and the Silver Penny.* (Also Titled) *Harlequin Dame Crump and the Silver Penny, Pig Won't Get Over the Stile Tonight*, by Barnaby Brazen.

1855 *A Merry Christmas and A Happy New Year; or, Harlequin King Candle and Queen Rushlight; or, Princess Prettydear of Taper Land.*

1855 *Harlequin King Domino; or, High, Low, Jack, and the Game.* (At the Marylebone Theatre).

1855 *The Vicar of Wakefield.* (By Tom Taylor with John Douglass?)

1856 (?) *The Lucky-Horse-Shoe.*

1856 *Hickedy Pickedy My Black Hen; or, Harlequin King Winter and Queen Spring.*

1857 *Georgy Porgey Puddin and Pie, Kissed All the Girls till He Made them Cry; or, Harlequin Old Daddy Longlegs.*

1859 *The Forty Thieves.* (An adaptation of an old extravaganza?).

1859 *Harlequin Earth, Air, Fire, and Water; or, Mistress Mary Quite Contrary How Does Your Garden Grow.* (Also at the Pavilion Theatre as, *Mary Mary Quite Contrary, How Does Your Garden Grow; or, Harlequin Silver Bells Cockle Shells and Primroses All of a Row.*)(With a scene staged by J. R. Douglass. This may be a mistake for J. and R. or for J. T., If so it is the first of seventeen- year-old John Thomas Douglass's writing, perhaps aided by his fifteen-year old-brother (Samuel) Richard.)

1861 *The Sleeping Beauty In the Wood; or, Harlequin Prince Pretty and the Seven Fairy Godmothers.*

After 1861 John Douglass seems to have turned the writing over to his son John Thomas Douglass. He may have contributed to the Christmas Pantomimes up to 1866.

JOHN THOMAS DOUGLASS (1842–1917) (Pseudonyms: Leonard Rae, and James Willing)

The plays dated 1861 were composed during the years immediately before but not published, or licensed, or produced until John T. was eighteen.

1861 *First Impressions Everything; or, the Young Lover and the Remembrance of Childhood.*

1861 *The Pirates of the Savanna.* (W. E. Suter also wrote a play of this title. Both plays were probably translations of a French original).

1861 *The House on the Bridge of Notre Dame* (From the French play by Barrière and de Kock.)

1861 *I've Beat All Three.*

1861 *The Fireman and the Volunteer; or, An Artful Trick and Love in the Dark.*

1861 *Twelve O'Clock; or, [and] The Midnight Angel* (From the French play by Barriere and Plouvier).

1861 *Cora; or, The Octoroon Slave of Louisiana.* (At the Pavilion Theatre).

1861 *Louisiana; or, The Slave Daughter. (Same play as the above.)*

1861 *The Sleeping Beauty In the Wood; or, Harlequin Prince Pretty and the Seven Fairy Godmothers* (with John Douglass).

1862 *Mark Ringwood; or, Two Chapters in the Life of a British Grenadier.*

1863 *Night; or, The Perils of the Alps.*

1864 *The White Scarf (Louise).* (From the French play of D'Alberte.)

1864 *Mark Winslow; a Tale [Story] of the Cornish Coast.*

1864 *The Market Cross.*

1864 *The Forty Thieves.*

1864 *Second to None; or,The Lady of the Lone House* (with, or by T. H. Glenny?).

1864 *Dame Durden and Her Five Serving Maids; or, Harlequin Robert and Richard Were Two Pretty Men.*

1865 *The Assassins of the Roadside Inn. (from the French play Robert Macaire).*

1865 *The Brigand in a New Suit for Easter.*

1865 *£200 Reward (Pavilion Theatre).*

1865 *Pat-A-Cake Pat-A-Cake Baker's Man: or, Harlequin Bah! Bah! Black Sheep. (With Brittain Wright).*

1866 *Abon Hassan, the Cockney Caliph.*

1867 *Der Freischutz; or, The Bride, the Bullet and the Bobby.*

1867 *Oranges and Lemons Said the Bells of St. Clement's! or, Harlequin and the Good Fairy of the New Year.*

1868 *A Royal Marriage.*

1868 *Dead Calm; or, The Fisher's Story.* (Possibly Mark Winslow revised.)

1868 *Advertisements.* (A revision of an old farce?).

1868 *Tell Tale Tit; or, Harlequin Dickory Dickory Dock.*

1869 *For Sale.* (With Alfred Rayner).

1869 *The Young Man of the Period.*

1869 *In and Out of Service.*

1869 *Jack the Giant Killer; and, The Seven Champions.*

1870 *Guy Fawkes; or, A New Way to Blow Up a King.*

1870 *Venus Versus Mars.*

1870 *A Chapter of Accidents (Wooing Under Difficulties).*

1870 *The Vicar of Wakefield, (Vicar Primrose),* (from old version by Tom Taylor? From Oliver Goldsmith).

1870 *Ride a Cock Horse to Banbury Cross; or, Harlequin and the Silver Amazons.*

1871 *Germans and French; or, Incidents of the War of 1871.*

1871 *Warranted Sound and Quiet in Harness* (Greenwich, licensed in 1865 as *In Jest or in Earnest; or, Warranted Sound and Quiet in Harness*).

1871 *Aladdin and the Wonderful Lamp.*

1872 *Brave as a Lion* (from a French play).

1872 *Thompson's Visit* (from a French play).

1872 *Cinderella and the Little Glass Slipper.*

1873 *What Will the Neighbors Say?*

1873 *Harlequin Whittington and His Cat.*

1874 *This Side Up* (by Leonard Rae, taken from Albert Smith's story *The Scattergood Family*).

1874 *Hal O' The Wynd* (from *The Fair Maid of Perth* by Sir Walter Scott).

1874 *Harlequin Robinson Crusoe and His Man Friday.*

1875 *Rank and Fame.* (by Leonard Rae and Frank Stainforth, from the French play *L'Officier de Fortune*).

1875 *Children in the Wood; or, the Wicked Uncle.*

1876 *Open Sesame; or, Harlequin the Forty Robbers of the Magic Cave.*

1877 *Queen of an Hour* (With Frank Stainforth).

1877 *Harlequin the Enchanted Prince; or, the Beauty and the Bears.*

1878 *Eliza and Uncle Tom* (by Leonard Rae from the French play *Le Chalet de L'Oncle Tom*)

1878 *Ali Baba and the Forty Thieves (same as above, but at Park Theatre).*

1878 *Harlequin Robin Hood; or, The Marrie Men of Sherwood Forest.*

1879 *Under two Reigns* (by James Willing, with W. Percival).

1879 *Poor Relations; or, Jane Eyre* (by James Willing from Bronte, Park Theatre).

1879 *Blue Beard Re-Wived.*

1880 *Delilah; or, Married for Hate* (by James Willing, from Ouida's *Held in Bondage*, Park Theatre).

1880 *Harlequin and the Wide-Awake Sleeping Beauty.*

1880 *Harlequin Little Red Riding Hood; or, Little Boy Blue and the Fairies fo the Coral Reef* (by Leonard Rae, with W. Walden, Park Theatre).

1881 *Harlequin and Sinbad the Sailor; or, the Genii of the Diamond Vally.*

1882 *Humanity; or, An Incident in the Life of Grace Darling* (by Leonard Rae withHugh Marston, Leicester and Standard Theatres).

1882 *The Ruling Passion* (by James Willing, with Francis Edward Stainforth, in *The Home Library of Powerful Dramatic Tales,* no. 5, 1886).

1882 *Little Red Riding Hood; or, Harlequin Boy Blue, Miss Muffit, the Wolf, and the Bears.*

1883 *Glad Tidings* (by James Willing and Frank Stainforth).

1883 *Harlequin Puss in Boots.*

1884 *A Bitter Wrong; A Wife in England, No Wife in France* (with George Lander, from a true story).

1884 *Daybreak* (by James Willing).

1884 *Harlequin Cinderella; or, the Fairy of the Little Glass Slipper.*

1885 *A Bubble Reputation* (by James Willing, Shrewsbury Theatre).

1885 *A Day of Judgment* (by James Willing, called Day by Day in 1889).

1886 *A Dark Secret; or, A Tale of the Thames Vally* (by James Willing, from a novel by Sheriden Le Fanu *Uncle Silas*).

1886 *Harlequin Aladdin; or, the Genie of the Ring and the Slave of the Lamp.*

1887 *The Royal Mail.*

1887 *The Tongue of Slander* (with T. G. Warren, from an incident in a story by Charles Gibbon).

1887 *Fee–Fi–Fo–Fum; or, Harlequin Jack the Giant Killer* (with Frank Marshall).

1888 *The Lucky Shilling* (by James Willing).

1889 *Her Father* (with E. Rose, Vaudeville Theatre.)

1890 *No Man's Land* (based on R. L. Stevenson's *Treasure Island*,)(Leicester Grand Theatre).

1892 *Wilfred's Vow* (Novelty Theatre).

1893 *Nance; or, Reclaimed* (Pavilion Theatre).

1894 *The Birthright; or, The Brigand's Ransom* (Huddersfield).

1894 *Down on His Luck* (Oxford).

1896 *A Bunch of Shamrocks* (with F. Bateman, T. R. Edinburgh).

1897 *From Scotland Yard* (With F. Bateman, at Accrington).

1897 *The Cross for Valour*.

1897 *The Burglar's Baby* (with C. Williams, at Ealing).

1898 *The Joy of the House* (Norwich).

1899 *Known to the Police* (Portsmouth).

1899 *Mistress of the Seas* (West London Theatre).

Other titles attributed to J.T. Douglass include: *The Man with the Pigeons; Saved; or, the Innundation*; *The Sea-Girt Cliff*; and *A Lost Child*.

AMY STEINBERG (Alice Rachel Koning Mrs. J.T. Douglass) (1850–1920).

1888 *Our Climate*.

1889 *My Uncle. (Terry's)*.

1890 *My Mother* (Toole's).

BIBLIOGRAPHY

Allen, Cecil J. *The Great Eastern Railway*. London: Ian Allan, 1955.

Anderson, James R. *An Actor's Life*. London: Walter Scott Pub. Co., 1902.

Booth, Michael R. *English Melodrama*. London: Herbert Jenkins,1965.

Clark, G. Kitson *The Making of Victorian England*. Cambridge: Harvard U. Press, 1962.

Coleman, John *Fifty Years of an Actor's Life*. London: Hutchinson and Co.,1904.

Disher, Maurice Willson, *Blood and Thunder*. London: Frederick Muller Ltd., 1949.

_____ *Victorian Song*. London: Phoenix House, 1955.

Donohue, Joseph *Theatre in the Age of Kean*. New Jersey: Rowman and Littlefield, 1975.

Douglass, Albert *Footlight Reflections*. London: Samuel French Ltd.,1934.

_____ *Memories of Mummers and the Old Standard Theatre*. London: The *Era*, 1924.

Fleetwood, Frances *Conquest, the Story of a Theatre Family*. London: W.H. Allen,1953.

Hart, F. Jerome and John Parker *The Green Room Book*. London: Pitman,1907.

Howard, Diana *London Theatres and Music Halls*. London: The library Association, 1970.

Jackson, Allan S., and M. Glen Wilson *French Theatrical Production in the Nineteenth Century*. Rare Books of the Theatre Series Number 10. New York: American Theatre Association , 1976

Mackintosh, Ian and Geoffrey Ashton *The Georgian Playhouse*. London: Arts Council of Great Britain, 1975.

Mander, Raymond and Joe Mitchenson *A Picture History of the British Theatre*. New York: Macmillan, 1957.

Morley, Malcolm *The Old Marylebone Theatre*. St. Marylebone Society, No. 2, 1960.

_____, *The Royal West London Theatre*. St. Marylebone Society, No. 6, 1962.

Newton, Henry Chance. *Crime and the Drama or Dark Deeds Dramatized*. London: Stanley Paul, 1927.

Nicoll, Allardyce *A History of English Drama*, Vol. 5, Cambidge: Cambridge University Press, 1962.

Parker, John *Who's Who in the Theatre*, London: Pitman, 1947.

Pascoe, Charles Eyre *The Dramatic List*. London: David Bogue,1880.

_____, and William H. Rideing, and Austin Brereton. *Dramatic Notes*. London: David Bogue,1883.

Reid, Erskine, and Herbert Compton *The Dramatic Peerage*. London: Raithby, Lawrence, 1892.

Reynolds, Harry *Minstrel Memories*. London: Alston Rivers Ltd., 1928.

Rose, Millicent *The East End of London*. London: Cresset Press,1951.

Rowell, George *The Victorian Theatre*. London: Oxford U. Press, 1956.

Tallis, John *Tallis's Drawingroom Table Book*. London: John Tallis and Co., 1851.

____ *Tallis's Illustrated London*. London: John Tallis and Co., 1851.

Speaight, George *The History of the English Toy Theatre*. London: Studio Vista, 1969.

Trewin, J. C. *The Edwardian Theatre*. New Jersey:Rowman and Littlefield, 1976.

Wilson, A. E. *East End Entertainment*. London: Arthur Barker Ltd., 1954.

PERIODICALS

The Builder. London, 1858–1922

Dramatic Notes. London, 1879–1893.

Entr'Acte. London, 1869–1907.

Entr'Acte Almanac. London, 1873–1906.

The *Era.* London, 1838–1939.

Era Almanac. London, 1868–1919.

General Theatrical Programme. London, 1883–1886.

Illustrated London News. London, 1835–1895.

Illustrated Sporting News. London, 1865–1870.

Illustrated Sporting and Dramatic News. London 1874–1945.

London Daily Telegraph. London, 1883–1897

The Referee. London, 1880–1888

The Theatre. London, 1877–1897.

Under the Clock. London, 1884–1885.

INDEX